When People
Wrote Letters

To Gene —

Martha Tuck Rozett

Book design by Melissa Mykal Batalin

Printed in the United States of America

The Troy Book Makers • Troy, New York • thetroybookmakers.com

To order additional copies of this title, contact your favorite local bookstore or visit www.tbmbooks.com

ISBN: 978-1-61468-041-3

When People Wrote Letters

A FAMILY CHRONICLE

Martha Tuck Rozett

Acknowledgments

MANY PEOPLE – friends, family members, and students – have listened to me talk about this project, read the manuscript, and offered advice and encouragement over the years. My heartfelt thanks to you all. I am grateful to the Schlesinger Library at Harvard University, which has provided Edith Stedman's papers with a home in perpetuity and made them available to curious readers like myself. I would also like to thank the staff at The Troy Book Makers in Troy, NY, for helping me bring this project to completion. And finally, to the ghosts of the people who inhabit these pages, forgive me if I have not portrayed you exactly as you would have wished.

In transcribing and excerpting the letters and other documents, I have retained the original spelling and punctuation as much as possible.

Contents

Family Tree

Issac Stedman
b. 1605   d. 1678

Thomas Stedman
b. 1640   d. 1707

Joshua Stedman
b. 1674 (?)   d. 1762

Issac Stedman
b. 1706   d. 1757

m. Huldah Trowbridge
b. 1715

James Stedman
b. 1752   d. 1757

m. Mary Barrett
b. 1759 d. 1853

Issac Stedman
b. 1780

James Stedman
b. 1789   d. 1858

m. Betsey Richardson
b. 1792   d.1872

Nathaniel Stedman
b. 1798

Vernal Stedman
b. 1814   d. 1889

m. Elvira Karhal
b. 1822(?) d.1896

Olive Stedman
b. 1817

m. Henry
Williams

James Seldon
Stedman
b. 1820

Mary Elizabeth
Stedman
b. 1829

Ella Faustina Stedman

George Herbert Stedman
Ⓐ b. 1846   d. 1903

James Howes
b. 1764   d. 1846

m. Priscilla Sears
b. 1768   d.1855

Stephen Howes
b. 1792   d. 1865

m. Deborah Mayhew
b. 1795   d.1861

10 children including
Samual Munson Howes
b. 1833

Priscilla Howes
b. 1816   d. 1887

m. Augustus Fifield Holt
B *b. 1816*

Gratia 'Kitty' Holt
b. 1847   d. 1911

m. George Herbert Stedman
A *b. 1846   d. 1903*

Frank Holt Stedman
b. 1874   d. 1945

m. Marian Murray
b. 1883   d.1954

**James Herbert
Stedman**
b. 1878

Edith Gratia Stedman
b. ~~1798~~   d. 1978
1888

Edith Gratia Stedman
b. 1912   d. 1984

**Mary Elizabeth
'Betty' Stedman**
b. 1914   d. 1991

m. Eugene Tuck
b. 1909   d. 2000

Frank Holt Stedman
b. 1915   d. 2002

Joseph Burt
b. 1738

Gratia Burt
b. 1786   d. 1874

m. Fifield Holt
b.1784   d. 1830

Augustus
Fifield Holt
B b. 1816

Gratia
Ann Holt
b. 1818

Mary
Burt Holt
b. 1821

m. Edmund
Messer

Elizabeth Holt
b. 1825

m. William
Babbitt

Joseph Holt
b. 1828

m. Julia
Rollins
b. 1829

Emily Burt
Berry
b. 1854 d. 1934

PART ONE

Family History

ONE

The Letters
April 2000

Aᴀᴛᴇʀ ᴍʏ ᴍᴏᴛʜᴇʀ'ꜱ ᴅᴇᴀᴛʜ my father reduced the accumulations of a
lifetime – two lifetimes – to the contents of a one-bedroom apartment
in New York City. It is now six weeks after his death, and I have begun the
sifting and sorting process once again. The clothing is gone, and in the back
of a closet I find two shoeboxes of letters my parents wrote to one another
during the early 1940s. With them are the Spain letters, my mother's weekly
chronicle of the year she spent in Madrid. She was a nineteen-year old
college student in 1933-34, and she wrote home to her parents in Boston
every Sunday without fail. I'd known about the letters for as long as I could
remember, but my two younger brothers and I were under strict orders not
to touch – let alone read – them should we find ourselves in the attic of our
childhood home. The attic, as I recall, was a wonderfully dangerous place,
accessible by a ladder that swung down from the ceiling and unfinished in
places so that if you stepped off the narrow beams you'd plunge through the
floor into the room below – or so we were told. The letters, I assume, were
considered too private and too adult for our young eyes. They had been

moved from a succession of apartments to the small house on Long Island with the dangerous attic to a much larger home that my parents lived in for the rest of Mom's life and finally to this room where I am sitting in bed becoming acquainted with the people my parents were before I was born.

Their story – my story – is in many ways a quintessentially American one, a story of the mixing of traditions and religions in early and mid twentieth century America; a story about what people remember, what they save, and how they 'write themselves' in letters, memoirs, and family histories. It is also a meditation on a form of communication that has lost its prominence in our culture. The long, leisurely letter, a way of communicating for centuries, now seems on the brink of extinction. This is a pity, for the letter as a form of self-expression arises from a different motive and serves a different purpose from the journal, the autobiography, the blog. Letters combine spontaneity with reflection, description with inquiry. They mingle the practical day-to-day ("Did you receive my package?" "Have you seen the doctor yet?") with self-revelations large and small. Letters are nearly always about the writer *and* the recipient, and it goes without saying that the writer always knows exactly who his or her audience is. When people wrote letters, they committed a version of themselves to paper to be read and reread. They said things they might not have said in conversation lingering over a turn of phrase yet hurrying to finish so that the letter could go into the mail. They said as much or as little as the space on the page allowed. And then they folded and sealed the letter, addressed it, and sent it on its way, in the knowledge that a day or perhaps a week or more would pass before it would be read.

TWO

Betty's and Gene's Courtship Begins
1940-1942

NOT LONG AFTER her twenty-sixth birthday, my mother, Betty Stedman, arrived in New York in the fall of 1940 to assume a position in the school textbook department at the publishing house then called Harcourt Brace. She was visiting a friend at the Barbizon Hotel, a chaperoned residence for young women, when she was introduced to Eugene Tuck, a thirty-one-year-old graduate of Harvard Law School with a small law practice at 120 Broadway. Gene was a native New Yorker, the son of Latvian Jewish immigrants, who had gone to City College where he wrote for the college newspaper. During the summers and on weekends throughout the 1930s he supervised synagogue youth groups and worked at summer camps, composing comic skits and directing and performing in plays. Had he been free to choose his career without regard for the practical business of making a living, he would have been a writer. Gene lived in Brooklyn with his mother and elder sister Jane, both of whom were public school teachers who had steady employment throughout the Depression.

Evidently some time had passed after Gene and Betty met, because while Betty was in Chicago on business a letter, postmarked October 25, 1941, was forwarded to her by Harcourt Brace. This is the first of Gene's letters—nearly two hundred of them – that Betty preserved. The witty, self-consciously casual tone suggests that Gene was prepared to be turned down and didn't want to seem vulnerable.

> *Dear Betty,*
>
> *If the name strikes no chord in your recollection, I am the cherubic young man who infested the Barbizon last year.*
>
> *Unless you are (1) Married (2) Engaged (3) Not in the market for new male investments or (4) just plain disinterested – will you have dinner with me some evening next week? Drop me a line and let me know what evening is convenient for you and where and at what time I should call for you.*
>
> *Hope to see you soon.*
>
> > *Cordially,*
> > *Gene Tuck*

Judging from the letters, the romance blossomed during the next few months. The postmarks on the envelopes, which Betty nearly always saved, provide a rough chronology of events. Gene adopts a similarly arch tone in a letter apparently written not long after that first dinner:

> *I hope you are aware that you are being treated to your first dose of my illegible handwriting. My mother has always been convinced that the only reason why I was not at the very top of my class at school was because the profs could not read my exam papers. She made such a fuss about it, that believe it or not, I printed the entire Bar Examination. Of course, I have always consoled myself with the thought that all great men have illegible handwriting. The older I get, however, the more I am convinced that I am the exception that proves the rule.*

Elsewhere in the letter Gene playfully alludes to the men she will meet on the road, presumably on one of the many trips she was making that year as a textbook representative. All of the other publishers' reps were men, and Betty became adept at keeping them at bay.

> *By the time you receive this, I suppose you will have already donned your winged feet. I can see you flitting gaily away from the lecherous old men at the first sign of a glint in their rheumy eyes – nice watery old eyes. Now, my little one, you had better not be too prodigal. Remember that it may not be very long before all of us virile young men are unavailable – shall we say. You may have to fall back on said lecherous old men. And, in falling back on them be careful not to injure them. They may be fragile.*

By the end of 1941 the virile young men, including Betty's brother Frank, were joining or being drafted into the armed forces. My father never concealed the fact that he avoided military service as long as he could. He had graduated from law school ten years earlier, but because of the Depression and the anti-Semitism widespread among the big New York law firms he had only just begun to establish himself in his profession.

In February 1942 Betty's travels have taken her to San Francisco and then on to Hollywood. Gene's handwritten letter addresses her as "Dearest," reports on the contents of her mailbox, which he has been checking for her. He offers to make a deposit in her bank account if she is short of money and urges her to accept. From this I infer that the relationship had developed and that my parents had become a "couple." In a typewritten letter written at about the same time, Gene alludes to war news in Java and observes, "inefficiency is the price of democracy. To think of all the years and the lives that will have to be given to win back all that lost territory."

The only clue to the date of an illustrated letter is the following:

> *Due to the fact that a certain famous lady-killer was born a couple of hundred years ago tomorrow, I am facing a long week-end and am not at all interested in doing anything about it.*

It must be the February Washington's Birthday holiday (or was it Lincoln who was the lady-killer? In the 1940s both holidays were observed). This is the first reference I found in the letters to the imaginary family Gene invented for himself and Betty.

> *I have been considering designing a family tree for us – an obvious form of sublimation. First there will be a girl who will be a good deal like her mother – not so vivacious perhaps – but one cannot have everything. In fact she will be a rather sober and dependable creature, which will be a rather good thing because she'll have to help mother bring up the rest of the family. She will be blonde, of course, with her mother's eyes but not with their twinkle. She will do well at school, be very obedient and whatever little petting she does during adolescence will be done discreetly, miles from the family sofa.*
>
> *Then we will have a son, who will be the capable one – industrious, resourceful, highly practical – not terribly imaginative and not particularly emotional – affectionate in a very dutiful sort of way – with a very strong sense of duty – a responsible fellow – who will begin to shift for himself at a very early age. He'll be tolerant of and amused at the harum-scarum behavior of his scatter-brained parents – who will grow no less scatter-brained with the years but rather more so.*

The letter continues for another page, with two more children, and primitive little stick figure drawings of all four. Mary is washing dishes, and the first son is wearing an academic cap and gown with the caption "Harvard summa cum laude." Reading this in April 2000, I felt a strange shiver of recognition. I would become that sober and dependable eldest child (and wash a lot of dishes in my adolescence, although to be fair, my brothers always took equal turns). There would be three of us in rapid succession, not four, as the letter envisioned.

Having created his cast of characters, Gene continues to spin out comical stories about them in subsequent letters. Here is an undated one:

Dearest,

Just got your cute little note not to speak of Aunt Sally's Creole Pralines which were delicious and a welcome relief from Mary's cooking. The poor little dear tries so hard but the little ones have been living on castor oil and I have become a walking advertisement for Bi-su-dol. The family intestinal tract is beginning to resemble a battle-scarred section of the Eastern Front, and every evening when I pass the bottle of castor oil around and hold the respective noses as it goes down, I try so hard to cheer the children up by telling them that Mother will soon be home.

As far as spoiling them is concerned, I have had the time of my life and I'm sure it will take you months to get things back into status quo. Of course Mary's cooking and the castor oil have checked us considerably.

March 15 was the day on which income taxes were filed in those days (there were lots of Ides of March jokes). As a trusts and estates attorney, Gene was intimately acquainted with the tax code and the behavior it inspired, as his letter mockingly indicates:

Dearest Pooch,

'Tis income tax time in old New York and the deductions are flying so thick and fast and crop up in such strange places and in such numerous disguises that some of them can scarcely be recognized. I wonder whether the process of evolution will ever carry us to the point where the human tax-payer will understand that there is no essential distinction between direct and indirect taxation and will pay his income tax just as cheerfully as he pays his cigarette tax....

For myself, I am beginning to grow soft. I took less than half of my usual deductions and disregarded several contributions that I could legitimately have taken – thus reversing the process applied in previous years. In fact, I did everything except wave an American flag in the face of the Collector of Internal Revenue and shout "Take my daughter and half my kingdom but let my people go." Beautiful – this patriotism, if one could forget for a moment some of its by-products like corpses and broken bodies.

Gene ends his letter with another reference to the imaginary children:

The kids are awful lonesome for you – and little Mary our eldest is getting awful sick of cooking for her finicky old man and taking care of the littler brats.

In April 1942 Betty was traveling for Harcourt Brace by car, which she did whenever possible until wartime gasoline rationing made it impossible for her to continue. In a note addressed "Dear Funnyface," Gene asks Betty to let him know when she'll be returning, and includes another of the little stick figures in the margin. This one is a tiny figure driving a shoe-shaped convertible, with the caption "God's gift to school superintendents," an allusion to the purpose of Betty's trips, which was to persuade the superintendents to adopt Harcourt Brace's textbooks for their districts.

I've tried to imagine life on the road in the early 1940s while reconstructing the itinerary of Betty's next trip for Harcourt Brace from the letters. On October 7, 1942, Gene sends her a letter care of her Chicago friend, Lois Lord; the next day, he sends one to the Loraine Hotel in Madison, Wisconsin, with a note to "hold till arrival." The October 14th letter is addressed to a hotel in Oshkosh, Wisconsin; the Oct 16th letter to Green Bay, Wisconsin; and by October 20th Betty expects to be back in Chicago. There are a couple of letters without envelopes or clear postmarks in this batch and a final one postmarked October 24th and sent to Racine, Wisconsin. Gene's letters refer to other stops in St. Louis, Missouri, Urbana, Illinois, and Davenport, Iowa, as well. The sequence begins rather like a scene from a movie:

Dearest Pooch,

Did you see the little drama that occurred on the platform of the train or did your porter complain to you bitterly about me? When I reached the platform, the gate was closed – sort of a half gate, and the train had just begun to move. The porter was standing there and I asked him to open it but he refused. Very good, said I, then I'll hop over it. "Don't do that – you can't do that" cries my good brown friend, and promptly grabs me by the arm and hangs on for dear life. The train was picking up speed and there was nothing to do but to give the poor fellow a good shove and hop over the gate. I looked back and there was such a hurt expression on the poor guy's face, that my heart has been aching for him ever since. I caught a glimpse of your face peering out of the window as I hit the platform, but you were gone before I could even wave to you. It was kind of a crazy thing to do, I suppose, but I had visions of myself having to remain on the train until Pittsburgh or Buffalo or some such place. As a matter of fact, later in the day just for fun, I called Grand Central and discovered that there were no scheduled stops before Chicago. I almost got around to seeing Chicago after all, perforce.

While Betty is in the Midwest, Gene has given up the weekend job of leading synagogue youth groups with which he'd supplemented his income for the past eleven years, but a few days later he asks for it back, because "I need the dough." His sister Jane has suddenly announced that she is getting married the following week, and he's busy looking for an apartment for her and figuring out how he and his mother will help pay for the furnishings. They'll need to try to break their lease and find a smaller apartment too, now that they won't have Jane's salary to help with the rent. And his colleagues have all gone off to war: "I feel like the last surviving soldier in a fort, with the Indians all around and Katie the frontierswoman loading my long rifle" (Katie is his elderly secretary). "One by one, the boys are dropping off and now I have no one to consult with."

Although none of Betty's letters from these trips were preserved, we get glimpses of their contents from Gene's responses. She must have told him about being pinched in an elevator, for he responds with:

Every traveling salesman can recognize a delicious morsel when they see one. Answering your questions seriatim: I have loved no brunettes; I do not cheat my clients, although I occasionally cheat other lawyers' clients. There are no draft developments – Allah be praised. As for the children, I have been too busy "marrying off" my little sister to pay much attention to our children but I hope to devote myself to them shortly.

I am looking wan and losing weight, losing my sense of humor and generally going mad for loneliness. Darling, I swear,

At this point he is interrupted, and when he resumes writing he can't recall what he was about to swear. Since the letters don't resume until March 1943, I'm going to pause here as well. Years later, when Betty was asked about something that happened in the past, she would say with mock seriousness, "History does not relate…." For a few months in 1942 and 1943 History remains silent.

THREE

Dinners at Farwell Place
1964-1968

PART OF WHAT INTERESTS ME about family history is the many forms it
takes. The oft-retold anecdote, the diagrammed family tree, the objects
or scraps of paper that meant something to the person who saved them
long ago, and especially, the letters sent home to family members, friends,
or sweethearts – these relics tell their stories very differently from the way
a biography or autobiography does. My title could just as appropriately
have been "What They Saved," for in the course of this narrative, I will
summon as witnesses such artifacts as carefully preserved newspaper
clippings, a high school graduation address and examination questions, a
lengthy horoscope, a little handwritten literary magazine compiled in 1868
by a maiden aunt thought to be not quite right in the head, a long account
of a sea voyage whose author was allegedly eaten by cannibals, and many
photographs.

The story I want to tell begins as an epistolary account of my parents'
courtship: a match between the descendant of an old New England family
and the son of East European Jewish immigrants. But what follows is a

miscellany, a quilt composed of found objects, a series of windows into my heritage but also our collective American past. And it is also the story – or part of the story – my great aunt Edith Stedman undertook to tell in the unfinished autobiography she gave me before she died. Edith wanted her life to be remembered, and to that end left copies of all her papers, along with a trove of photographs, letters, and travel journals to the Schlesinger Library at Harvard/Radcliffe.

I got to know my great aunt during my college years at Radcliffe, from 1964 to 1968. Then I married and moved to Ann Arbor, Michigan, to go to graduate school. I saw Aunt Edith infrequently, for I was busy with my own career, and seldom returned to Boston to visit her. She had given me copies of her published and unpublished writings, and told me stories which I now wish I'd written down. By the time of her death in 1978 the flourishing of women's history had created a growing readership for accounts of unusual career women like Edith Stedman. But I was otherwise occupied teaching and writing about Shakespeare and his contemporaries — and besides, it would have been difficult for me to undertake the project of editing and finding a publisher for her autobiography during my parents' lifetime because of their complicated feelings about her. Edith would not, I imagine, ever admit to being anti-Semitic, but her resistance to my parents' courtship looked a lot like anti-Semitism at the time. It wasn't until after my parents' deaths that I revisited the autobiography along with the other letters and documents I had found in my father's closet.

Edith's story, it now seemed to me, belonged with the other stories, the shreds of history I had begun gathering about her New England forebears and the episodes in my parents' lives that intersected with hers. The autobiography proceeded in linear fashion from her birth to her old age, its focus squarely on her experiences and accomplishments. *My* telling of the story of my family, I decided, would draw attention to the fragmentary nature of family history and would be based, whenever possible, on the letters that were once so much a part of people's lives. A story told partly through letters is necessarily incomplete. When the characters are traveling away from home, they write letters to family and friends, letters that, in the best tradition of travel narratives, describe the dislocations and adjustments and discoveries of living abroad. But when the journeys end and the letters cease, the details become scarce. And even when the letters are long and chatty and summon up a time and place, the story is univocal, for in almost every instance only half of the correspondence has been preserved.

Edith was the younger sister of my maternal grandfather, who died shortly before I was born. She was a formidable Boston spinster of strongly held ideas and remarkable accomplishments. After a career that combined travel with various roles in the early development of medical social work, she had settled in Cambridge, Massachusetts, the city of her birth. Her last and longest job was as the director of Radcliffe's Appointment Bureau, or career service, an office she created from scratch during the Depression in order to help the students earn money while in college and find employment once they graduated. Every college and university provides such a service now, but in the 1930s, it was quite a novel idea. When Edith retired in the mid 1950s, Radcliffe provided her with a small pension and a small, early nineteenth century row house on Farwell Place, just off Brattle Street (the house has long since been demolished to make way for a university building).

Without ever acknowledging her strained relationship with my parents, Edith seemed determined to make a fresh start with me, and the time I spent with her was as much a part of my college experience as the classes I took and other aspects of college life. Dinners at Farwell Place followed a familiar pattern: she would send me down Brattle Street to S. S. Pierce to buy packages of Stouffers frozen cheese soufflé (no longer in existence, alas) and spinach soufflé. While the soufflés baked in their tin foil containers (for an hour and fifteen minutes in those days before microwave ovens) we drank gin and sweet vermouth and she held forth about her projects, past and present. Occasionally one of her friends would be there, and I would listen as the witticisms flew back and forth. After dinner I would be set to work scrubbing those tin foil containers at an old-fashioned sink before returning to my dorm. I remember staying overnight in the guest bedroom on Farwell Place once or twice when dorm life became too much for me, and I also remember thinking "I should keep a record of some of these trenchant, epigrammatic pronouncements" – but I didn't.

FOUR

New Sharon, Maine

Our family took a number of vacations during my childhood and adolescence, which I ironically referred to as "family unity trips." At my request we took a final trip together during the week between my last exam and Radcliffe's graduation ceremonies in June 1968. I would be getting married and beginning graduate school later that summer, and in anticipation of the end of this first chapter in my life I decided I wanted to see the place where I had been conceived, and where my mother's family had lived for many generations. And so my parents, my brothers, and I made a pilgrimage to Cape Cod Hill in New Sharon, Maine. I don't remember much about the trip, for despite my desire to visit the past, the present seemed more compelling; Robert Kennedy was assassinated and the country was thrown into a state of grief.

Once I had children of my own, I wanted to preserve a record my mother's early history for their benefit in a taped oral history about her childhood. Here she is, telling me how to get to New Sharon.

To get to New Sharon take the turn off the main road north of Augusta, toward Belgrade Lakes. You'll find New Sharon between Farmington and Skowhegan, and when you get there, the road winds westward up Cape Cod Hill. The cemetery there is filled with members of the Howes family. The Stedmans are originally from Sidney, Maine. To get there, you take the middle road past the grange hall, turn right at the general store, and the first farm you see on the right is where the Stedman burying ground is. Olive Stedman is buried there. We lived in the white farmhouse that James Howes built in 1799. Much later, my Uncle Bert constructed a little stone bungalow nearby called the Retreat right next to another farmhouse that belonged to the Holts; my grandmother Kitty Holt Stedman was born there.

We lived in the old Howes farmhouse for about two and a half years, from 1918 to 1921. My father, who had given up his position as minister of St. Mark's Church in Waterville, Maine, hoping to be posted as a chaplain in the Navy, came back to New Sharon to farm as the war was ending. He grew rhubarb and other vegetables but his main crop was potatoes, which he grew in a field full of rocks, and every spring more rocks would heave out of the ground during the thaw. The other farmers were skeptical about the potato project, but Daddy got a bumper crop, to their surprise.

In a red velvet-bound Stedman genealogy I found among my mother's papers her father's life is described as follows:

Frank Holt Stedman (1ˢᵗ) was born in Cambridge, Mass Feb 12, 1874. Prepared for college at Cambridge Latin School and at Phillips Academy in Andover. Entered Harvard with the class of 1900, but was compelled to withdraw on account of financial reasons. President Charles F. Thwing of Western Reserve University, Cleveland, Ohio, who was born in New Sharon, Me. and was an old friend of the Holt family offered him a chance to work his way through if he would come to Ohio, which he did, graduating with the class of 1903. He returned to Cambridge and entered the Episcopal Theological School, graduating

*in 1906. Ordained by Bishop Lawrence in 1907, he accepted a call
to become the rector of St. Peter's Church in Delaware, Ohio, where
he married Marian Murray on June 14, 1909. He served as rector of
various churches in Ohio, Wisconsin and Maine, resigning from St.
Mark's Church, Waterville, Me. in 1918 during the World War to do
war work for the Y.M.C.A. among the shipworkers at Bath, Me. From
1921 to 1931 he labored as a missionary in Texas, returning to Boston
in 1931 to be rector of St. Peter's Church and also to be a hospital
chaplain under the direction of the Episcopal City Mission. He retired
from the active ministry in 1942 and died in New Sharon, Maine, Sept.
14, 1945 aged 71.*

There is no mention of the farm or the potatoes. It seems odd that Frank
Stedman's ministry in Texas is described as missionary work. The turn of
phrase suggests a parochial New England sensibility that regards the deep
South as a foreign land, its Baptist and Methodist inhabitants in need of
enlightenment from the civilized north.

Frank and Marian had three children, Edith Gratia ("Little Edith"), born
Sept 11, 1912, Mary Elizabeth, called Betty, born July 17, 1914, and Frank
Holt (2nd), born July 29, 1915. They moved around a great deal: Little Edith
was born in Cincinnati, Betty and Frank were born in Milwaukee, and by
the time Betty was two, they had returned to Maine. Here, again, is Betty,
reminiscing:

*My earliest memories of New Sharon are of the kitchen in the old
farmhouse where we were living. I remember the woodbox, which
seemed very high to me at the time. There was an orchard going down
to the river, and one apple tree that I especially loved to climb. The
winters were cold and long and snowy; sometimes, the snow was six feet
deep, and we could sled across the top of the apple orchard. Mother used
snowshoes. We had two horses to pull the hay wagon, a cow that had
to be milked every morning, a dog and some cats. There were kittens in
the barn and I remember once that Edith, Frank and I were up in the
hayloft playing with them one afternoon when the hired man moved*

the ladder. We called and called and finally, as it became dark, Mother came out to the barn looking for us and helped us down. Another time I was chased by an angry old sow and a bull – I was scared pink and ran along the board on the top of a fence, with the sow on one side and the bull on the other. I was always doing things like that.

Daddy would bring ice back from the river to the ice house; I can remember the feel of the sawdust we used to keep the blocks of ice apart. I also remember the castor oil mother would give us as punishment, and the time we went to Cousin Clara's in a sleigh filled with straw and a smelly old bear rug on Thanksgiving Day. It was a crisp, frosty day and we took the back road, the river road. A big tree had fallen across the road blocking our way. We all waited, very excited, while Daddy walked to the Adams farmhouse to get men and a saw to cut the tree so that we could get through.

My brother Frank and I began school at the same time, since the school had been closed for two years because of the flu epidemic and fuel shortage. We would carry our lunch in pails and slide down Cape Cod Hill on our sleds to the village and then, at the end of the day, we'd have to pull them back up. It was a long mile and a half on the return trip. The schoolhouse had two rooms. I sat in the front row for Grade 1 and then moved to the second row, which was Grade 2. I already knew how to read because my mother had taught us using flashcards—it was called the Calvert System.

My brother had asthma and so it was decided that we would move to Texas, where the warm dry climate would be better for his lungs. I remember traveling on a train for two days and nights to get there. Who had ever heard of Texas in those days? It was like going to the Wild West, and mother said we should expect to see rattlesnakes curled around lampposts. In Stamford, Texas, the members of the Episcopal Church had built a new rectory for us, and the railroad ran between the rectory and the church.

Betty's father must have arrived in Texas before the rest of the family, for a letter survives that Betty mailed from Marian's hometown, Delaware,

Ohio, on June 7, 1921. It was addressed to Rev. F. H. Stedman, Stamford, Texas—evidently no further address was needed. The letter reads as follows:

> *Dear Daddy. I love you. I do not go to school. The school is out next week. Mother's sty is a lot better and Edith has one. I hope you are well, Daddy dear. How do you like it there? I wish you many kisses good bye good bye. I like your letters. With love, Betty.*

Betty sent another letter four days later, also preserved. She tells her father that she had to stay home from the moving picture show because she had cut her foot and must not walk on it. She adds: *"Mother says you must not worry about it. We are getting lonesome for you."*

FIVE

Beginning in 1635

IF YOU GO BACK FAR ENOUGH, you can trace the Stedmans to an Isaac Stedman who left England at the age of thirty in the year 1635 and came to the colonies with his wife Elizabeth, on a ship called the "Elizabeth." Tradition has it that he was a miller in Biddenden, Kent, who subsequently built a mill in Scituate, Massachusetts; that mill remained standing into the twentieth century. Other accounts tell us that he later settled in what would eventually become Brookline, Massachusetts, but was then called Muddy River, and was a merchant until his death in 1678. His will, which can be obtained from the Scituate Historical Society, states that he left large holdings of land in Boston, Cambridge, and the vicinity to his two sons, Nathaniel and Thomas. To his wife, as "a token of my Love to her" he left the property she brought to their marriage, their house, and "one Cow, and two sheep and one hog & also pasture and winter keeping for the Creatures" for as long as she remained in the house. Should she move to Boston, she would receive five pounds yearly in provisions such as wood, corn and meal. To his three daughters, he left forty pounds apiece, although the will notes precisely how much of those monies he has already loaned to their respective husbands.

There were many Isaac Stedmans and Elizabeth Stedmans; these and other names recur again and again. Betty made several efforts to sort out family relationships using the "roll" of New Sharon, Maine. I have used her records and others to create my family tree. For many of the people on the family tree, we know little more than their names. But for others, glimpses of a life lived have survived in photographs, letters, memoirs, and other documents and mementos that someone saved and passed on to the next generation.

Among the documents the Stedman family saved was the family genealogy bound in red velvet, which I alluded to in the last chapter. It begins with this passage attributed to the eighteenth-century political theorist Edmund Burke:

> People will never look forward to posterity
> who never look backward to their ancestors.

And look backward to their ancestors the Stedmans certainly did. Glimpses of their story can be found in another genealogy of the Stedman family, a small typed booklet that also quotes Burke, who noted that "the ancient and illustrious family of Stedman [was] known in England since 1191."

The 17th century Isaac Stedman from Biddenden was the great great-grandfather of the first James Stedman, the subject of the only narrative in the booklet longer than a few sentences. In this account we meet James's wife Mary, one of the many strong, enterprising women I encountered while compiling this family history. James and Mary arrived in Maine in the 1780s, according to the narrative:

> *At the close of the revolutionary war James Stedman removed to Maine.*
>
> *He sailed as far as Augusta, then, in a canoe, paddled up the Kennebec River to Lovejoy's Landing (8 miles), on the west side of the river. Here there were a few families settled.*
>
> *Pushing his way thro' the forest he began clearing land about three miles from the river. He staid nights at Mr. Hastings' or Mr. Lovejoy's*

and walked the distance night and morning, by "spotted" trees, to his work.

He worked the first season felling trees and building a log house of one room, and then returned to Massachusetts, and the next season brought his widowed mother, Huldah Trowbridge Stedman, to live with him.

After a season or two he again returned to Massachusetts and was married to Mary Barrett, of Chelmsford, Mass., who came with him back to the "wilderness" and helped him build up his arm and fortune, truly, for her grandchildren have heard her tell how she helped him build "log fence," rolling up the charred and blackened logs with the strength of a man.

In time a new log house was built. His mother lived some years, and could take care of the house and little Isaac while his wife helped in the clearing or ran after the gun while he kept a bear at bay, and, with a pitchfork for herself, carried his gun to him and together they dispatched his bearship.

She often told stories of her life in Massachusetts and of the British officers who were in Concord, where she lived for a time. She must have been very homesick, for, when Isaac was six months old, she went home to Massachusetts, in a sailing vessel, but suffered so much on the voyage home (being six weeks on board vessel on account of avoiding British cruisers) that she never undertook the journey again.

Not having neighbors nearer than three miles, at river and pond, she used to "go visiting" of an evening, on an ox-sled, marking the way by "blazed" trees, and it would take nearly all night, for it was the fashion then to cook goose or spare-rib, after the company come, and have supper no matter how late.

She is described as a very interesting person and even in her old age was a bright and entertaining talker and visited by friends from far and near. She died Feb 7, 1853, aged 94 years.

In the course of time James cleared a large tract of land comprised in farms in what is now known as Sidney, Me., and it was divided among his four sons. His son Isaac built a large and substantial

*dwelling (near the site of the log house) and the old people resided
with him until their death.*

I wish I knew more about Mary. She lived for nearly a century, a
remarkable life span in those days, and gave birth to ten children, only four
of whom survived infancy.

My mother's family could trace their descent from the Mayflower, which
in some New England circles remains to this day a mark of great distinction.
They took particular pride in being descended from Priscilla Sears, the
great, great, great, great, great granddaughter of William Brewster, one of
the original settlers of Plymouth in 1620. According to family tradition,
James Howes, a soldier from Massachusetts who had served in the
Revolutionary War, went to New Sharon with a friend in about 1789 or
1790 and built a log cabin on the side of a hill, not far from James and
Mary Stedman in Sidney. Like James Stedman, James Howes remained in
Maine for a season, and then returned to Cape Cod to fetch his bride. He
and Priscilla traveled to Augusta by boat, then by canoe up the Kenneback
River to Belgrade, and finally to New Sharon. Priscilla rode on horseback
with her featherbed, her silver, and her china; James walked. They named
the hill Cape Cod Hill and in 1799 built a farmhouse. Six generations of
Howeses and Holts and Stedmans lived on Cape Cod Hill in that house
and elsewhere in New Sharon, right up until Frank Holt Stedman's death
in 1945. It was also in 1945 that my father and mother, on a visit to Maine,
decided that now that the war was over it was time to start a family. Nine
months later, on July 1st, 1946, I was born in Manhattan, where my father
had resumed his law practice.

My collection of relics and records includes a treasured object created by
the second Priscilla, granddaughter of the first. Priscilla Sears Howes was
one of eleven children, according to a Howes family bible that recorded
over a century's worth of birth, death, and marriage dates. Shortly before
her marriage to August Fifield Holt in 1841, she embroidered the alphabet
on a tiny square of cloth, about three by four inches. The colors are all faded
now, and the sampler was placed in a wooden and glass frame many years

ago. According to a tag affixed to the frame, the sampler was passed down through the oldest child in each generation to Frank Stedman and then to Betty's sister Edith, who gave it to Betty at some point. The tag reads:

Sewn by Priscilla Sears Holt of New Sharon, Me. in 1840. Given to Gratia Burt Holt on her marriage, 1870. In turn, given to the Rev. Frank Holt Stedman on his marriage in 1909 and passed by him to his daughter on the occasion of her marriage in 1936.

I'm inclined to believe that the family bible gives the correct date for Priscilla's marriage, and that she was not yet a Holt in 1840. Nevertheless, the instinct for preserving the past is very much in evidence in the tag my grandfather affixed to the sampler. I remember seeing it for the first time at some point in the 1960s. Why do you suppose people save some things and not others? The oldest object in my possession that had belonged to the Stedmans is a child's small wooden potty chair, supposedly more than three centuries old. It sat in my parents' bedroom during my childhood, and now it sits in my upstairs hall.

SIX

Vernal Stedman's Letters
1833-1843

D URING OUR 1968 VISIT to Cape Cod Hill an elderly relative of
my mother's gave her some old family bibles and a wooden box,
about the size of a dictionary, which he extracted from a hodge-podge of
crumbling books and papers in an ancient barn. I, in turn, found the box
after my mother's death in 1991. The letters and mementos it contained had
remained undisturbed for over a century – or at least I like to think that
they had. My great, great grandfather, Vernal Stedman, the author of most
of the letters, was a traveler in his youth, just as Betty and her aunt Edith
were. I suspect that Vernal's parents, James Stedman and Betsey Richardson
Stedman, began saving the letters, and that Vernal's sister Olive eventually
became the family archivist responsible for adding more memorabilia and
preserving the box for posterity.

Nineteen-year-old Vernal writes home from Bangor, Maine, on October
the 20th, 1833:

Respected parents.

I now take my pen in hand to inform you of my health which is good at present, and hope these few lines will find you enjoying the same blessing. I have nothing of any great important to write but however I will give you a broken sketch of my transactions since I left home.

Evidently Vernal is traveling with another person, perhaps the Orin T. C Alden mentioned later in the letter, for he uses the pronoun "we." He and his companion have arrived in Bangor by stagecoach and are staying at an inn, where, as was customary in those days, travelers sometimes had to share rooms, even beds, with strangers.

...in the morning the gentleman which slept with the fellow spoken of lost three dollars. He had his thought about it as well [as] we, but there was nothing done about it. Orin T. C. Alden hired with a man for $15... [and] I hired with a man for a few days until I could get acquainted with the times but did not stay but 4 ½ days. From thence I started and went to Oldtown where I found all hands and in good health.

From Oldtown Vernal returned to Bangor, where he was hired as a carpenter at $16 per month and would receive "instruction" in the building trades. Vernal tells his parents that he expects to be home "the last of November" and adds in a postscript "I wish it could be so that you would come down with the horse and wagon so as to see the place and carry me home at that time." At nineteen, he is an independent young man, but not so independent that he won't attempt to get his parents to provide transportation home.

The letters are written on large sheets of heavy, cream-colored paper, about twelve inches in width by fifteen inches in length. The paper was folded in half, to make four pages, of which the last was left blank. With the blank side face down, and the letter held horizontally, the two sides were folded toward the center and then the top and bottom were folded inward, to create a small packet, about three by five inches. A red wax seal was affixed to seal it closed and the front was addressed to the recipient, in this case to "James Stedman, Center Sidney, Me." Postage stamps were not widely used as yet, but handwritten numbers on the letters indicate that the postage ranged from ten to twenty-five cents, large sums in those days. The letters often have stamped circular postmarks with the date and place.

We don't know what Vernal was doing for the next six years, but by 1839 he was traveling much further afield. Here is the first letter from those travels that was preserved:

> Key West, Dec 15th 1839
>
> *Dear Father and Mother. It is with pleasure that I take my pen to inform you of my health and prosperity if such it may be called. We left Bath* [Maine] *on Saturday the 16th ultimo* [i.e. last month] *and arrived here the 7th of December. The reason why we touched in here was because the wind was such that we could not get by the shoals that are near here. The Schooner left here the 11th for her destined Port. After we left the mouth of the river we had it pretty cold and squally four or five days I was some sick during this time but not so sick as I expected to be. Nothing of any great importance occurred on our passage. It was fifteen days after we left the river* [that] *we saw any land....*

In the early 1830s Key West was growing rapidly. It had become the site of a United States Naval Base and a designated port of entry in the 1820s, and from 1831 until the Civil War it was a major source of salt for American consumption. The Cuban cigar industry also spread to Key West, and so there must have been a great deal of money in circulation for building houses. Vernal writes:

> *I commenced work here on this Island the 12th for a Gentleman by the name of Amos Tift formerly of Connecticut. I hired for the small sum of thirty-five Dollars per Month and all found I should not have hired for so low wages but I have heard of so many that have gone to Texas and other Southern Ports that I feared I might not better myself by going farther. My employment mostly will be house building and steady employ as long as I see fit to stay. I like the appearance of my*

employer very much. As yet I board with him & he keeps me well though for beef we have turtles as a substitute. His cooks are colored and wait on us very politely. This island is about four miles long and one wide. The trees and other vines are all new to me, the cocoanut tree is very beautiful, beside many that I have not yet learned the names of. This island lies about half way between Cuba and Florida. Its population is about seven hundred. The people are supported mostly by the misfortunes of others. They are called wreckers for they go round these bays and reefs in search of wrecks. When they find one they take the goods in here and sell them at auction. They lawfully have [i.e. keep] one half. There was one merchant ship of New York wrecked here a few days before I arrived, her hull was turned the day before we came in. We were in plain sight of her. I hear that there is two wrecks just on this morning & boats are out after them. Thanksgiving day on the water [it was] as warm as midsummer is with you. There never has been such a thing known as frost here. I have heard tell of the steady sweet warm weather but I did not believe much about it but since I have been here it has been the pleasantest weather I ever knew. Everything is growing beautifully [and] we have bananas and oranges in plenty. A fourpence is called picayune [and] a ninepence is called a bit. I work within a stone's throw of the water I am as well as I ever was hearty as a bear. I have one hour to get my breakfast in and two hours for dinner so that I don't have to work but about half of the time. I have written in great haste for the mail boat is to start one hour sooner than I expected. The mail comes in here once in a month so that unless you write soon after receiving this I shall not get your letter short of two months. Do write all the particulars that you can think of and tell us who stood up with Alfred Bacon to his wedding. Please direct your letters to Key West by the way of Charleston South Carolina because that is the only regular line for our boat. Give my sincere respects to all inquiring friends tell them not to wait for me to write because I have nothing that would be interesting to them.

Yours truly,
Vernal R. Stedman

A letter Vernal sent six months later, on June 15, 1840, also from Key West, is written more carefully, in a somewhat more elegant script.

> *Respected Parents:*
>
> *It gives me much satisfaction to have the privilege of answering another letter from you which I read yesterday. It found me quite well as to health & tolerably well contented. I should be well contented were it not for the mosquitoes. They are very troublesome. I have slept under a mosquito bar this three months. Olive I was very sorry to hear that you was sick but I hope these few lines (which I am writing by lamp light) will find you & all the rest of the Family enjoying good health & a decent flow of spirits. The mail is to leave this place on the fifteenth of every month for Charleston but the mail did not come last month so that your letter was a long time getting here. I have hardly yet made up my mind whether I shall stay here all summer or not.*

Vernal reports that he is helping to construct a "fine house" for which he is being paid $2.50 per day, and adds that the work is much easier than in the north. In response to his family's queries, he describes the churches in Key West.

> *It is the Episcopalian doctrine that is preached here full of forms and ceremonies, would keep one hopping up & down every minute. Through the winter season there was a Methodist Prayer Meeting every Sabbath eve in a Gentlemans house* [and] *after I found it out I used to attend quite often. There was two or three that took an active part in the meeting. There was one staunch old fellow like old Capt. Butterfield* [who] *put it down by the word of mouth strong & heavy & helped them sing.*

Vernal goes on to describe the food—green corn from Havana, new potatoes, and watermelons "near two feet long," from which he saved some seeds to bring home to his brother, James Selden, whom the family called Selden. Many kinds of fish are caught "in almost any quantity that you wish." This letter uses all three available sides of the folded paper, and in it Vernal tells his family a little of the history of Key West.

> *This place is called the Key of the gulf. It has been settled about 15 years by the inhabitants which are now here but previous to this it was a complete rendezvous for pirates. Its location for that business must have been first rate for hardly a vessel can pass betwixt this and Havana through into the great Bay of Mexico or betwixt this & Florida without being seen. There is about 10 wrecking sloops that belong to this port that constantly lay outside up & down the reef waiting for vessels that go ashore or strike the hidden rocks (this reef extends near two hundred miles the entrance of the gulf). When a vessel gets anywhere on the reef twill not be long before assistance will be offered. If the Capt accepts assistance the sloops go along side and take out enough cargo to lighten her & get her off. They take the vessel cargo into warehouses built for the purpose and go through out the vessel and examine her by a committee. If she can be made sea worthy this is repaired if not she is condemned and burnt. The salvage or price the wreckers have for their trouble is settled by the court or rather by the Judge of the court. The wreckers frequently get on large ships ten thousand Dollars salvage, anyhow it generally costs the vessel one half of her cargo. Two wrecks were brought in last week. The cargo is always sold at auction to pay expenses. I have seen nice mahogany timber, cargoes of molasses from 17 to 20 cent per gal, also sugar and coffee.*

Vernal is clearly intrigued by the business opportunities in Key West, though he says toward the end of the letter that "I have had good chances to make money but dare not run any risks." He closes his letter by wishing his family "all the best of Heavens blessings, peace and happiness."

The next letter in chronological sequence is addressed to Vernal's uncle, Nathaniel Stedman, in Waterville, Maine. Written on July 17, 1840, it deals with "a little business of mine" which he wants his uncle to attend to involving some mortgage notes. The transactions seem rather complicated, but evidently Vernal felt that Nathaniel was the one to undertake them, for, as he says, "I am sorry to trouble you but I know of no other one that knows as well about it as you." He closes with some family news:

> I saw a man the other day from Arkansaw Territory he said that he worked with John Stedman for a considerable time. He said that John went to Texas last fall on horseback. I shall probably be back next spring. I do not work all the time on account of the heat. When I work I have three Dollars per day. Please write me as soon as you receive this & let me know the news. I have not heard from home since the first of April.
>
> Yours affectionately,
V. R. Stedman

Ten days later Vernal writes to his father to tell him that he ran into some acquaintances from Belgrade, Maine; like John Stedman, they had been in Texas. One of the acquaintances is on his way back to Maine and has agreed to transport the letter (which is stained and difficult to read) along with "two grey mixed round tailed coats and three gauze handkerchiefs." He adds that one of the coats "may fit you if it does please accept of it. If not sell them for what they will fetch." He bought the handkerchiefs for his mother and his sisters Olive and Mary at auction, no doubt one of the auctions he describes in his earlier letter. Vernal visited Havana on the fourth of July but says very little about what he saw: "I went over for the sake of a change and to have a resting spell & see the place which I was much pleased with." He goes on to describe an opportunity to make some additional money:

> Two or three days ago a large barque deep loaded with sugar and coffee touched on the reef in plain sight of this place. I was offered a sailors share if I would assist in getting her off. I accepted and we ten of us started out for her but to disappoint us when we got within a mile of her she floated which spoiled our fun. We might have shared 400 or 500 dollars....

The letter ends, as usual, with love to his grandmother and to "all inquiring friends."

January 16, 1841, finds Vernal still in Key West building houses for wages of $3 per day, although so many "down easters" from Maine have been arriving in Key West that the day rate has dropped to $2.50. Evidently the matter of Uncle Nathaniel and the notes has not yet been resolved, and so he asks his father to look into it. He closes by saying that he expects to return north in April or May since there won't be much work in the summer months, and besides, "I am rather short of clothes." This is a brief letter, for "my hands are stiff." He closes the letter: "Your unworthy son, V. R. Stedman."   Did Vernal return to Maine for the summer? The next letter, written almost a year later from New Orleans on December 26, 1841, suggests that he did, for he notes that he "wrote you a few lines from Bath [Maine] on Friday 5th. We sailed the next day at three P.M." This must have been November 5, for elsewhere in the letter he says that he had boarded a ship seven weeks earlier, and he has been spending his time "spinning street yarn" and "making chests drawers and wash stands on board this and another ship." The journey was longer than expected:

> We were becalmed several days near the berry Islands & plenty of natives came along side with fishes, Turtles & Conks, in exchange [for which] the Captain gave them meat. When we passed Key West and Sand Key 'twas about sunrise [and] we could see Sand Key light from the deck. I went aloft as high as I could get & could see the light house & dwelling house but nothing of Key West. From there we shaped our course for the mouth of the Mississippi but not being able to get the sun for two days we run too far to the northeast. So one day about noon we fell in with a pilot boat just off Mobile bar as we were heading straight on. From there we. . . tacked ship and again shaped our course for the river and in three days entered. Lucky for us that it was day time.

The decision to go to New Orleans may not have been a wise one, for there was not as much construction work available as he had hoped for, and he says "if I do not get a cabin to build which I have in view, I shall start for Mobile with a view of getting from there to Key West." The letter provides a fascinating glimpse of New Orleans as a busy trading port.

> *Mr. Abbot wished me when I wrote you to mention the prices of some particular articles. I will mention a few. Hay per hundred from one Dollar [to] one twenty five, potatoes from 1.12 and a half to 1.50 a barrel, Apples Greenings and russets 75 cts to 1.37 and a half per barrel. In fact all provisions are at the same ratio. Fowls per doz 2.25 to 3.75. There is more provision landed here every day from up river than ever grew in Maine in one season if I do not mistake. To say nothing about Cotton, Tobacco, Molasses, Rice. As near as we can calculate there are this very day over a thousand ships waiting, the most of them for cotton freights to rise; they occupy about three miles in length from four to six vessels side by side at each tier. This is a fine country for railroads for from here to the mouth of the river it is as level as the blueberry bog & I am told that it is the same for several hundreds of miles up the river. The color of the river is the same as the color of water standing in a clay pit. [It is] perfectly dense [and] you cannot see into it any farther than you can into the solid earth it self.*

Vernal writes to his father again on January 6th, 1842, with the news that he has left the ship he had been living on and hired for a month on another ship. He is "feeling very anxious to hear from you all" and writing in hopes that "if you write immediately after the reception of this I may get yours before I get through with my work."

> *My wages is thirty four Dollars per mo and I found that I have a fair chance to work and live on board [the ship]. I shall forget how it seems to live in a house after a while if I keep on in this way. I have not been in a Dwelling house since I left.... My work on board this ship is mostly on the cabin she has one spar that I intend to make. It is her fore yard its length is sixty two feet its diameter fifteen inches. It is computed that upwards of sixteen hundred died here the past summer of yellow fever. I can hardly meet a lady in the street without she is dressed in mourning.*

When it is convenient please send me some papers. I intend to send you and others some before long. There is a temperance society lately established here by the name of the Lafayette temperance society. I am told it prospers well but have seen but little of its proceedings in print. Write me all the news for I feel very anxious to hear. Give my respects to grandmother, to cousin Ann and the rest of my cousins.

Yours with much respect,
Vernal R. Stedman

Two months later, Vernal is on a sugar plantation in St. Mary's Parish, Louisiana, when he writes to his younger brother Selden on March 13, 1842. The letter contains many details about the money he has earned so far this winter, and then goes on to describe his trip one hundred and ten miles up the Mississippi River by way of several "Bayo"s. The river was "as level as a mill pond and cleared on both sides of the river from one to three miles back, which is as far back as can be cleared for swamps on these plantations."

I have counted a number of negroes houses from one to thirtyfive to a plantation [and] I have probably seen a hundred darkys planting cane at one time. On going down the river I saw two alligators — the stream was not over four rods wide where I saw one of them. He was on a big cypress log near the shore asleep. Our boat was nearly opposite him before he awoke [and] when he awoke he dove into the water. I had a good view of him, his length was some where from eight to ten feet or twelve feet. It was late in the afternoon when we passed down this bayo or I should probably have seen a full dozen of them.

Vernal ends his letter with some brotherly advice:

I hope Dear Selden you will write me as soon as you receive this and let me know the news. I hope I shall learn from you that you have been steady at school this winter & have learned a heap of knowledge for if you live you will see the need of it. I hope you will stay at home with

Pa this summer & plough a good part of the upper field & plant it to potatoes, that is the best thing you can do. In my opinion a rolling stone gathers no moss. My affections are to be tenderly remembered to sisters and brother likewise if I have any friend that inquires for me.

Yours from your affectionate brother,
Vernal R. Stedman

I wonder what Selden made of these admonitions. Perhaps he thought it was unfair that Vernal was in Louisiana observing alligators while he had to stay home and plow the upper field!

Over a year later, there is another letter from St. Mary's Parish, dated May 8, 1843. Vernal has been steadily employed building houses, for which he is very thankful. He reports that his health has been good, despite "the unhealthy climate and hardships… that is, being exposed to the sun and sometimes rain." Often he has to walk more that five miles a day to work and back in "the heat of the sun and sickly season." But his constitution is strong, for "people have often told me that I stood the sun equal to an alligator." Vernal is planning to return to Maine, and in anticipation thereof has shipped his tool chest and fourteen thousand pounds of sugar, worth about $560, to New York. He has insured his sugar for half again as much as he paid for it, so that "if it goes to the bottom 'twil fetch more than if it goes safe." He informs his parents that the merchants in charge of the sugar are the firm of Peck & Sayre and adds that "should any thing befall me on my passage home so that I never return, you will know how my business stands." After telling his parents that the last house he finished is called the best house on the Bayou and that he is well regarded in the building trade, he ends rather poignantly:

When I was at home last my mother told me that she was much disappointed in me for she had thought that I would make something [of myself]. Well, I must inform her that she is not the only one that is disappointed, for I used to think myself that I should be something although I have born these things in mind I find myself quite the same thing.

Yours truly, V. R. Stedman

Perhaps his mother was disappointed because she wanted her older son to remain in Sidney to carry on the family farm; going off to Key West and Louisiana may have seemed like shirking responsibility by nineteenth-century New England standards, although it is clear from the letters that many young men were doing so during the 1830s and 40s. But Vernal has acquired considerable skills as a carpenter, and if his shipment of sugar did arrive intact, he would have a valuable commodity to sell. As far as we can tell, he returned from Louisiana at the age of twenty-nine or thirty and settled in Boston in the carpentry trade.

When next we hear from Vernal, in a letter dated Boston, July 20, 1845, he is writing to his brother Selden in Center Sidney. The letter alludes to his earlier efforts to find Selden a position in the furniture business doing specialized labor constructing piano legs. Pianos had been imported from England until the 1820s, when Boston firms started manufacturing them. Evidently, the piano legs were produced by subcontractors, and Vernal, by now a skilled carpenter, has found employment in this business. He describes his most recent interventions on his younger brother's behalf:

> *I have secured for you a job on four square legs, which may last for all that can now be known, as long as you will want them. The job was procured through the influence of Mr. Frost our foreman. The legs are first pieced out to Mr. Burrell and then from him to you. He will pay you five dollars per set [after] he finds you shop room and furnishes you with legs... and suitable instructions concerning them. The shop is on Sea St. Follow Beach St. out from my Boarding place till you strike Sea St. & you are at the shop. It is a little over a third of a mile from my Boarding place. I expect you can Board with me if you like to. I pay two seventyfive for my Board the same that I paid all winter. Bartlett allowed me eighty Dollars for my horse. There is fair places where you can Board for two fifty, that's the lowest. If you board here I shall charge you but two fifty. Persons who are acquainted with making this kind of legs generally make two sets a week, some [make] more. I suppose for the first six months you will be able to average about 1½ sets per week without working as hard as you have this season so far. If such be the facts you will easily see that your prospects are rather flattering.*

You will have to furnish you own tools and bench [but] *I have already made some arrangements about a bench to hire or make worth 10 or 12 dollars which will be good enough to make legs on. My bench cost me thirtysix Dollars all mahogany except the legs which are black walnut* [with a] *front plank four inches thick. As for tools you will not want a great many 3 or 4 double ironed planes, some saws, files, scrapers, chisels, etc. If you can find any of my chisels at home you better take them.... Your tools I will buy for you. I will now write a few lines to Father to show him the reasons of your changing places, as I understand them, though you have no doubt told him.*

Vernal is now in his early thirties and permanently settled in Boston. He has married a young woman named Elvira Kaharl, and together they write a letter to his father on June 8, 1846. Vernal alludes to their recent return from Sidney by ship ("Elvira was rather seasick").

Our barrel present arrived safe and we have had a jolly time eating fried pork and hasty pudding. Elvira has met with a serious loss since our return in the death of her only sister. She was here on a visit seven days before she died [and] *four or five of the family have lain sick most of the time since our return. My grand object in writing is to invite you to come up here and see these children* [for] *we are rather lonesome. I want you to come up this month as it will be quite as agreeable to us & much more pleasant for you before the hottest summer weather. If you could send mother up here soon I could wait for you until about the 6 of July when I should like for you to be here. One thing I should like for you to see is the fireworks which it is said will be the best ever displayed on the continent. I want Olive and Mary both to come but I can't plan the time so well as you can your selves. Selden has commenced boarding with us this day. Good bye for tonight if I do not write more Elvira will.*

Elvira's postscript to Vernal's letter begins on the reverse page. It is a sad letter, a reminder of how frequently and quickly illnesses led to early deaths in those days.

...my time has been very much taken up since I came home, since my return sickness and Death has visited our family and taken an only Sister in the bloom of youth, although sick but one week. Her sufferings were great. She was deprived of her sense the most of the time caused by inflammation on the brain. Her disease was Scarlet Fever and Canker Rash. My feelings will not admit me to say much concerning her Death. I leave the subject to speak of the rest of the family. I expect soon to follow a little Brother to the other place prepared for all the living. I have just heard from home and him, he cannot live but a short time unless there is a change. There is great danger of the mortification, should that take place he cannot live but a short time. The rest of the family are very comfortable and will I think recover. I hope you will as soon as you receive this letter make arrangements to visit us I am very lonesome and I hope you will think of me and come up as soon as possible.

I would like to think that James and Betsey responded quickly to the lonely young couple and came to Boston for a visit. But June is a busy time on a farm, and they may have written back to say they could not come. None of their letters survive, alas, so we can only speculate.

SEVEN

Olive and Mary Stedman

W HAT FASCINATED ME about the wooden box containing Vernal's letters was the accidental nature of its contents. Why had these pieces of paper been singled out to be saved? Or was it sheer happenstance that a letter, or a pamphlet, or a scrap of newspaper founds its way into the box along with more important documents, while other equally revealing fragments of the past might have been used to light a fire or line a drawer or discarded because they seemed too unimportant to be preserved for posterity? The wooden box contains a few disconnected glimpses of the lives and interests of Olive and Mary, the two sisters who stayed home in Maine while Vernal traveled south to the Keys and beyond.

Olive seems to have spent most of her life in Sidney, except for a short period between 1846 and her marriage in 1849; the certificate recording her marriage is in the wooden box, along with a lacy greeting card in a beautifully embossed envelope addressed to her. At the age of twenty-nine, she left rural Maine to seek her fortune in manufacturing. She writes home to her parents on January 2, 1847 from Lowell, Massachusetts, a manufacturing city north of Boston, where she is working as a seamstress. She apologizes for not writing sooner, for

> *My time has been entirely taken up with needlework during the week, and Sunday mornings, when I am not too tired to go to meeting. I have my Sabbath school lesson to get or go without it. I hope you have not worried any about this child —she is well entirely. This is one reason why I have staid so long from home — my health is good here, better than it used to be, I can assure you. I feel very anxious about home. I hope you are getting along well enough without me however... I suppose you would like to know how I have prospered since I left home. It would take me a week to tell you all about my voyage and wanderings, prosperity and adversity since I left home. I will wait until I have a more convenient season. I suppose I should have done better to have worked in Augusta. I could have made as much. We have to work cheap here, [for] dressmakers are as thick as Uncle said the Methodists were in Ohio.*

Olive reports that she spent Christmas Day with Vernal and Selden in Boston; she left Lowell at seven in the morning and arrived in Boston at nine. She found her two brothers in their workplaces, where Selden had made a bureau for his employer "who said it was a nice one." In the evening she went to the Tremont Temple in Boston for a temperance lecture, which she describes as:

> *...not such a performance as you have down east, no no, it was grand. A young lady sung several beautiful pieces of music. When we could get through the crowd we went home... [several others] had collected to have a sing [and] they delayed it until we came home...we had a splendid time.*

Further along in the letter Olive says that she is trying to summon the courage to move to Boston, where she would be able to make more money than in Lowell. Vernal has offered to help her get established, just as he did for Selden. Olive ends her letter with thanks for Mary's gift of yarn, love to all, and these parting words:

> *I wish I knew how you were getting along if you need my help I will come home. I should like to look in upon you some evening when you are not thinking about your, Olive B. Stedman*

I suspect that Olive did not, in fact, move to Boston, since the wooden box contains no other letters from her and we know that she married Henry G. Williams of Sidney in May 1849.

The earliest item in the box is a torn scrap of paper dated Sidney, 24 May 1812, containing the last few lines of what seems to be a letter followed by poem of conventional nineteenth-century religious sentiments:

> *Return saith Christ thou precious youth,*
> *To me the way of Life, the Truth*
> *Partake my grace enjoy my Love*
> *And set your hearts on things above,*
> *Lord I would hear thy gracious voice*
> *And in thy service might rejoice....*

It continues in this vein for another twenty-five lines or so. The initials elaborately inscribed at the bottom of the page, "HR," suggest that the author, or copyist, may have been Olive's grandfather, Henry Richardson.

The wooden box also contains newspaper clippings containing sentimental poems (one has Olive's name handwritten on it) and seven tiny booklets, the size of small playing cards, with titles like "Conscious Effects of Faith," "Is it True?," "God With Us or, the CXXXIXth Psalm" and "No Sect in Heaven." These seem to have belonged to Olive, whose name appears written in pencil on some of them. Someone saved two copies of a piece of sheet music, dated 1858, with the hymn "Rest for the Weary," a clipping of a poem by John Whittier written in 1876 and a poem entitled "Sherman's March to the Sea." It would be interesting to know how significant the little booklets were to the Stedmans' spiritual lives.

Olive's younger sister Mary was referred to in later years as "Crazy Aunt Mary," and family legend has it that she that she used to sit in a sleigh in New Sharon and take imaginary journeys all year long. She never married and lived with family members for most of her life. I have a certain sympathy for Mary, who had literary aspirations which went unnoticed, I'm reasonably certain, except perhaps within the family circle. The wooden box contains a small lined copybook with elaborately engraved front and back covers bearing the name of its maker, one Edward Fenno of Water Street, Augusta Maine, with writing in Mary's hand from 1847-48. There is an essay entitled "The Sabbath," another called "The influence of associates," and then "Autumn," "Perseverance," and "Politeness." At the back of the copybook are penmanship exercises, with beautifully inscribed words for the letters of the alphabet, for example: Ammon, Banner, Camden, Emmons, Franklin, Gammon, Indiana, Jamestown, Kingsfield, Lincoln, Manchester, Nomination, Ohio, Penny, Queensdale, Romans, Smithfield, Templeton, Union, Vermont, Washington, Xenophon.

The last letter in this fragmentary story was written nearly twenty years after Olive's letter from 1847. Mary writes from Hill, New Hampshire., to her seventy-four year old mother, now a widow and still living in Center Sidney. In Mary's description of the letter-writing habits of the people around her, one is reminded of how time-consuming this activity was in the days when people wrote letters.

May 14, 1866

Dear Mother,

I thought I would write to you this time for fear you would think I used partiality, and I knew that you are always pleased to get a letter from Vernal, and would likewise be glad to get one from me.

It is a most splendid day, and I have been to Church this forenoon (am feeling very well for me) and though I would write you in "still hours" while the rest is in bed not so much because I wish to be quiet but I thought I would try what they teach here, that a person can write better on an empty stomach. I have known some of them to go without eating dinner if they have letters to write in the afternoon and if they eat dinner at 2 to write late in the evening. But I am afraid I shall not be inspired for I am thinking of dinner all the while. I imagine you would if you had only two meals and knew you could have nothing more. I have often thought of you and wondered how you would get along.

There is an old lady here nearly as old as you are, an "old maid" that has lost the use of her limbs and cannot walk a step or use her hands much. She thinks it [was] occasioned by poison given by a person to kill her. She keeps a girl to wait on her. I am doubtful if she is ever cured and I guess the Dr. thinks so too but he will keep her because she has plenty of money.

I should like very much to be at home today and see how you all get along without me. But if I was there and you knew it I shouldn't have the fun of knowing…but enjoy yourselves as fast as you can for you won't have the privilege long. I expect to be able to come home by the end of the month.

I got a letter from Elvira last week she said Vernal could not leave before the middle of the month to visit me and she meant to come with him if possible, so I shall look for them this week.

The letter also contains some medical advice, and I infer from the earlier allusion to the doctor and the old lady that Mary may be residing at a sanitarium or hospital in New Hampshire. She offers her mother a "fomentation" that may be good for the hips, stomach, or side, or when "your food distresses you."

I have tried it all this week, at night on going to bed, for my left side that troubled [me] about bringing a long breath, and this week I am to try it over my liver in the forenoon. Wet a cloth in hot water or cold if you please, fold it several times, and apply it to the part affected covered with several thicknesses of dry cloth, then hold a jug of hot water or a soapstone over it for 15 or 20 minutes and it will answer just as well as a mustard draft and a great deal better for you would take cold even if you wash the place after in cold water, don't be discouraged but follow it up. I think it would be the best thing for your hips or back that I can think of, for I don't see as I am a bit clearer headed or can think of anything more to write than I should have if I had a good hearty dinner....

The letter resumes after dinner.

I feel better now, have made a good dinner of mush bread and squash pie. The other day we had some roast veal stuffed, real nice, we have had dandelion greens and spinach several times and asparagus. I hope you are much better than you were when I heard from you last. . . I feel and think a great deal more about you than I can express. Hoping to see you soon, I am with much love, the same,

Mary

Poor Mary. She remembers how happy her mother was to receive Vernal's letters, and tries in her own sad way to emulate him, but the letter reveals a much more circumscribed life than Vernal's adventurous and prosperous one.

Mary's girlhood literary aspirations evidently continued into her later years, as indicated by another item preserved in the wooden box. It is a collection of sheaves of lined paper, bound with ribbons, entitled:

"The Literary Gem"
Published by the Pemigewassett Literary Association
Jan. 28, 1868,
Vol. 1. No. 9.
Edited by
Mary E. Stedman
Motto
"I'll try"
Terms
Your Patience and forbearance

Its contents include "little Gems" like "Real difficulties are the best cure for imaginary ones, because heaven helps us in the real ones and makes us ashamed of the others." There are also poems, "Musings and Memories," and a "Dear Gem" letter about "wimmins rites" (a pun on "women's rights?), a monologue in dialect in which a woman recounts the way she caught a much-sought-after rich man's son. Was the thirty-nine-year-old Mary the sole author of all these Gems, I wonder, or were Polly Peppergrass and Dolly Doughsticks the *noms de plume* of other aspiring writers? Did my grandfather Frank Stedman, who was born six years after the "Literary Gem" was published, have a warm spot in his heart for his Aunt Mary, and if so, is that why he named his second daughter after her? My mother once told me that she was named after "dotty" Aunt Mary and another aunt named Elizabeth Holt, who will make a very brief appearance in the next two chapters.

EIGHT

Kitty Holt and her family

T HE LARGE CARDBOARD BOX in which I keep all of the things my great aunt Edith gave me during and after my years at Radcliffe yields new discoveries each time I open it. Just recently I came across a tiny Book of Common Prayer (the prayer book of the Episcopalian church). It is inscribed as follows:

> *Martha –*
> *From Aunt Edith*
> *10 January 1966*
> *your grandmother's prayer book*

The inscription was an error – Edith meant to write "your great grandmother," for the prayer book had been give to her mother Gratia ("Kitty") Holt Stedman in 1902, according to another inscription on the flyleaf. Edith's actions were seldom without significance, and I suspect that the gift was meant as a reminder of my Episcopalian heritage. If I were psychoanalytically inclined, I might say that her conflation of me and my mother ("your grandmother's prayer book") was an unconscious return to the early 1940s, when, in a troubling development for Edith and her brother, the Episcopal minister, my mother was being courted by my Jewish father.

I have always wished I knew more about Kitty Holt Stedman, if only because her portrait hangs on my dining room wall. Kitty is the link between the Holt and Stedman families. She was the third in her line to be named Gratia; her aunt, Gratia Ann Holt and her grandmother, Gratia Burt Holt shared the name, which has been passed on through seven generations of Holt-Stedman descendants. Kitty and her two younger sisters, Mary and Elizabeth, were well-educated women for their day. Their father, Augustus Holt, had been a bookseller for a time, and the family home was filled with books. They read the *Atlantic Monthly* and *Harpers* and *The Boston Transcript* regularly, and Kitty was also an accomplished musician. She left Maine to study at the New England Conservatory of Music in Boston and there, at the age of twenty-three or twenty-four, she met George Stedman, Vernal's son. We get a tiny glimpse of their courtship from this letter, written by George in 1870:

> *My darling,*
> *I forgot last night to say that Thursday Evening I want to go to the Lodge, as there will be an interesting occasion at that time and I've invited my Uncle to come out—so if you will make it Friday or Wednesday it will be better for me – will you drop me a line or step in, if uptown near Lawrence and Co—letting me know when it will be most convenient, all around, for me to call— Yours as ever,*
>
> > *GHS*

The handwriting is beautiful, and George's initials are inscribed with a flourish. How unfortunate that the letter doesn't reveal more.

The Holts, like the Stedmans, were an old New England family. A cousin of Kitty's, Emily Burt Holt Berry, who was blessed with a remarkable memory, composed a lengthy memoir in 1932, toward the end of her long life. She describes the travels of the Holts during the mid-nineteenth century.

In 1784, just after the Revolutionary War, my grandfather Fifield Holt, was born. His parents were then living in Nashua, N. H. Fifield Holt obtained an education at various schools…and graduated from Middlebury College, Vermont, in 1810. His ambition was to be a Congregational Minister; he probably earned his way through college by teaching school and, in the course of his travels, he met Gratia Burt, also engaged in teaching.

They were married in due time; he was installed as pastor of the Congregational Church of Bloomfield, later called Skowhegan in Maine. It was his duty to do a certain amount of missionary work in Franklin County; he sometimes preached in New Sharon and Farmington, making friends in those places. They lived very happily there; five children were born to them. Augustus, the oldest, was born in 1816, with Fifield as a middle name. Gratia Ann followed in 1818. Next came Mary Burt in 1821 and Elizabeth in 1825. My father, Joseph, was the youngest, born in 1828. A baby had been born and died to whom they had given the name of Gratia's father; when the youngest one came he was given the same name, Joseph Burt.

Fifield died young, leaving Gratia to raise their young family. Here, again, is Emily's memoir:

In 1830 grandfather Fifield Holt died from an attack of erysipelas for in those days its treatment was not understood, by country doctors at least. My grandmother, Gratia Burt Holt, was at that time a very good-looking woman with brown hair and eyes. She was quick, energetic, a fine cook and a good manager. She owned a small farm and a very good house. Here she was left with five children, ranging in age from two to fourteen. She took the new minister, Mr. Hathaway, as a boarder, set her fourteen-year-old son, Augustus Fifield, to running the farm and set about educating and supporting her family.

Augustus would have liked to follow in the footsteps of his father and he wanted to be a minister but he was obliged to carry on the farm, get what education he could and help his mother to bring up the other children. Later, he became interested in Priscilla Howes of New Sharon, married and raised a large family. He was always interested in education, politics and all good causes.

In her autobiography, Edith muses that:

...of all my ancestors, the one that I would most like to have known was my own maternal grandfather, Augustus Fifield Holt, a man very much after my own heart...

I don't think the stony pastures of New Sharon were his cup of tea, and as soon as he could he seems to have left the farm in charge of a hired man and gone on the road for a textbook house. He was interested in all kinds of causes. The principal one was working on the underground slave railway, and he became a friend of William Lloyd Garrison. I have a letter that he wrote when he was quite an old man from Elmira....

Edith had typed out a copy of the original letter, now lost, in which Augustus Holt describes an incident that had happened many years earlier when he was involved with the Underground Railroad. It was addressed to her mother in 1876 or 1877. Had Kitty heard the story before? Or was her father recounting it to her for the first time? The letter reads:

Arlington House,
Coburg, Ont.

My dear:

I am spending this delightful day at this excellent house where in all regards I am perfectly comfortable and where the dear ones of home with me should be content. It was to this spot in 1844 that Bro. Langdon, Ed. Messer and I sent a band of fugitives of 39 from Elmira, hotly pursued by slave hunters from the south.

It was a stirring scene as on that clear star-lit night at the quiet hour of 12 our two companies of fugitives, one let by Bro. Messer, the other by a colored preacher coming from different point 9 miles distance both met at the exact hour. Bro. Langdon and I came from Elmira 9 miles in a carriage well filled with supplies for their journey. We rode to the appointed spot and gave the signal to which Messer from behind a fence responded in person and blowing a whistle, a like answer came from a swamp a mile away, bringing the other band.

We distributed among them a good supply of clothing and making up to each $5.00 and to each of the pilots $10.00 which I had begged from friends in Elmira.

Then a Virginia newspaper was produced containing an advertisement of the company giving a minute description of each individual and as it was read, each responded to his real name. Then all knelt down on the grassy carpet by the way side and [after] Bro. Langdon, in such a prayer as I hardly ever heard before or since, commended them to the care of the fugitive's Friends, they started on their way in double file singing a plaintive negro melody. They traveled by night on the public roads, sheltered and cared for by day by some good friends who kept the underground R. R. Station until they reached the neighborhood of Oswego, then full of slave catchers.

A small schooner was chartered which came around to the cove where they went on board and the free winds of Heaven wafted them to this part [i.e. Canada] where under Victoria's flag they found that protection which the Stars and Stripes could not then afford. We used to get occasional letters from them and of their prosperity. Since the war doubtless many of them have returned. I have just seen [the play] Uncle Tom's Cabin that brings all these scenes up fresh to mind. Most who were actors in the stirring events of those days have passed away. I was a young man of 27 but now am among the few old men of that day. I hope, when you have leisure you will read Henry Wilson's History of the Rise and Fall of the Slave Power in America. No other history gives a truthful account, in fact no one else had undertaken it.

I go tomorrow to Peterburo, Toronto, then to Hamilton, London, Chatham and around via St. Thomas to Buffalo and thence home. Write me at the continental Hotel, Buffalo, N. Y. On rec't of this, give my very best regards to M. and Mrs. Weston and the family, your father,

Augustus F. Holt

You can see why this letter would have captured Edith's imagination. The only other documentary record regarding Augustus's activities is a beautifully engraved invoice, from a butter and cheese business he seems to have undertaken in New Sharon. This may have been one business of many that failed, for Edith comments that "My brothers knew my grandfather and he seems to have been great fun, but certainly not a financial success."

NINE

Gratia Holt and the Journey West
The 1850s

WHILE AUGUSTUS REMAINED behind in Maine, his brother and sisters joined the westward expansion. As Emily Burt Holt Berry's memoir explains,

> In the middle of the nineteenth century Minnesota Territory was having a boom. My parents, Joseph and Julia, were married on April 1, 1853 and went to a place sixteen miles North of Minneapolis opposite a town called Anoka. Government land was taken according to the Homestead Law. A log house was built near the bank of the Mississippi River and a new pioneer life began. Settlers rushed in regardless of the fact that thousands of Sioux Indians were still living in this region.

Joseph's sisters, Elizabeth and her husband William Babbitt, and Mary and her husband Edmund Messer, had also moved to the Minnesota Territory, leaving their mother in Maine with Augustus. But at some point in the 1850s, Gratia Burt Holt, now nearly seventy years old and the beloved matriarch of this far-flung family, joined the others in Minnesota. Thus it came about that she wrote this letter to Kitty, who was about ten years old at the time. There were probably many more letters, but Kitty saved this one and it came into Edith's possession; perhaps she found it after her mother's death, just as I found my parents' letters.

My dear grand-daughter Gratia,

When I returned from your uncle Joseph's last week I was very happy to find a letter from you. I wish you would get your Parents to write me often. I am so glad to get letters from home. Glad to hear you are all well and doing so well. Hope you all will improve your time at school to best advantage and be some of the best scholars there is in school. Perhaps in a very few years you will come out to Minnesota to teach school. You would like to do so if your Father should move out here. I wish I could go down cellar with you and the other children and get some apples and cider. Think you would find me some good ones and I would enjoy eating and drinking with you.

Uncle Wm. has been out and marked out a claim for me and Uncle Ed has taken out lumber to build me a Shanty. What will your Father and Mother say to that, wont they laugh at the thought of my living in a Shanty. I am a very old lady now and cannot go about as I used to. I am going to send you children some Sunflower seeds they are very large double flowers as handsome as anything you ever saw, they grow very tall here.

Tell your father there is much inquiry about him whether he is coming out this spring. I wish he would write and tell me. Uncle Wm. talks of going to NY and Boston this month. I shall prevail on him to visit Maine if I can. I know you would all be glad to see him. I want you should be very good children and make your parents and friends happy.

I wish you children could all come and see us. We should be so glad to see you all here. I think you would have a fine time with your cousins. Your uncle Ed is gone out to Hutchinson about 70 miles west where they think of moving in the spring. They have a very pretty house here it is all finished but your uncle thinks they can go there and make considerable money by doing so. We all wish your Father was here and would go and make a claim. There is a good many going out there this spring.

Your aunts, uncles, and cousins send love to you all. We have had a very cold winter indeed more so than anyone here has seen in Minnesota. I am glad you have a team of your own to draw your wood I wish we had some of your wood or some like it we don't have such good wood here as you do. Write all of you very soon

to your Grandmother

I am trying to imagine Gratia reinventing her life in a shanty in the far West at the age of seventy. How many letters back and forth from Maine to Minnnesota preceded her decision to move? Despite her yearning for the wood and apples of Maine, she accepted her role as the stalwart backbone of an extended family.

The story of the Minnesota settlers resumes in Emily's narrative:

> *The Babbitts and Messers bought land in Minneapolis, making their home in that rapidly growing town. Frequent visits were made back and forth. Grandmother Gratia Holt was helpful with all the families, especially so with my mother, Julia, who had been teaching for about ten years. Grandmother Holt was an unusually fine housekeeper. She seemed as fond of my mother Julia as of her own daughters; this happy state always existed. I have never known another family so united.*

In hopes of keeping her family united, Gratia urged her son Augustus to move out to what then seemed to be "The Promised Land," although the promise proved illusory. Emily explains:

> *In 1857 came the "Financial Crisis" which ruined my father and hundreds of others. Large debts had been incurred; real estate was a drug on the market. My father was not one of those shrewd Yankees who lie low and finally emerge rich in the end. He had been borrowing money at 2% a month and debt was always a serious thing in our*

family. He prided himself on his honorable dealings and proceeded to give up his property and settle with his creditors.

. . .

Father persuaded Uncle Ed [Edmund Messer] to accompany him on a trip South with a view to finding a warmer climate for a future home. They were quite delighted with the country, especially the tablelands of eastern Tennessee.

Although Joseph Holt and Edmund Messer were eager to settle in a new part of the country, Edmund's wife Mary refused to leave Minneapolis, so Joseph and Julia set out on their own:

My father selected a site in the Tennessee mountains, not too far from Nashville and, I suppose, made a small down payment on it. He came back full of enthusiasm and began preparations for the change. My aunt, Mary Holt Messer, had learned by experience to take the management of her family finances into her own hands and refused to go south, holding on to their Minneapolis property which became valuable in later years.

If I am not mistaken, it was in 1859 that we and our belongings traveled by steamboat down the Mississippi River, ending our journey at Nashville. My father bought a big wagon and a pair of oxen, carrying us and our possessions up the mountain.

. . .

During our second year there, rumors of war began... A Confederate official or sympathizer came and warned my father and the other settlers, saying they must either join the Confederate Army or leave the country. They did not take it seriously. Of course, there were heated discussions but nothing was really done until a second officer came and threatened that, if they did not join the Confederate Army, they would be hung. Preparations were immediately made for a hasty departure for the North. Before then my brother, about a year younger than I, sickened and died. His death was caused by one of the diseases which prove fatal so often and is such a sad bereavement to the family.

The furniture and books, so highly valued by the owners, were packed in good order and left in the house; they were never heard of again.

Emily, who was six years old at the time, has vivid memories of the long journey back to Minnesota by covered wagon. They traveled by back roads to avoid notice, rejoicing when they finally crossed the Ohio River and were safely out of Confederate territory. Shortly after their arrival in Minnesota, Joseph enlisted in the First Minnesota regiment. He was thirty-three and eager to fight on behalf of the North. Emily recalls:

We arrived in Minneapolis after a long journey. On Monday morning, my mother began a year of teaching there. We made our home with my Aunt Elizabeth Babbitt. My grandmother Holt was also there but she had been thrown from a sleigh and broken her hip. Confined to her bed, she had become blind from reading so steadily while in a recumbent posture, they thought. My sister Alice was attacked by a contagious disease, scarlet fever, I think, and died at the age of four and a half. It was a hard blow for all of us to have her taken so suddenly. Henceforth I was an only child.

My father was assigned to McClellan's army which was trying so unsuccessfully to capture Richmond. At first "Little Mac" was extremely popular both with his soldiers and with the President and his followers. As time dragged on and nothing was accomplished, everyone became dissatisfied. Conditions were terrible. The countryside was a vast swamp. The soldiers were wading through water, exposed to an unfamiliar climate, without proper food; sickness followed as a matter of course.

. . .

Bowel troubles were disabling the men. My father suffered from this and from rheumatism and was sent to a hospital. Finally, he became an inmate of the Finley Hospital, in the environs of Washington, D. C., and as they saw no prospect of his being able to return to his regiment, he received an honorable discharge. Upon his discharge, my father went back to the old family home on Cape Cod Hill in New Sharon, Maine.

After the close of my mother's school in Minneapolis, she took my grandmother and me to join my father in Maine.

Thus in 1863, Gratia, in her old age, returns to New Sharon, the home of her ancestors.

In those days the railroad facilities were very crude compared with present day service; long distances without change of cars was unknown. Our first stop was at Bloomington, Illinois, to visit the Messer family. There was a small misunderstanding about the arrival of trains and we were put off at a small station, entirely closed, in the early hours of the morning in a snow squall. My grandmother was moved from train to train in a large wicker chair. Two trainmen or helpful passengers carried the chair, with her in it, to its destination, for wheeled chairs were not then available. Our relatives soon rescued us from our uncomfortable predicament, none the worse for our adventure.

. . .

My father met us with a team at Farmington, Maine; then we had a ride of nine miles to New Sharon where we were welcomed by Uncle Augustus Fifield Holt and family.

When the wandering branch of the Holt family returned to the family homestead in Maine, Emily met her cousin Kitty for the first time.

Gratia Burt Holt, always called Kitty, was a very pretty girl of sixteen and a great admirer of her Uncle Joseph who seemed a romantic character just home from the War.

Emily's memoir goes on for many more pages, but there are no further references to her grandmother or her cousin Kitty. She recalls sledding down Cape Cod Hill in New Sharon, climbing trees in the summer in the old orchard, and exploring the woods of Maine with her many cousins. Edmund Messer went on to have a successful career as an artist, and eventually, as the director of the Corcoran Art School in Washington D. C.

In his portrait of Kitty, which I look at every evening at dinner, I can see sees a strong family resemblance shared by her daughter Edith and her granddaughter Betty.

Gratia Burt Holt's story is told in another way by the anonymous author of a printed obituary that Kitty kept with the letter she had received as a child. It reads as follows:

IN MEMORY

Of

MRS. GRATIA HOLT

Who departed this life at New Sharon, Maine, February 14, 1874

aged eighty-eight years.

The subject of this notice was born at Westmoreland, N.H., January 16th, 1786, where she lived until her marriage in 1815, with Rev. Fifield Holt, pastor of the Congregational Church in Bloomfield, (now Skohegan), Maine.

In all the cares and pleasures, the joys and trials of a minister's life, in a comparatively new country, she was truly a "helpmeet." For sixteen years they were permitted to live and labor together there. Then the Master had need of him and he was called to the reward of the faithful, at the age of forty-six years.

This mysterious providence well nigh crushed her, and but for her five fatherless children she must have sunk beneath the blow. The widow's God sustained her and gave unto her many years of great usefulness, not only to her own family, but wherever duty called. The home of the poor and sorrowful, the bedside of the sick and dying were no strange place to her. The stranger and the fatherless who so often enjoyed her hospitalities in hours of suffering, will rise up and call her blessed.

The house of God was her delight, the hour of prayer a precious season to her. Morning and evening her little family were called around her and committed to the care of her covenant-keeping God. The family altar was sustained by her until in the providence of God, and in answer to her prayers, her eldest son was fitted to conduct family worship.

In 1842 she left the place so dear to her and removed with her son to New Sharon, Me., but still retained her relation with the church in Bloomfield she loved so well.

The succeeding twenty years she devoted to her scattered family, going wherever she could do the greatest good.

In the spring of 1862, in Minnesota, she was thrown from a cutter, fracturing or dislocating the hip, rendering her ever after a cripple.

In 1863, her eyesight failing, she returned to her home in New Sharon, desiring to look once more upon the friends and scenes of her earlier days. Her dark hour soon followed, and for ten long years her eyes were closed. But her Christian life shone brighter and clearer as the physical wasted away. Her unfaltering faith and trust were only equaled by her patience and submission. In all these years of decrepitude and blindness, never a murmuring word escaped her lips. It was enough for her that her Heavenly Father gave her the cup to drink. It was all right.

For two years she was confined to her bed, helpless, her mind wasting away as did her body, until a bare shadow of her former self remained. Though the events of the present were a blank to her, the memory of earlier years never failed. For years she longed for the summons to call her home, but was willing to wait God's time. Her end was peace.

Her remains were taken to Skowhegan, thereby gratifying her long cherished wish to be laid beside those of her husband, and among the dear friends of their happy days.

TEN

Betty's Childhood in Texas
1921-1931

WHEN MY BROTHERS AND I were children my mother loved to tell us stories about her childhood, stories that took on a mythic quality as they were repeated over and over. Interestingly, when I made an oral history tape with her brother Frank, several years after Betty's death, he remembered most of the same details. The stories were often part of family evenings, called "Friday night specials" when we'd gather around the fireplace and indulge in roasted marshmallows and other treats. I seem to recall that my mother also made a short-lived attempt to incorporate Bible stories into those evenings. Much later, when I was in college, I became fascinated by English and New England Puritanism, and wished that I'd learned more about the Episcopalian side of my family during those early years.

My mother's move to Texas at the age of seven loomed large in her chronicle of her childhood. Like the Holts' move to the Minnesota Territories seventy years earlier, it was part of the migration from New England to the open spaces of America, and like the Holts, Frank Stedman and his family would return to New England. As my grandfather moved his family from one small Texas town to another every few years, the family became intensely close – this closeness is everywhere apparent in Betty's letters from Spain. The frequent moves also helped shape Betty's personality; she was outgoing and gregarious, unfailingly courteous without ever being stuffy, and, as she once told me, she was never, ever bored.

Betty's oral history was a "letter" to her grandchildren that retold the stories I remembered from those Friday nights.

When we arrived in Texas we were considered rather odd, and were often teased and referred to as "northern children." Our father spoke with a broad New England "a" and wore a clerical collar; in the land of Southern Baptists and Methodists he was regarded as a "damned Yankee." Since there were so few Episcopalians, Father also had churches in Albany and Spur, two small towns. When we moved to Cisco, he had six small mission churches. They weren't self-supporting parishes, and so he would cover three each Sunday. We had bought one of the first Model T Fords, and once Daddy took me with him on his Sunday trip. We stopped for lunch in a hotel, and I was so disappointed because it was a very hot day and Daddy ordered me a lettuce sandwich with sugar and vinegar—not my idea of a restaurant meal!

Mother would bake six loaves of bread every week. We'd eat one loaf while it was still warm, and the six loaves would never last the whole week. She taught my sister Edith to cook and sew, but I was always off playing with the boys. I read about knights and ladies, King Arthur and the Round Table, and every Saturday I'd dress up. I recall Mother saying to Edith, "After all, you can't ask a pirate to wash dishes...." I used the lid of the boiler for a shield and poor Frank, being the youngest, had to use the lid of the chamber pot for his shield. When we played pirate I'd turn Mother's sewing table upside down and tie a piece of cloth to one of the legs for a sail. I was always the captain and Frank was my willing lieutenant.

In 1925, after two years in Cisco, we moved to Big Spring, in western Texas. It was a desert region on the edge of the frontier, with sage brush and mesquite trees. It would get up to 110 degrees in the summer and we would have terrible dust storms—sand storms, really. The sand would drift under the doors, into the sugar bowl, even, and the storms would last for several weeks. Mother's friends told her that instead of fighting the sand, she should play bridge until the storms ended and then give the house a complete cleaning. So that is what she did. The town was in the midst of an oil boom, and I remember there was a little section called Humbletown, where the employees of Humble Oil lived. The oilmen were the parishioners in my father's little churches; in one church, there was only one oilman who donated a pew—and so he sat during the services while everyone else stood. These oilmen were adventurers, rather like the pirates and knights of our games.

Just when we'd settled into a place, it seemed as if we had to move on. We moved to Taylor, Texas, in 1928, about six weeks before the end of my sophomore year in high school—that was hard for me. Even though we had lived in Texas for seven years, we were still considered strange northerners, particularly since nearly everyone else was a Methodist, Baptist, or member of the Church of Christ, and the only other clergy who wore clerical collars besides my father were the Catholic priests. The other kids weren't always kind to us, I'm sorry to say. The Baptist church was right across the street from our church and we would go out and play croquet after the 9:30 service on Sunday mornings. Our games became pretty noisy and the Baptists, who had their service at 11:00, would complain. They became even more indignant when Daddy started a Sunday afternoon baseball league for the neighborhood kids; they called him "the leader of the lawless element in town." Not long afterwards, one of the Baptist ministers ran away with the head of the church choir, leaving behind two large families. So much for self-righteous morality!

The organist at my father's church was dying of cancer, so she gave me a quick course in church organ playing and at the age of 14 or 15 I took over. Mother was the head of the women's guild and Edith ironed the vestments. Sometimes Frank would take a turn at playing the organ, *but when he hit a wrong note he'd go back and start again, confusing the congregation no end. So the job of playing the organ fell mostly to me.*

The Stedmans traveled often during those years in Texas. In 1924 they made their first trip back to Ohio to see Marian's parents, and in the summer of 1929 they traveled in a new car, a "Whippet," all the way to Maine for a long visit.

> *We went through Arkansas, Tennessee, up the Shenandoah Valley to Washington, and from there to Philadelphia, New York, Boston, and Maine. I had left Maine as a child of seven in 1921, and it was wonderful to be back on Cape Cod Hill.*

I have sometimes wondered if the family was tempted to remain in Maine, after traveling all that way. They returned to Texas, however, and by the following year, Betty continues,

> *The Depression had begun by the time I finished high school in 1930 and I wanted very much to go to college. It happened that the wife of the Bishop of Texas, Mrs. Temple, and three of her friends had created a scholarship to Wellesley College in Massachusetts in memory of a classmate who had died. It was Mrs. Temple's turn to choose the scholarship recipient. She asked Father if I would like to go to Wellesley and of course I said I did. To qualify, I would have to take a forty-day course in third year Latin by correspondence from the University of Texas and prepare for the College Board examinations, which very few students took in those days. Our little town had no library, but we had a family friend who would let me borrow books, and I went to work at an office in town to earn some money. Each week my brother would bet me a banana split that I couldn't finish the week's worth of Latin lessons and each week I won the bet. We'd go to the drugstore and with great ceremony he would buy a banana split for 25 cents. I'd have one bite and then he'd finish the rest. This ritual continued until I had finished the Latin course.*

Betty had taken Spanish in high school – the only foreign language Taylor High offered. After she graduated, she wanted to keep up her Spanish while learning Latin. At the time,

> *Taylor had a white school, a black school and a Mexican school— three schools for a population of 3,000! After I graduated my Spanish teacher would invite me to her house and have me talk to a Mexican boy to improve my skills. He was supposed to correct me, but he was much too polite to do so.*
>
> *After a year, on a day when it was 120 degrees I went to San Antonio dressed in a "pajama suit" to take my College Boards. The examiners issued us each a big blotter because we perspired so much.*

By the spring of 1931 Frank had graduated from Taylor High School and Betty had passed her College Board exams and was ready to begin college at Wellesley. It was time for the family to leave Texas for good:

> *Daddy's churches, along with the rest of the country, were affected by the Depression and he hadn't been paid his $100 a month salary for about six months. Daddy, Mother, Edith, Frank and I took turns driving through the night for two and a half days without stopping until we got to Cincinnati. All we had with us was $50. We stayed there one night, and then another with Mother's family in Delaware, where my grandfather was still practicing medicine (he would die a few years later, in 1935). Then we drove for a day and a half straight to Braintree, to Uncle Bert Stedman's house. We arrived with 20 cents left from the $50.*
>
> *After staying for six weeks with Uncle Bert and his family we moved into a house in Jamaica Plain in Boston, and I began my freshman year at Wellesley College. Frank got a job at the Boston Public Library to help with my college expenses; later, when I finished college, I helped with his.*

During Betty's first year at Wellesley she missed the open spaces of the West; the white houses and green lawns and tall trees seemed suffocating. She also found it difficult to keep up with the other students, for most of them had gone to much larger high schools. Spanish, the subject she liked best, was especially difficult. Despite the efforts of her high school Spanish teacher and the boy from the Mexican school, she had never been in a classroom in which Spanish was actually spoken. As Betty recalled years later,

> *I started out with an "F" and the teacher was unsympathetic when I asked for help. That made me mad, so I worked very hard and by the end of the year I was caught up.*
>
> *We had to take a course in Bible, one half year on the Old Testament and one half on the New Testament. I remember that the teacher was a Quaker lady who had been a missionary in China. She wore a high white collar and was very dignified. The course was quite a revelation, especially to those of us who had been reared in religious families. The Roman Catholic girls would become very upset and would go to the priest to be absolved after class. The Jewish girls, on the whole, found it interesting. We Protestant girls were asked to write out our creed, which I found very difficult. I had been an Episcopalian all my life, but I had never had to explain why or what it meant.*

I paused over this paragraph after I transcribed it, for it occurred to me that these "Jewish girls" were the first Jews Betty had ever met. I wonder if they really did find the Bible course "interesting." Perhaps they resented having to spend a semester studying the New Testament; perhaps they were very much aware of the differences between them and the Protestant and Catholic girls.

Betty's account continues:

> *After freshman year I worked at an Episcopal summer camp. When I returned at the end of the summer I found a letter waiting for me from Mrs. Temple saying that the Depression had hit Texas hard and the cotton crop had failed, and so she wouldn't be able to pay my tuition that year. My Aunt Edith was working at Radcliffe by then, and so I asked her if I could apply for a scholarship and*

transfer to Radcliffe. She said I couldn't because she was on the scholarship committee and it would constitute a conflict of interest. Sadly, I told Wellesley I wouldn't be returning, but the Dean told me to give them a week or so and they would see what they could do. Wellesley was wonderful; they gave me a full tuition scholarship and put me into a brand new cooperative house where we all had work assignments which lowered the cost of room and board.

Betty's gratitude to Wellesley endured to the end of her days; she attended every reunion, donated to the annual fund, and joined the Alumni Association and the Wellesley Friends of Art. Her life might have turned out very differently had Edith behaved differently. I have sometimes wondered if my mother's complicated feelings about her fascinating aunt can be traced to that time, and I have always wondered, too, if Edith used her connections to help me get into Radcliffe in 1964. If so, perhaps that was her way of making amends.

ELEVEN

What Betty Saved

T HE SMALL PACKAGE of treasured items Betty took with her when she left Texas for college is reminiscent of the contents of the nineteenth-century Stedmans' wooden box. As a fragmentary portrait of her girlhood it is both fascinating and frustrating. Both collections seem at once deliberate and arbitrary, official and informal. Marian Stedman had kept a small, wallet-sized *Baby Book* for Betty, distributed by the Kodak Company. In addition to photographs taken from 1914 to 1927, it contains a lock of "Baby's Hair," pasted onto the spot provided, lists of significant dates, such as "The first Short Clothes," at six months, "The first Steps," at 14 months, "The first Word" ("bye bye") at ten months, the first Christmas gifts, and faint pencil tracings of "Betty's foot" and "Betty's little hand" at sixteen and a half months.

Someone – probably Marian — carefully saved an envelope with all of Betty's report cards from the various schools she attended, and another envelope with the programs for piano recitals, her high school commencement ceremony, and a curious little certificate dated March 9, 1921, from the Modern Health Crusaders of New Sharon, Maine, stating that the recipient holds the rank of "Page" and has agreed to keep to the Crusaders' health rules listed below. The sentence "Bathe your whole body twice a week at least" was amended in pencil to "once a week." The young pages are also enjoined to sleep with the windows open, keep fingers and pencils and everything likely to be unclean or injurious out of the mouth and nose, and to be cheerful and clean minded. I'd love to know when the change from twice a week to once a week was made. Perhaps water was a precious commodity in dusty Texas, or perhaps during those Maine winters baths were kept to a minimum. The lessons remained deeply engrained, clearly, for when I was growing up, we scrubbed our faces and necks with washcloths each morning and evening, but were discouraged from bathing daily, and there was always much talk about conserving hot water.

Betty and her mother saved newspaper clippings too: one, entitled "School Honors are Announced" reports that Mary Elizabeth Stedman was named the Salutatorian of the Taylor High School class of 1930 with an average of 96.33 percent. Interestingly, this "northern child" was named "the most representative pupil of the class," an honor conferred by her classmates. The program for the high school commencement exercises was saved as well. Betty delivered the opening, or "Salutatory" address, preceded by her father, who delivered the invocation. Later in the program her mother, the "Local Regent" of the Daughters of the American Revolution conferred the D.A.R. Awards (Among the papers Betty preserved is a large certificate with elaborate calligraphy, dated April 13, 1929, stating that Marian Murray Stedman is an approved member of the Daughters of the American Revolution by virtue of her descent from Lieutenant Colonel John Murray). Betty's sister Edith, listed in the program as "Edith Gratia Stedman II," was a member of the graduating class as well. Betty saved her Salutatory address, which reads, in part, as follows:

As we gather here tonight, we cannot help but be mindful of the pleasures experienced and the helpful influences encountered during our four years in high school. Neither can we refrain from meditating upon the incentive that has made our high school education possible....

In reviewing our four years in high school we must realize that we will soon forget the lessons which we have learned from books, but we shall not so quickly forget the lessons that we have learned which are intangible, which can not be seen, but whose influence will be felt for many years. First among these intangible lessons is the principle of democracy. Someone has said that democracy in its purest form is to be found in the public schools of America…

Another lesson not to be found in books is the art of self-control. I feel that the class will uphold me when I say that one cannot get along in high school without exercising this art. We have learned, in a measure, to control our thoughts and our words and have begun to realize that our school life would have been in vain without this mental discipline….

The speech continues with paragraphs devoted to sportsmanship, friendship, leadership, and "the dynamic personalities of our teachers" who have encouraged the students "to be ambitious for a richer and fuller life" but to "keep ever in mind…that service is the greatest work of all." Undoubtedly Betty was eminently suited to the task of composing and delivering this speech—all those Sundays of listening to her father preach from the pulpit had prepared her for this role.

Betty had clearly made the most of her years at Taylor High School. A tiny clipping entitled "A Winner" announces that "Miss Mary Elizabeth Stedman, a member of the "Cotton Boll" editorial staff of the Taylor High School, was awarded third place in 'proof reading' at the state meeting which was held at Austin on Friday."

Mixed in among the records of her accomplishments is one lone relic attesting to Betty's social life, which I knew had been difficult. Smart girls from the North didn't fit in well in the South, and the daughters of a clergyman had to be above reproach. The little dance card from a Halloween dance, with a tiny pencil attached by a string must have marked an important occasion, or so I'd like to think. The twenty dances were spoken for by nineteen different young men; as was the custom, her escort, Chester Latham, claimed the first and the last dance.

Betty also saved a list of graduation gifts—seventy-nine in all, with neat little check marks next to the names to indicate that a thank-you note had been duly sent. Hankies, beads and stockings seem to have been popular gifts, but friends and relatives also sent dolls, pictures, powder jars, bloomers, a prayer book, "step-ins", "vanities," money ($5 or $10 or $15), books, perfume, brassieres, and a manicure set. I can't imagine anyone receiving seventy-nine graduation gifts in twenty-first century America, and certainly not gifts of underwear! Would these well-meant gifts have been presented to Betty by the ladies of the Episcopal Church Women's Guild? Or by her school friends and their parents? Or by relatives far away in Ohio and New England? Clearly graduation from high school was an important life passage in 1930 in small town America. When Betty married far from home during World War II, I doubt that she received seventy-nine gifts.

As a teacher of English, I was especially interested in an examination paper from Betty's English IV class at Taylor High School, dated January 21, 1930. The questions provide a glimpse of the way English literature was taught in those days. The instructions read:

Answer all questions:
a. Give Professor Long's definition of literature.
b. Name, define, and give concrete examples of the qualities of literature.
c. How does modern poetry differ in form from Anglo-Saxon poetry?

The exam continues with six more sections. Students were expected to "Give in full outline form the origin and development of the drama," and "Account for the pre-eminence of the Elizabethan period"; they were expected to know certain texts very well, like Bacon's essay on friendship and the essays of Addison and Steele. The following year on June 16, 1931, Betty took a Comprehensive Examination in English as part of the College Boards. As part of the exam, students were given the following topics from which to choose for an essay of 350 words:

1. "The past is the tradition of the present; the present, therefore, is the tradition of the future."
2. Aristotle said that great poetry is more true than history.
3. Literature: record, interpretation, or escape?
4. In a certain city a beautiful old house was torn down to make room for a modern apartment.
5. Some knowledge of science contributes to the enlargement of our vision.
6. A rocky pool
7. "Music, when soft voices die, Vibrates in the memory..."

There are still more, but Betty paused here, and chose number seven. I wish I knew what she'd written, and how it reflected her sixteen-year-old sensibility.

I'm certain that Betty must have written and received letters during her years in Texas, but alas, only two survive. A letter from someone named B. N. Hays of the Melasky Bldg, Taylor, Texas testifies that:

> It has been my privilege to know this young lady for the past year in a business way and I can very truthfully say that she is one of the finest young ladies that I have ever come in contact with.
> Although she has never actually been in my employ, I do know that she is very competent as a stenographer.

The other letter is a picture postcard of a snow-covered mountain sent to her from Japan by her Aunt Edith. The card is addressed to Miss Betty Stedman, Cisco, Texas, USA, and the message reads:

> Dear Betty,
> The snow is on the mountains here and it is very cold. The little Japanese children are running around all bundled up and shivering. I hope you are well and strong again. Your loving,
> Aunt Edith

Edith, as we shall see, was traveling in the East while working in China. To Betty and young Edith and Frank, she must have seemed like an exotic, distant reminder that there was an enormous world beyond Texas.

TWELVE

Gene Tuck Reminisces
About his Childhood in the 1920s

I N 1959 OUR FAMILY MOVED to a large house in an affluent Long Island suburb, and during my first week in eighth grade, a classmate asked me about my religion. My brothers and I were accustomed to responding to such questions by declaring proudly that we were "half Episcopalian and half Jewish," as if religion were an ethnicity, rather like being half Italian and half Greek. We knew other children of mixed religions, so this did not seem strange to us. One of our closest friends in the town where we had lived previously was half Catholic, half Jewish, though his family, unlike ours, settled on the Ethical Culture Society as a neutral middle ground. The eighth-grade classmate, filled with a misplaced zeal instilled by Lutheran confirmation classes, responded to my declaration of mixed heritage by promptly informing me that I was destined for Hell. From that day forward, I considered myself more Jewish than Episcopalian, certain, as only a thirteen-year-old can be, that Jews were smarter than Christians.

We went to church once or twice a year during my childhood, and even more infrequently to Central Synagogue, an imposing Moorish edifice in New York City that my father attended each year on the anniversary of his mother's death. Hanukah and Passover were duly celebrated, but Christmas was a big event, as it was for all of the other families in our suburban town and, indeed, throughout America. We sang Christmas carols in school, baked Christmas cookies (a custom I continue – my only link to the festivities of my childhood) and my mother sent and received hundreds of Christmas cards, which were displayed prominently in our front hall, along with the Christmas tree.

While I was experiencing teenage alienation from my Christian classmates, my Jewish father, who never really took to suburban life — particularly in a town that prohibited Jews from belonging to the country clubs — was writing witty satirical essays on the suburban lifestyle, the woes of commuting by train to the city every day, and other subjects. I found a kindly rejection letter from an agent, along with a set of carbon copies of the essays, in the closet that held the letters from the 1940s.

One of the essays provides a glimpse of my father's childhood, which was in many ways just as insulated from cultural and religious differences as my mother's was in the small towns of Texas. In New York City, each immigrant community occupied its own territory. I doubt that he knew many Christian children, and when he entered City College in 1929, nearly his entire class was Jewish. Here is his description of what it was like to grow up just north of Central Park, before it became the Harlem of today, from an essay about the games of childhood entitled "Immies and Other Memories" (immies were marbles).

> *To an adolescent in mid-Manhattan of the [nineteen] twenties, his street was his hometown, different in character from the "village" in the next street, enemy territory inhabited by despised inferiors. There were legends describing "street wars" of the "old days," bloody battles with flying milk bottles as weapons – stories to be told around the lamppost on summer evenings where we would congregate after the evening meal.*
>
> . . .
>
> *Our playground was at our door. Horses were not as pampered and particular as automobiles and did not require that every snowflake*

be banished from the city street within a day or two after its fall. Like manna, snow was a heavenly gift, to be hoped for and cherished.... After a week or so it froze into blocks – perfect material for building forts and remained in place for days as monuments to the indefatigable efforts of their youthful architects – forts that could be attacked and defended in blazing snowball fights, their stout walls stormed and their attackers repelled. No giant shovel propelled by a truck or tractor disturbed them and there they remained, growing smaller and sootier each day until they quietly melted into early spring.

Solidly frozen snow covered the street from curb to curb, serving as a perfect sleigh-run. In flat Manhattan, the force of gravity was not available to lend its motive force to a boy on his "flier," but with typical resourcefulness we found "belly-whopping" a solution to this problem. In order to "belly-whop" you had to run as fast a possible with your sled held at "port-arms" and after gathering enough speed, you plunged to the ground on your sled for an exciting twenty-five foot run. Occasionally, we would take the long seven block walk to Central Park, our sleds on our backs, to trudge up a small hill innumerable times for the breathtaking thrill of plummeting to the bottom.

· · ·

Holidays were celebrated in very special ways. Thanksgiving was a time to don old clothes – preferably a dress of your mother's with a long skirt dragging along the ground – and to beg passersby for pennies. On Halloween we turned our jackets inside out, filled one of our long black stockings with flour and beat our friends with it until their coats was well as ours were white. In tougher neighborhoods stockings were filled with stones instead of flour to produce a more lasting effect. July the Fourth was the most memorable holiday of all. Pennies were saved to buy fireworks, illicitly imported from New Jersey by youthful smugglers furtively ferrying them from Fort Lee to resell at a profit.

· · ·

Independence Day ushered in the long golden days of summer – two sunny months without school or homework.... We needed no well-equipped, safely fenced and professionally supervised playground. I recall with wonder and admiration the planning that went into the organization of a track-meet on our street. Not all the usual events were included, of course. High-jumping was impractical and discus throwing unheard of. But the dash, the broad-jump and the relay were routine, and the three legged and potato race not uncommon.

"Box-ball" is a term that has now disappeared from the sports vocabulary, but in the nineteen-twenties, it was a cherished part of a boy's daily life.... It was a form of baseball with each base at the corner of a fifty-foot square or box, its base-lines marked off with chalk from curb to curb. The rubber ball was served by the pitcher on a single bounce and was to be hit as a "grounder" with the palm of the hand. A fly ball landing outside of the box was "out." The batting order and box-score, written in chalk on the pavement, were washed away by the rain or by the street-cleaner with his wheeled barrel and enormous brush. Fifty feet of curb on either side of a residential side street uncluttered by parked cars is not longer to be found in mid-Manhattan and box ball is a relic of the horse and wagon era. Even if its driver were asleep at the reins, no friendly nag would harm a base-runner intent on scoring. The player's greatest hazard was an occasional pile of horse-droppings neatly deposited athwart the base line. We felt no resentment toward the animal for this indiscretion, nor for his contribution to the ever-present stream of water running along the curb... an unavoidable hazard of a game of "immies."

"Immies" were large glass multi-colored marbles, projected by the player along the curb by a snapping movement of the thumb and index finger. Your opponent's immie was yours if you hit it with your own. If it was a "realie" it was worth five ordinary "immies." A "realie" was a particularly pretty marble and a prize for the avid collector. There was a vigorous trade in "immies" and everyone had his particular gems, too precious to be risked in a game and kept safely at home in an old cigar box to be fondled, shown off and admired.

"Stick-ball" was another favorite sport. It required only a broomstick, a rubber ball and a piece of chalk to mark the bases. We assumed that the principal function of the manhole cover was to act as home plate.

We never saw it used for any other purpose. If a ball landed in a cellar vault, the batter was limited to two bases.

The short flight of stone steps leading to the front door of a tenement house provided the arena for "Stoop-ball," a game native to a tenement society. It was a game of skill requiring the player to hit the point of a step with a rubber ball from a standing position at the curb. Only if the point of the step was hit would the ball arch up in a fly which, if caught by the player, would gain points and permit him to continue. If missed, the player would yield his place to his opponent.

. . .

"Johnny-on-a-Pony" was a spectacle that many of my generation will remember with mixed pain and pleasure. It was literally a back-breaking experience. Members of one team would leap upon the backs of their crouched opponents bouncing and rocking violently while thrice shouting "Johnny-on-a-pony, one, two, three" before alighting. If the crouchers caved in, they lost the round.

Summer brought with it a yearning for trees and grass and plans were made long in advance for a hike in New Jersey's Palisades, and when the great day arrived, off we would trudge to the ferry – a motley crew dressed in all varieties of camping attire and burdened like pack-mules with axes, knives, canteens, knapsacks, leggings, cooking utensils, and enough food for a week. Our wilderness goal was a dusty river road crowded with other intrepid pioneers from Manhattan's streets, some reclining on rocks along the side of the road accompanying their rendition of popular songs with ukeleles.

. . .

Every Saturday afternoon at the local movie we would suffer with Pearl White through her harrowing perils, thrill to the daring exploits of Tom Mix and William S. Hart, or gaze spellbound upon the tragic and noble poses of John Barrymore. For a six-cent admission charge we would watch in horror while Pearl White was strapped to a railroad track or tied to a plank to be cut in half by a giant circular lumber-mill saw. The house lights would go on just as Pearl's decorative frame was about to be severed lengthwise. Next Saturday she would, of course, be rescued by a dark and handsome stranger to the tuneful strains of a tinny piano banging out appropriate suspense-producing selections.

. . .

After Labor Day, our favorite targets were straw "katies," those hard-brimmed flat straw hats which we would flip off the heads of passersby by means of a strong black thread stretched across the sidewalk, a boy at either end lolling on a stoop or leaning languidly against a lamppost. After jumping on the prize and yelling "get a new hat," we would take to our heels leaving its angry owner sputtering over his shattered headpiece, his plans for reviving it for another summer by a lemon-juice rub gone a-glimmering.

Another piece of deviltry consisted of filling an old change-purse with horse-dung and watching from a nearby cellar-vault while its lucky finder opened it, fully expecting to see a fat roll of bills.

As we marched through our early teens and the day drew near when we would discard our knee-pants and black ribbed stockings and don long trousers and vests, we became more serious. We organized "social and athletic clubs" which conducted weekly meetings with meticulous and tiresome attention to parliamentary rules. Dues were collected, ball teams and debating teams were formed, and we even produced a one-act play and published a two-page mimeographed newspaper.

In the mid-twenties our neighborhood was changing. Family after family moved out and our tightly organized, highly structured society of teen-aged boys dissolved and drifted away. Some of us went to college and on from there, but not many. I have often wondered what happened to the companions of those formative years when I learned to be a leader in some areas, but more often a follower, and to live within an established set of mores in preparation for survival in a more complex and impersonal society.

In his final years, my father's dearest hope was to live into the next century. He was a trusts and estates attorney, and he knew that changes in the tax laws due to occur in early in the year 2000 would be favorable to us, his heirs. And so, by sheer force of will, he held death at bay until

March 1, 2000, just as he had planned. He had lived in New York City and its environs for all but a few years of his life. The New York of horse-drawn wagons and immies and stoop ball and "Johnny-on-a-pony" had long since disappeared, but the city with its theatres and restaurants and busy streets continued to be, in his opinion, the center of the universe.

PART TWO:

Edith Stedman's Autobiography

THIRTEEN

Edith's Childhood

W HEN I GOT TO KNOW my great aunt Edith in the 1960s, her little
house on Farwell Place was filled with historical artifacts, not the
least of which were several different typed versions of her autobiography, a
work in progress that she occasionally shared with me (though it is to her
credit that she never asked me to help with the typing). I have a version
with some pages missing; the Schlesinger Library has a slightly different
one. Edith was blessed with the degree of self-importance that I have
always assumed autobiographers need to possess in order to believe that
their stories are worth sharing with the world. She knew she was living in
interesting times, and she began saving copies of letters she wrote during
World War I. Her description of her childhood and college years contains
much less detail; presumably these are memories she gathered together
much later in life, for they have a retrospective tone, as if recalled from
some distance.

Edith didn't know her grandfather Vernal Stedman, but her
autobiography gives us a glimpse of him as a prosperous man in his later
years. The opening chapter begins with these words:

The obvious thing seems to be to start with what one knows best, and that is one's own life. I was born on December 29, 1888 in a three story house with a mansard roof, built by my grandfather, Vernal Stedman. His father had had a farm on Norfolk Street with orchards and fields around it. At this period Cambridgeport [Massachusetts] *was still rural and fishing boats landed on the lower Charles.*

It was still farmland, as well, and Vernal had extensive land holdings near what is now Central Square, Cambridge. A record of the land sale survives:

Dr. Samuel Grover sold two houses on Prospect St., Cambridge for $1500.00 to Vernal Richardson Stedman—land with dwelling house— northerly house in block of 2 houses on Prospect St Ward 2 Book 1075 p 459 April 26, 1869. More in Bk. 1072 p 258 Oct. 14, 1868.

Vernal's obituary provides a brief account of his life after the youthful adventures in Key West and New Orleans:

March 8, 1889
We greatly regret to announce the death of Mr. V. R. Stedman, senior partner of the firm of Stedman and Company, manufacturers of wound strings for musical instruments at Cambridgeport, Mass.
Comparatively few men have left a better record than that which now belongs to the memory of Mr. Stedman. He was one of the heroes who redeem humanity from the stigma of ignoble selfishness. His life, though comparatively obscure except for among his friends and acquaintances, was a life full of devotion to duty, to family and to the dictates of an enlightened conscience. For a long period, as far back as the time of the Gilberts of Boston fame — he worked at the bench in a piano factory, afterwards pursuing the business of action-making with marked success for nearly 30 years. His reputation as an action-maker is well remembered. During the past 10 years he has been engaged with his son, Mr. George H. Stedman in the manufacture of strings for

violins and guitars, etc. Throughout his entire career he remained quiet, unassuming, benevolent, faithful and honored by all with whom he came in contact, and largely befriending, in his own modest way, the unfortunate and the nessitous. He was, in brief, a good and true man – one of those honest, duty-loving citizens who are the real strength and glory of the nation. No nobler inheritance than his example could fall to the lot of those who survived him. Mr. Stedman was in his 75th year.

After Vernal's death his widow, Elvira, continued to live with her children, Ella Faustina Stedman and George Herbert Stedman, and George's wife Gratia ("Kitty") Holt Stedman. Edith's earliest memories are of the big house in Cambridge where her grandmother had a floor to herself.

Edith writes about her mother and father in the first few pages of her autobiography:

My father, George Herbert Stedman, was born in Boston and graduated from the Boston Latin School. He was uncommonly talented and there still exists a portfolio of his drawings, most of them cartoons. I am sure he wanted to study art but instead had to go into business with his father who was a manufacturer of piano strings. I imagine he loathed it, for after his father's death a very prosperous business bit the dust and at the time of my father's death I think he was an accountant or something of the sort in the Lawrence Mills. Anyway, we were brought up on Chamber's Encyclopedia, a wedding present from old Mr. Lawrence.

. . .

My two older brothers, Frank and Bert, were eleven and fifteen years my senior when I appeared on the scene on December 29, 1888. My mother, named Gratia for her grandmother but always called Kitty, was forty-two at the time and had a difficult delivery – my advent must have come as a surprise, but my father was delighted to have a little daughter. It was almost a generation gap between me and my brothers, and the older one, Frank, I scarcely knew for he was away at school (Andover, Harvard and the Episcopal Theological School) as

I was growing up. My other brother, James Herbert, called Bert, was married when I was ten years old and shortly after that bought a house in Braintree.

. . .

When I was about nine we moved from Cambridge to Belmont. In those days Belmont was a town of about 5,000 people and was almost completely agricultural with a number of large market gardens. Although it had only been incorporated about a hundred years previously, actually it was very much older having been carved out of bits of Waltham, Watertown and West Cambridge and its earliest settlers were members of the Massachusetts Bay Colony in the early seventeenth century. It was an almost entirely Anglo-Saxon, homogeneous society but it was far from classless. It is difficult, looking back, to describe where the lines were drawn and where they overlapped. Although there was a considerable amount of wealth in the town I think the real hierarchy consisted of the old families whose names had persisted for generations. My brothers, as eligible bachelors, belonged to the Tennis Club and my mother and aunt to the Thursday Club, one of the oldest literary clubs in the country, which met at Mrs. Winthrop Cheney's and was considered a sacred institution.

Our house in Belmont was in the "newer section" and was a nine or ten room wooden building with a verandah around two sides and a smallish garden. The first two floors were centrally heated, but the heating did not go up to the top floor where the maid slept, but that was taken completely for granted. She was Irish, as were most of the maids, and I don't think that, until I went to college, I ever knew as a friend a Black or a Jew or a Roman Catholic. Families in Belmont were divided pretty much between the Unitarian and Episcopal churches. We went to the Episcopal Church although my father was a Unitarian. However, he liked the rector's sermons and would come in time for that and, as soon as it and the offering were over, would stomp out.

. . .

I think I was confirmed when I was about fourteen. But the following day I had dogmatic doubts and went to call on the rector. He was hoeing in his garden and refused to discuss theology and set me to work picking up weeds and that was that.

. . .

We lived very simply. Everything was bought in bulk, flour, sugar, apples and potatoes by the barrel. Fruits and vegetables were canned in season. Saturday night's supper was invariably baked beans and brown bread, the curse of generations of Americans. Monday was wash-day, and the Saturday night meal was finished up then in order to save time. There was one woman in the neighborhood who had the effrontery to buy her bread from the baker's cart and she was considered therefore completely feckless and beyond the pale.

. . .

My father and I were great friends, and he saw to it that as a child I learned to know Boston and all of the historic sights. It was great fun going with him to places like Faneuil Hall and the Market, and one Washington's Birthday he took me to a Governor's reception so that I could see the State House. We rode on the Swan Boats in the Public Garden and he took me to my first theatrical performance which was Joe Jefferson in "Rip Van Winkle." He himself was a fan of Dickens and evenings when homework was done he would read aloud to us. If my brother was there, we sometimes played old-fashioned whist. At other times, my father would take me for long walks either to the old parts of Boston or the country.

The "far from classless" society in which Edith spent her childhood, where the most significant differences among her neighbors concerned whether they were Unitarian or Episcopalian, whether the bought or baked their bread, surely helped to shape the woman she would become. For her, as for Betty two or three decades later, Jews and blacks and Catholics were grouped together as "others" seldom thought about, much less encountered.

FOURTEEN

Edith at Radcliffe
1906-1910

B Y 2005 I HAD been working on and off on "When People Wrote Letters" for a few years; my brother Jonathan called it "my hobby." That June, I paid a visit to the Schlesinger Library on the day after my son's graduation from Harvard and found a row of college yearbooks. There, in the class of 1910, was Edith, in cap and gown and a white cravat that made her look rather like a nineteenth-century British judge. The yearbook entry records that she was a member of the class basketball team, the college hockey team, and the scenery committee for the "Idler," a performance group. Each student chose an epigram to accompany her list of accomplishments and Edith's reads as follows:

> *"His spirit was so stout,*
> *No man could make him face about."*

Was this a signal that "stoutness," in the sense of conviction and stubborn determination, were qualities she valued and aspired to? The quotation is from John Bunyan's *Pilgrim's Progress*, required reading for young Protestants of her generation, and so I think it must have been.

The first turning point in Edith's life occurred when her father died. The autobiography explains that

> *My father died when I was fourteen, and I had to grow up overnight. I became the head of the family which now consisted of my mother, by this time a semi-invalid, myself, a very capable maid, and a black cat. I wanted to go away to college but that was out of the question, so I entered Radcliffe College.*
>
> *Admission was a simple enough performance in those days, and I am not sure that I had any overwhelming desire to go to college. At that time it seemed to me the most desirable thing in life was to be a salesgirl at Jordan Marsh. But, it was assumed that I would go to college, and so I went.*
>
> . . .
>
> *Somewhere along the line I worked out a philosophy for myself – Don't expect too much, and if you get more it is an extra dividend. I don't recommend it for I could not completely carry it through and as a result I have dived constantly between extreme enthusiasm and immeasurable pessimism.*
>
> . . .
>
> *I don't think I ever would have managed that first year at Radcliffe if some of the upper-class women hadn't taken me in hand and I'll never be grateful enough to them. Dorothy Kendall, who was a senior and a very good student, made me study with her in the Library or took me home and sat me down where she could keep an eye on me. After that class had graduated I was passed on to some of the Juniors, among them Leila Tuckerman Page and Elizabeth Singleton. Leila had charm enough to call the birds out of the trees but she wasn't all that good a student herself so we struggled together, but her intentions were good. She was simply lovely to look at, and had the most disconcerting fashion of sitting in the front row of class and looking up at some instructor, with whom she had danced the night before at a coming-out party,*

making tears run down her cheeks. Her lovely blue eyes drenched in tears would be too much for the instructor and he would falter and look as if he would like to run. Elizabeth had a fine mind and did her best for me then as she had done ever since. Years later, when she became Headmistress of the Girl's Latin School in Chicago, she hired my niece Betty who had just graduated from Wellesley College.

. . .

On my first day at Radcliffe College I must have looked like something out of <u>Little Women</u> for I still had my hair down and wore a white Peter Pan collar. We were not allowed in those days at Radcliffe to go to Billings and Stovers as we might run into a Harvard man. Should we meet one, we were cautioned to keep our eyes on the ground. We were also not allowed in the Yard, and had to wear gloves at all times. I wasn't any natural born charmer, but I had one rather durable beau at Radcliffe. He came to our house for one Thanksgiving dinner and had promised to help me on a long paper I had to write for Phil 4 on Rashdall's Theory of Good and Evil. After an enormous dinner one of my brothers meanly offered Henry a cigar and in order to prove his manhood he unwisely accepted it. I was sure it was his first, for after a few puffs, he turned green and both the dinner and the Rashdall paper were lost as far as I was concerned.

. . .

I liked sports and played a lot of tennis, hockey and basketball (made the varsity) and even took part in a rather lumbering way in one or two of the Idler plays. It was all very funny because Miss Irwin, a Victorian of the old school who was Dean my first year, sent for me as I had flunked Biology at the end of the first half. She asked me why I had failed, and when I said I didn't recognize the bisection of a tapeworm a shudder of horror went through her because it was an indelicate subject. Later, when she saw me in one of my less attractive roles on the stage, wearing the only pair of trousers the Green Room possessed, very baggy knickerbockers, she sent a message to have me removed immediately, evidently thinking that my derriere was too prominent. That was the end of that, and I was relegated to scenery and lights.

. . .

I did take a course in Anatomy with Dr. Hapgood and I surprised myself by getting an A and I adored it. We had a bag of bones from a skeleton, and it was like playing jack-straws because we threw the bones in a heap and then had to name all of them. I was quite good, and Dr. Hapgood, knowing of my interest asked me to go along with him when he was called to set the broken arm of a Radcliffe girl who lived in Elliot House. Nothing pleased me more. He allowed me to hold the arm and feel the crepitus where the bone was broken before he put the splint on. Miss Hoppin, the head of house, raised a frightful fuss because I was there unchaperoned with the doctor and a half-dressed student.

. . .

I became interested in social work quite casually, and used to spend Saturdays down in the North End working for the Family Welfare Society, where my job consisted principally of taking poor little waifs to Carney Hospital to have their tonsils out. In those days they etherized the children, yanked out their tonsils, and then left these poor limp little rabbits on a bed for three hours until they could be taken home looking pale and bloody. I always gave them an ice-cream soda on the way back and delivered them to their mamas.

The North End in the days when I knew it was an absolutely fascinating place, and a part of another world. Scollay Square was the starting point filled with tattoo parlors and dentists offices where they displayed teeth that had been pulled in glass cases on the sidewalk. From there you went down Hanover Street, and the names of some of the more fascinating streets leading off Hanover were Prince Street, Half-Moon and Salutation. Salem Street was almost entirely Jewish. There was an old synagogue there with ancient long-bearded rabbis in skull caps; shops of all kinds selling kosher foods and old clothes, and sidewalk barrows selling markdowns. Most of the rest of the district was Italian. The shops at Easter were filled with sugar lambs and eggs and all sorts of symbols, and there were always religious processions and festivals.

The family that I knew best were the Cuddis, and I think they lived on Salutation Street. Anyway, Mrs. Cuddi was a very motherly soul who had a brood of children and she named the last one after me. The bedroom in an Italian flat was most imposing. There was a big brass bed with a huge eiderdown over it, holy pictures all around, crucifixes and holy water stands.

I was always treated as one of the family. I can't think how many flights of stairs I climbed in those days, but it never occurred to anyone that it wasn't safe to go anywhere. I do hand it to my mother for letting me have my head as much as she did for she must have worried a good deal about my wanderings around the city. But she was very sensible about it. Oftentimes I would bring some of my Italian children out to Belmont for a picnic.

. . .

We knew an extremely good doctor, Dr. Hagerty, and as I knew my tonsils needed taking out and that my mother worried about it I went to him one day and said to him "Do you mind taking my tonsils out tomorrow?" He said, "No, but don't eat any breakfast." So on one excuse or another without telling my mother I went over. He put a large pickle fork with a string tied in it between my teeth, boiled up his instruments on the kitchen stove, gave me some chloroform, and that was that. Then he laid me out on his surgery sofa. Of course, the sight of me covered with blood scared my mother to death and did away with all the good effects I had hoped to accomplish. However, I got a five dollar gold piece from my brother for being "a brave girl" and Dr. Hagerty let me make rounds with him in his old horse and buggy. That was great fun, and I wanted more than ever to go into medicine, which I had long dreamed of studying. But having flunked biology, and discovered that after three weeks of chemistry my senior year I was scared to light a match over the wretched burners, I decided I'd better settle for something else.

After graduation I couldn't take a job, as my mother wasn't well and anyway I wasn't trained for anything practical. However, I was taken on as a volunteer at the Massachusetts General Hospital. The social service department under Miss Ida Cannon was fairly new at that time and there were some rather famous characters in it.

Edith had landed, quite remarkably, in the forefront of a new field. Ida Cannon had established the first social work department in a hospital in the United States and in effect created the concept of medical social work. She wrote a seminal book on the subject and served as a consultant to hospitals and city administrations throughout the country. At Massachusetts General Hospital she assembled an impressive staff of women who helped develop connections between social work, psychiatry, and internal medicine. Edith would use everything she learned there throughout her career.

Miss Edith Burleigh was working with Dr. James Jackson on neurological cases, Gertrude Farmer, who had reddish hair and lined face and a sharp tongue and was the kindest person on earth, worked with TB's. Mrs. Hodder had started the new department for unmarried mothers and I was turned over to her. I seem to have spent a good deal of time chasing around to a restaurant called Marston's to fetch back apple dumplings for them for their lunch and doing all kinds of errands, both around the hospital and elsewhere. I was always sent off with bundles of clothes to some unmarried mother who had just had a baby. One bit of education was picked up through the head of Welcome House who used to spend her evenings in some of the more disreputable Scollay Square cafes, keeping an eye out for the recalcitrant members of her fold. She took me with her once. Needless to say, we had soft drinks, but it was quite a new world to me and I found it vastly interesting.

. . .

After my father died I was terribly concerned lest something should happen to my mother. I would listen at her door at night to be sure that she was breathing, or I would come running home from school afraid that she would not be there. Worry was not only forced on me but I think it is an integral part of a New Englander's makeup, a substitute, I suppose, for action. But I remember as a small child ill in bed saying to my mother "Won't you come and sit beside me and worry for a while?" thinking, I am sure, that if you worried a little you placated the gods, a little like the Chinese idea of putting girl's clothing on boys so they won't be snatched away.

My mother and I were very close, not only because after my father's death I felt she was my responsibility, but also because she was fun and took a tremendous interest in all my projects. She was terrified of thunderstorms and for some reason always seated herself in the darkest possible corner with a pile of pillows, saying, "Now children, there is nothing to be afraid of, just see how beautiful the lightning is." No one, including herself, was fooled by this optimistic stratagem.

Except for the two summers when I did volunteer work at Children's Island in Marblehead Harbor during my undergraduate years, and occasional visits, we were never separated. When I did go away for very short stays with friends, she wrote me every day, subtly reminding me to remember my manners and that as a guest I must be polite and considerate. She died in my arms in 1911 after several severe heart attacks. My brother Bert sold the house almost immediately and, with the help of the nurse and our dear faithful maid, I cleaned up everything, storing the furniture that I wanted to keep and giving away the rest. I did it all systematically and stoically until I came to her glasses in their case and then I broke down completely and realized for the first time that I was nobody's child although I was grown up, and that there was no one left who loved me no matter what happened. I was on my own and I headed straight for Sherborn Prison in four weeks' time.

FIFTEEN

Four Years of Prison

THE NEXT CHAPTER in Edith's autobiography is entitled "Four Years of Prison," although she only spent three years in her first paid position. Her experiences there had a profound influence on the rest of her life as a pioneer in the field of social work.

The House of Mercy, jails, and the Good Shepherds, all penitential way stops for beginners in crime, were familiar enough; but I had never been in a proper prison; and as we drove from the grimy, old, Framingham [Massachusetts] *Railroad Station through the town and toward the country, I began to wonder what I was in for. It was a hot July day in 1911. The fields were beginning to look dry, and even the leaves on the trees seemed to be drooping with boredom. Suddenly, around a bend of the dusty road, the big, red, Victorian bulk of Sherborn Prison* [the Massachusetts Reformatory for Women] *loomed up with both the State Flag and the "Stars and Stripes" floating listlessly in the still air. High walls around the buildings, then a small lodge, and a driveway circling through an arch gave entrance to the Prison and the*

Superintendent's House. The driver of the hack unloaded my trunk and with a cheerful wave at the barred windows he turned to me and said, "Well, I hope you enjoy yourself, Miss."

At twenty-two I was by far the youngest of any of the prison employees. Partly because of my greenness and partly due to the fact that I had done volunteer work for nearly a year in the Social Service Department of the Massachusetts General Hospital for the new Superintendent, Mrs. Hodder, I was to live in her house. How lucky I was, I didn't realize at the time. It was a huge red-brick affair, most attractively furnished with double drawing rooms at the right and a dining room with a conservatory leading off it on the left. My room, looking out over the fields, was very big and comfortably furnished— mostly with Victoriana (a walnut double bed, wardrobe, and marble-topped washstand). A big piazza ran across the front of the house, which had a well-kept lawn. Our three house servants were all in for murder. Two of them, middle-aged women, had neatly polished off their husbands, who from all accounts got no more than they deserved. The third was just a girl who had done away with her illegitimate child. A nicer lot of people I have never known—completely honest and reliable and surprisingly lacking in bitterness.

I was taken over the institution the next day: East and West Wings, isolation quarters for new arrivals, the infirmary and nursery wing, and an almost outmoded cell block of three tiers, which Mrs. Hodder later turned into a gymnasium. The final stop was at the solitary padded cell in the basement for complete incorrigibles. Then, I was solemnly handed a bunch of keys on a long, leather strap to be hooked onto my belt with the warning that I was never to be separated from it. Actually, I got so lost and mixed up the first few days that some pitying prisoner would always tell me which key to use!

Mrs. Hodder was to become another of many important, charismatic women friends and role models in Edith's life. She was, says Edith,

... a remarkable woman with a cosmopolitan background, beautiful to look at with wavy brown hair and big brown eyes. She had great dignity combined with compassion and an intuitive understanding of human nature born of the tragedies in her own life.

I was intrigued by this reference to "tragedies" and found a reference to Jessie Donaldson Hodder in Estelle B. Freedman's book *Their Sisters' Keepers: Women's Prison Reform in America 1830-1930.* Evidently Jessie Hodder's husband, Alfred, had contracted a bigamous marriage and died, probably by suicide, before Mrs. Hodder could conclude her legal case against him. Their daughter died young and Mrs. Hodder was left to raise her son Alan by herself (page 219, note 32). Alan donated his mother's papers to the Schlesinger Library at Harvard. They include records of her twenty years at Sherborn Prison (she was superintendent there until her death in 1931), speeches, and reports on visits she made to European prisons in 1921.

Jessie Donaldson Hodder (1867-1934) was a pioneer in prison reform, and Edith's autobiography provides glimpses of the changes she made while at Sherborn. Until she arrived in 1911, the women prisoners had to walk with their hands behind their backs and turn their faces to the wall if they met anyone in the corridors. They had supper at five, after which they were locked up for the night. Edith reports that

Chapel services were always well attended. There was no nonsense about ecumenical feelings – after all, it meant going somewhere. The women's favorite hymn was "I Sing Because I'm Happy; I Sing Because I'm Free" (this with wardens lining the walls). Mrs. Hodder changed all that by getting a proper musician appointed to the staff; and before long, the prisoners were doing Gilbert and Sullivan to which guests were invited. Their favorite was <u>The Pirates of Penzance</u>, particularly the "Policemen's Chorus"; for, by some sleight of hand, the music director got hold of some old Boston policemen's uniforms and the cops were invited. The prisoners were in great form; for with no animosity, they kept

*picking out the particular coppers who had pinched them. You might
say that there was real rapport between the cast and the audience.*

. . .

*The prisoners had never been let outside the walls before, but Mrs.
Hodder soon took care of that, and I was turned out daily with a gang
of twelve or fifteen to work in the fields and gardens. All my life, jobs
seem to have been thrown at me for which I have had no training, and
this was no exception. Mrs. Hodder put the women in bloomers and
middy blouses, and all the little street walkers of Boston (who didn't
know any more about thinning carrots and weeding onions than I did)
were sent out in squads. I did have a whistle and, of course, my jangling
keys, but I wasn't much older than some of them, and it never occurred
to me that they would try to escape.*

. . .

*According to law, no baby could be born in prison but was expected
to come into this world at the State Alms House. This was all very fine
and good, but the time element had to be considered, and the prison ran
it on the close side. When our doctor gave the word, Mr. Flett, who was
the farm manager, and I drove the pregnant prisoner to Tewksbury. I
don't suppose it was more than fifteen miles or so; but with an old horse
and carriage, it seemed an eternity. I was always scared stiff; for my
knowledge of obstetrics at that period was nil. However, I daresay Mr.
Flett could have coped for he had a fairly large family. Of course, it was
a real outing for the expectant mother.*

*There was a terrific hierarchy among the prisoners...those in
for murder, forgery, or abortion were in the top echelon. Adultery
outranked prostitution; but drunk and disorderly or vagrancy had
precious little standing.*

With her characteristic flair for character portrayal, Edith describes an
elderly alcoholic who spent her winters at Sherborn and her summers at the
Deer Island House of Correction, with only a few weeks on the streets each
year. While in residence, she would work on sections of a large patchwork
quilt she was making for the Catholic chaplain.

When it came time for her to go, she would fold it up carefully and give it to one of the wardens with the instruction: Mind that none of youse touch it. I'll finish it when I get back." Another pet of mine was a thoroughly naughty youngster who sang like an angel. After one or two brief prison sentences, she settled down, married a nice man and named her first child after me.

Edith's greatest challenge occurred when six young women arrived who were considered "too incorrigible to handle" by the State School for Girls. Edith tried to teach them to read, write, and sew, but since she had never learned to sew herself, she was hardly a successful role model. So, with Mrs. Hodder's encouragement, she found a simple one-act play, and the prisoners performed it for an audience consisting of the wardens.

Mrs. Hodder began gradual changes – attractive blue weekday uniforms with white for Sundays, a library service, classes for the illiterate and those who wanted more education, privileges for good behavior – developing an extraordinary spirit within the prison. Occasionally, a prisoner would go beserk; and then Mr. Flett had to be called to put her into a strait-jacket and turn her into the padded cell. Against all warnings, Mrs. Hodder would go alone into that place for a long talk with the offender which generally quieted her down.

During her second year at Sherborn, Edith traveled to Europe with Mrs. Hodder. The trip, financed by her brother Bert, was to last three months. She kept a detailed travel diary chronicling the journey, illustrated with maps and pictures. They sailed to Madeira on the Cunard Line ship the "Ivernia" from New York City on October 10, 1912, and from there went on to Gibraltar, Naples, Capri, Pompeii, Florence, Rome, and Milan. Mrs. Hodder returned to the States, and Edith continued to France and England. Her return trip was an eventful one. According to newspaper clippings Edith pasted into her travel diary, the "President Grant," a six-masted steamer, "fought hard" in a terrible "battle with the sea," a storm so violent that it had caused two ships to run aground in New York harbor.

The ship called into port at Halifax to refuel, as it was running short of coal. Bert sent Edith a telegram from Boston on January 10:

> From papers note stormy passage you have had. Think it far better for you to come from Halifax to Boston by rail. I have reserved a section for you…. Wire me at once.

Seven of the ship's 800 passengers disembarked to continue by rail, including a Miss Stedman, according to one of the newspaper articles. Edith made her way back to Boston and resumed her work at Sherborn.

Upon her return, Edith was promoted to the position of Head of the Social Service Department, where she managed to wangle a part-time secretary to assist her. She began taking case histories and visiting the homes of many of the prisoners for further information. She would travel throughout Massachusetts, calling on the local chief of police, who would drive her around the district. Most of the homes she visited were filled with undernourished children, many of them "dimwitted, the result of inbreeding and often incest." Although she was successful at Sherborn, her career there ended abruptly in 1913.

> My three years in Sherborn ended rather badly. My brother [Bert], who had never wanted me to go there in the first place, had become an honorary member of the Massachusetts Prison Commission and as such, of course, was one of Mrs. Hodder's superiors. I used to dread the monthly meetings of the Board, for most of them couldn't see or understand the progress that she was making and were forever thwarting her most forward-looking ideas. It put me in a very awkward position, to say the least. Then, on top of that, my brother was fool enough to loan a considerable sum of money to an ex-convict from the men's prison at Charlestown. This man had been an experienced candy maker, or so he said, and my brother gave him enough to set him up in business. Of course, the inevitable happened. The man made off leaving behind a lot of equipment. My brother certainly had no interest in the candy business but he thought it would be a wonderful idea for me to

leave Sherborn and take the whole thing over and be independent. That fact that I was a complete ignoramus he dismissed airily with, "Oh well, you'll learn." Torn between two loyalties I decided to resign. Mrs. Hodder had been more than my chief. She had taken the place of my mother, and I loved and admired her enormously. It was a very difficult break but probably wise.

SIXTEEN

The Priscilla Sears Candy Shop

EDITH FOUND A small storefront on Avery Street in Boston for her candy shop and named it after her ancestor Priscilla Sears, through whom the Holts traced their descent from the Mayflower. At first, Edith enjoyed running her own business in Boston:

> It was fun supervising the decorating of the Priscilla Sears Candy Shop. The walls were a soft grey with white window trim and charming chintz curtains. There was only room for a soda fountain, a long candy case, and a high backed bench for elderly customers. The candy boxes were also grey, with a line drawing of Priscilla in blue. There was very little storage room, and the candy was brought in each day from the small factory, which at the beginning only employed two or three workers. I had a girl to help with the selling and a trained soda jerk, but they had to have relief so I quickly learned to pack and wrap, and mix candy, all with soft centers for the elderly, and mix sodas with the best of them. We were open evenings, as I remember, until 9 p.m., and most of that fell to me. Before Christmas and Easter, all hands had to work all night filling orders to be mailed or called for.

When I left Sherborn my brother Bert naturally thought that I would live with him in Braintree with his wife and small daughter Gratia. He was one of the early manufacturers of rubber tiling, with his own mill in South Braintree, and was making more money than was good for him. Later, in the Depression, he lost everything and was a most unhappy man. He had a grand house with a large music room and a pipe organ, but I loathed the whole setup, for I had grown up and wanted my independence, and our wills clashed. He had to be right and he taught me the destructive power of the pronoun 'I,' a lesson that I hope I shall never forget. However, he had always been extraordinarily generous to me, putting me through college, sending me abroad, and giving me a car on the promise that I stop smoking.

After a short stay in Braintree I took a room in a lodging house at 36 Newbury Street in Boston, near the shop, in one of those old brown-front affairs with large rooms and high ceilings. Marjory Gregg, a Radcliffe graduate and a teacher at the Windsor School, also lived there and we became friends. The Delands lived opposite and I came to know them very well. I had met Mr. Deland while I was at Sherborn in connection with one of our more intelligent prisoners, a very clever forger who showed promise as a writer and whom Mrs. Hodder had introduced to him in the hope that Mrs. Deland might become interested in her. I had wanted to meet Mrs. Deland even since I had read her book <u>John Ward Preacher</u>. She was one of the most popular novelists of her day; her books <u>Tales from Oldchester</u>, <u>Dr. Lavender's People,</u> <u>Helena Richie,</u> and <u>The Iron Woman</u> were widely read here and abroad, and she told me once she had never had a rejection slip. She had known all kinds of interesting people: Julia Ward Howe, Edward Everett Hale, and Phillips Brooks. I fell very heavily for her charm, and she, in turn seemed fascinated by my tales of Priscilla Sears and the candy shop.

There is an elegant formally posed photograph of Margaret Deland among Edith's papers, with the inscription: "This doesn't look like me—because it doesn't show how much I love you—but all the same, I do."

Edith recalls that the Avery Street candy shop soon became a gathering place for the newspaper crowd.

I was often offered free tickets for the theatre by the newspapermen. Once I was even asked to write a review of a rather poor play, which the drama editor didn't have time to cover. I never felt so important in my life as I walked into the press room after the show and was given a typewriter to do my review. I could only type with one finger and in my ignorance supposed I had to write the names of the entire cast. I had barely finished that and was laboriously condemning the play when the drama critic came along, snatched the paper out of the typewriter, and did a lightning review of an unseen play.

The newspaper crowd introduced me to a side of life I had never know, freewheeling, free thinking, and free living, and there wasn't a bar they didn't know, though they always took their jobs seriously. I had a car, and after the paper had been put to bed and the shop closed some of us would go adventuring. By today's standards we were extremely restrained, but I found that I could easily have been as susceptible as some of my Sherborn friends.

This is really one of the most difficult parts of my life to write about, and yet in a sense the whole story hangs on it, for it represents me in all my conflicting moods. I did not like my work much, I was at odds with my brother (rightly or wrongly), my values were rapidly changing, and I was confused and unhappy. For the first time in my life I was living in complete freedom as far as accountability was concerned and was playing around with a group of people from the newspapers and theater of a sort I had never known before. I suddenly became aware of my own biological urges and susceptibilities, and the conflict between my feelings and my puritan upbringing and values was tearing me apart. Though I was terrified of the consequences, that did not prevent me from playing as close to the edge as I dared. As with most New Englanders, sin and indigestion were awfully closely tied—you paid a price for both, and you could never either overeat or sin with complete abandon. I was a strange combination of recklessness, prudence, and a desire for all kinds of experience.

About this time an older friend of mine, whom I greatly admired, told me quite casually one day (I can even remember the exact spot on Park Street) that she was the mistress of a well-known Bostonian and that I might be occasionally useful. Being useful turned out to be picnics in the country in his big car with a food hamper put up by the Somerset Club and afterwards reading a book in the back seat while they disappeared. On one occasion she took me with her to a hotel. I had always been a hero-worshipper, although none of my idols had ever wanted to be put on a pedestal, and when two or three of them crashed in quick succession I felt betrayed. I was still in my early twenties and although there was nothing after my Sherborn years that I didn't know theoretically, I was singularly naïve and began to think perhaps this is the way the world really is. Going down a Back Bay alley and having a door silently opened to you, or being lifted out of a car in the country so that you left no footprints appealed to my sense of adventure. On the other hand I hated the secrecy and sordidness of the whole thing. There was no one to talk to and I began to feel guilty and to hate myself. I was rootless and often deliberately reckless and unhappy. A sense of guilt, it seems to me, has nothing whatever to do with any act in itself; to me it is a relative, personal thing. Among the things I felt guilty about was breaking my promise to my brother about smoking.

Two things happened about that time. First, the Avery Street shop was going so well that my brother decided to take on another, much larger one, at the corner of Milk and Arch Streets, which, of course, meant an awful lot of extra work. At the second shop we had a very long soda fountain with boys behind it, small tables where people could be served sandwiches, and a cashier's booth which I sometimes had to occupy. We had a trained manager from Bailey's Candy Shop but even so, I spent a certain amount of time in both shops. Businesswoman that I was, I was still dumb enough to entrust the first $500 I had ever saved to a slick Greek banker who promised to double it. Of course, I lost it all.

The second event was that after a year at Newbury Street Marjory Gregg and I were tired of living in a rooming house, and, by great good luck, discovered a fourth-floor apartment on the top of Beacon Hill. There was a ladder leading to the flat roof and a view of the Charles River. We grabbed it fast, got furniture from storage for our four rooms, and went prowling around the antique shops. It was the first real home I had had since my mother died and it was a marvelous feeling. On hot nights in the summer we used to lug a couple of watering cans to the roof, strip to the buff, and give each other a shower.

This was a more normal life than I had lived for a long time, but I couldn't shake off the old feeling of remorse and regret, and was often moody and depressed. Also, there were frequent flare-ups with my brother, and a growing distaste for my job. One Christmas Eve Marjory and I wandered over to Louisburg Square and then to the Boston Common to see the lights and hear the carols. Suddenly, over the brow of Beacon Hill, a medieval procession came into view, as a long line of choir boys with a tall, kindly, white-haired old priest, made their way to the steps of the State House. After they had sung a few carols, the priest spoke for a few minutes of what Christmas should mean to all of us. Then the procession reversed itself and went back to the old greystone Episcopal church of Saint John the Evangelist on Bowdoin Street. Marjory and I followed as if mesmerized, and listened to the midnight mass beautifully sung, with a wealth of color in the vestments and candles, and the lovely smell of incense. The next day it all seemed like a dream, but the beauty and pageantry of the scene remained. It made me feel that I was leading a pretty aimless and rather shoddy life. Business or money didn't really interest me, but I didn't know what I wanted. Finally, one day I got up my courage and asked to see one of the Cowley Fathers [an Episcopal monastic order]. After I told him about myself, I felt an enormous load roll off my shoulders. I sent him a five pound box of chocolates and started going regularly to church. I am sure part of this turnabout was my aesthetic appreciation of the service, but there was also a genuine desire for a different set of values.

Thursday evenings in the shabby old basement school room at St. John's were unlike anything else. The church had originally been a mission of the Anglican Cowley Fathers in Oxford, England, and although it was now autonomous, the senior clergy were all Englishmen. There might be a lecture or a story by one of the fathers or a letter received from a distant parishioner. Then the hard benches were pushed *back, coffee and cake were passed around. The Right and Wrong side of Beacon Hill came together quite unself-consciously and a bum from Scollay Square got the same treatment as a Boston Brahmin. After the social amenities were disposed of, Father Powell would clap his hands and say "Now then, upstairs all of you." This meant fumbling up an old wooden staircase to the dim church with its faint smell of incense, lit only by the sanctuary lamp. Everyone knelt for a few prayers and after the blessing staggered out into the darkness of the dreary street with its rundown lodging houses. I will always be grateful to the help St. John's gave me at a difficult time in my life, and I did go there regularly until I took off for France.*

When the United States declared war on Germany in 1916, I couldn't take it anymore. I made up my mind that I wasn't going to stay out of what was the greatest cataclysm of my age, but it wasn't until 1917 that the way became clear. Mrs. Deland's husband had recently died and she founded what was called the American Authors Unit, which I suspect she financed herself. I think she had been asked by one of her publishers to do a book on conditions in Europe. The Unit consisted of her friend and companion, Sylvia Annable, who had been Mr. Deland's nurse, and myself. The idea was to offer our services to the YMCA for six months. Of course there was endless red tape and correspondence but all seemed to be going smoothly until I was refused a passport by Washington. At that point I began to smell a rat. My brother, probably for a variety of reasons, had intervened in Washington. We had a flaming row and I said rather dramatically that if he kept me out of this war I would never see or speak to him again. Mrs. Deland used her connections, and to the great relief of the postman and all my friends, the passport finally came through.

One of the main themes in this part of the autobiography is Edith's resentment of her brother Bert's belief that he knew what was best for her. A strong-willed young woman, she succeeded in evading his interference. These experiences didn't keep her from interfering in Betty's life many years later, however.

SEVENTEEN

Edith in the War Zone
1917-1919

E DITH HAD HER HOROSCOPE prepared before she departed from Boston for France to participate in what she called "the greatest cataclysm of my age." The horoscope is a substantial document, some seven pages in length, and is suspiciously accurate in its description of the determined young woman off to take part in the Great War. The author, Edith's Radcliffe friend Ruth Delano, predicts that persons born under Edith's sign are:

> ...open-minded, sympathetic and generous, honest, somewhat ruthless in expression of opinions. People born under the second decanate of Sagittarius are naturally self-willed, and inclined to exhaust their physical and mental reservoirs by unwisely and enthusiastically draining them out, without taking much thought as to how they are to be refilled. Conservation of nervous energy is most necessary for people of this decanate. Self-control is of prime importance to those born under these degrees.

Jupiter in the ascendant gives good nature, benevolence, tact, and honor. You are not unlikely to have a habit of foreseeing events—a kind of minor prophet, though the mantle of prophecy doesn't rest heavily upon you. You are sympathetic and humane, and rather more than a little a philosopher, though too much inclined to an active striving life to draw up by the wayside and spend your time in meditation.

Ruth Delano is prone to giving advice; the horoscope warns Edith that she is "apt to over-estimate your powers of endurance, and underestimate your really unusual qualities of mind." She must beware of "fits of depression, moodiness, and saying 'what's the use.'" To keep the tendency to moodiness from "get[ting] the upper hand," she is advised to "try always to be as optimistic as possible." Career advice follows: "If you were a man you would do well in the diplomatic service," but [you should] never to try to make money through speculative matters—you would always lose." Furthermore, Edith is advised not to marry "unless you have congenial tastes along artistic and literary lines." I suspect that Miss Delano writes from her own knowledge of Edith when she describes her thus:

You find it difficult to work as a subordinate; you may have differences with employers, superiors, and parents, and you certainly will have frequent changes of occupation. It is a fortunate position for independence, for public life…that means strange plans, unexpected journeys, and unexpected gains.

. . .

Your Moon in the eleventh house shows many acquaintances among women, inferiors, clubs, the general public &c…. Moon in your chart is in evil aspect to the two malefic planets, - Mars and Saturn. These aspects give sorrow in home, liability to have one's plans thwarted by elders, and misfortune through women.

And yet, the horoscope assures her,

You are sufficiently protected by strong positions and good aspects of the benefic planets to escape any serious ill effects from the base aspects of these bad 'uns.

Not surprisingly, there is an entire page on travel, and some predictions for the remainder of the year, though the Miss Delano remarks apologetically that "I'm not strong on the predicting part of this business...." The horoscope concludes with more thinly veiled advice-giving aimed both at Edith and at her domineering older brother:

People born under the fiery signs are strongly individual, active, full of initiative, and must work out their own salvation in their own way. They are not easily dominated by others, and...ought to have their own way. Their job is to learn to control themselves.... Leave them alone, and they will learn their own lessons in their own way.

Evidently, Bert finally realized that he needed to leave his younger sister alone, and Edith went off to France with Mrs. Deland to join the YMCA Women's Auxiliary. Her story resumes in a series of letters written to Marjory Gregg, who was still living in the apartment they had shared on Beacon Hill. The first is dated December 23, 1917, shortly after Edith's arrival in Paris.

Dear Marj,

People have been ever so nice and Miss [ ] has promised us a canteen of three hundred men near the Bastille. They are all enlisted men not the highbrow type and have been very much neglected in the past.

You don't know how far away America seems, if I don't get letters soon I shall feel as if I had no native country.

. . .

I am in my uniform all the time. It is quite good looking as to color but the material isn't awfully good –too light weight and chilly and the pockets are already sagging. However I have the Y.M.C.A. insignia on both my hat and right sleeve and the other morning as I was walking down the Champs Elysee a little American sailor passed me and gave such a funny, shy salute – it was very nice. I was at one of the Canteens last night where a young Jewish lawyer now an enlisted man in the Engineers offered me a piece of Schraffts chocolate, a strip of gum, and the Boston American, all of which I accepted.

I note in passing that the sailor was identified as "American," while the lawyer was identified as "Jewish." How did Edith know he was Jewish, I wonder? Did they introduce themselves to one another by name? Or was she judging from his appearance? His gift of chocolate was clearly significant, for, as the letter continues,

The two things here at present that seem the most desirable are sweets, jam, chocolate etc – you want them all the time – and soap. Laundry is hideously expensive partly on account of the price of soap. You know it is wartime here but the discomforts are accepted in a way that they would not be at home.

. . .

It is so cold here in this room that I can see my breath but I only wish you were here to be uncomfortable with me...In some ways it is a good thing that we aren't going out to a village just yet for the winter is pretty hard at first for those that aren't acclimated. I'll write you again in a day or so. I wish that I could send you a sprig of mistletoe that I have in my buttonhole.

The letters to Marjory continued at the rate of one a week, sometimes more. To our modern ears, they sometimes sound a bit like love letters, although it is impossible to know whether Edith and Marjory's relationship was what we would call a romantic one. Throughout her life, Edith formed very strong attachments to women friends and mentors like Mrs. Hodder and Mrs. Deland. Had she been born a half century later, she and others of her generation might have acknowledged their friendships to be sexual in nature. One doesn't always know what to make of the relationships between correspondents at a time when people used heightened emotional language in letters.

In a letter Edith sent Marjory in January 1918 she refers for the first time to Eleanor Roosevelt, the wife of Theodore Roosevelt, Jr., son of the former president. In a series of newspaper articles entitled "Average Americans in Olive Drab—the War as Seen by Lt. Col. Theodore Roosevelt," Ted, as he was called, spoke about his family's role in the war. Theodore Roosevelt Sr., believed strongly that all Americans should defend their country, and asked President Woodrow Wilson to allow him to organize a private volunteer army, at a time when the U.S. was still officially neutral. Not surprisingly, the request was refused. When America finally entered the war, all four Roosevelt sons enlisted (Quentin, the youngest, would die on July 14, 1918, shot down behind German lines). Ted recalls that

> *Our last days in this country were spent with the family. Archie and I went with our wives to Oyster Bay, where father, mother, and Quentin were. My wife even then announced her intention of going to Europe in some auxiliary branch, but she promised me she would not start without my permission. The promise was evidently made in the Pickwickian sense, as when I cabled her from Europe not to come the answer that I got was the announcement of her arrival in Paris. There were six of our immediate family in the American Expeditionary Forces, my wife, one brother-in-law, Richard Derby, and we four brothers....*

Eleanor had evidently joined the YMCA unit to which Edith was assigned, and they worked together for the next two or three months organizing the leave center at Aix, an entirely new and unprecedented venture.

> *January 30th 3 AM*
> *En Train*
>
> Dear Marj:
> *It is absurd to be writing to you so soon again...I am on my way to Aix with Eleanor Roosevelt, and as there were no sleeping accommodations we are sitting up in true French fashion.*
>
> . . .
>
> *Aix is going to be an interesting job, because we are starting it. Eleanor is an awfully good sort, and we are going down ahead of*

the other woman workers, so that when they arrive there will be jobs waiting for them. It is going to be quite a proposition to make a compulsory leave centre so attractive that Paris won't be sighed for.

We have just been held up for some minutes at one of the big stations where hundreds of soldiers were waiting to entrain at this heathenish hour, all laughing and joking, with so many middle-aged men among them. It is a queer sensation to be going through this French country in the moonlight with signs of war here and there. I am perfectly sure that we are just going to miss a big air raid on Paris. It has been threatened for some time.

You know you are hungry all the time here. Last night I went with some of the Y.M.C.A. office crowd—a good collection—to a place for dinner, and when we finished we began all over again. Today I made Mrs. Deland give me a parting lunch which cost her great sums.

The soldiers are entraining with loud shouts, and I suppose their train will be given precedence over ours.

How I wish you were with me. The things I enjoy I know you would, and then it would be double fun all around. Mrs. Deland is a regular person to do things with, and we have awfully good times wandering around together. I was in civilian's clothes today, having my uniform pressed, so I bought some brandy to refill my flask. The bar keeper put a small amount in a quart bottle and the paper came off, so we walked the streets, me with the bottle under my arm. The more I write to you the worse the habit becomes.

2 P.M. Dead with sleep, but Aix is lovely and there are wonderful possibilities in the Casino. Fancy the Y.M.C.A. taking over the bar, baccarat tables, etc. My knees got awfully nervous on the train and I didn't sleep at all.

Edith continued her letter in a brief postscript the next day; she and Eleanor Roosevelt were hoping to get to Chartreuse before the rest of the group arrived. "Lots of work of the kind I like and plenty of thrills," she observes, and then, in an afterthought, "Picked up an early yellow primrose today –primavera, they call them."

Nine days later, on February 9th, Edith is busy "with gas-fitters and furniture-men" arranging rooms for the women workers. The following day, the letter continues with more details about the leave center:

We worked like galley slaves yesterday, attending to bread, sugar and coal cards, plumbers, furniture-men, and paper-hangers. We went to a street auction, left a perfectly strange man bidding on a kitchen stove for us. We are furnishing the American Leave Club of ten huge rooms at Chambery and the Casino at Challes. It's an enormous job because labor and supplies are so dear and hard to get. We ransacked mediaeval arched lofts and found all sorts of loot in the way of gilt mirrors and fine old bits of carved furniture which we were able to rent at a very nominal sum. Mrs. Roosevelt is a corker, tremendously business like and very nice. Almost the hardest thing is to find places for the women workers.

Yesterday afternoon we were going out to Challes so we invited Mere Marie du Sacre Coeur and Soeur Constance to come along. They had the time of their young lives. It was the first time that Soeur Constance had ridden in an automobile and Mere du Sacre Coeur hadn't been to Challes in twenty years in spite of the fact that she has lived in convents in Russia and America. We bought some candy that they enjoyed like small children. They went with me to look at a house for the workers while Mrs. Roosevelt was struggling with the plumbers in the casino, and they perfectly adored planning where the women could eat, sleep, etc. Soeur Constance drew me aside and told me to be very sure of the price before I made any decision.

. . .

As we left Mere Marie turned to some children and said that an American transport had gone down and that they must pray for the souls of the American soldiers and sailors who had been lost. We are hoping that this first tragedy may stir things up at home a bit.

We decided on the house directly. It was a peach of a place set high on the side of the mountain in the midst of vineyards. Just outside the entrance gateway was the village wash pool with a weather-beaten old shrine over it. The garden was delightful, full of spring flowers…it sloped away in the sun to an old arbor and here the stone wall stopped suddenly like the ramparts of an ancient castle and the whole valley lay spread before you, overtopped by the snowy Alps.

The house was a rambling stucco affair with an outside stairway and in a little niche at the top was another shrine of the Virgin with 1776 painted under it…. On the way up we had to stop and let a little boy with an inquisitive family of lambs go by us on the narrow road.

The only thing I would leave this job for is one at the front. It is hard interesting work with all sorts of experiences and I am keen on it. The opening here is going to be a wild scramble and we are awfully worried about it.

Lovingly yours,
Edith

On March 3rd Edith sends Marjory a letter of thanks for a package of summer clothes, which arrived in the midst of a heavy snow storm.

This I believe is your birthday and I wish we were together. I hope you will like your token when you get it which may not be until I come home. I keep it in my own pocket.

We came over here [to Chambery] for a celebration at the French Foyer du Soldat. I drove the Y.M.C.A. wagonette filled up in the back with secretaries—nice ones—all egging me on. In some strange way the darn thing got on fire on the way over but we all turned to and put it out with snow. In the process Dr. Denison and the regular chauffeur passed us in their car with very scornful looks. We are still waiting for the men to arrive and these days of enforced idleness are very stupid. I am going back to Aix tomorrow and hope very much that if men aren't coming right here I can go where they are. Mrs. Roosevelt and I want to run a doughnut and coffee rout out from Toul, she making the doughnuts and I peddling them around to the boys back of the 3rd line in a little Ford. The idea is too good to be possible. She and I have been sitting up until this pleasant hour cheerfully discussing everything and everybody. I know you will like her, she's a regular person. I do hope to get closer to the Front after another month.

We are treated at Aix to a never ending collection of worthies from the States on tours of inspection – we don't dare offend any of them and today our treat consisted of four fat pompous civilians from Pittsburgh and its environs representing some mysterious Order of the Moose. Fatuous fools – one looked at me up and down and asked me if I enjoyed my work. I wish they would stay at home.

. . .

Did I tell you that some of the first men to come to Aix were in that American offensive last week and that some were killed? It brought the war very much closer to think that the boys we had given cocoa to and had seen off at the train had gone over R.I.P. It's such a pity that the Protestant mind balks at prayers for the Faithful Departed; in cases like that it's instinctive.

. . .

I'll tell you something cheerful…You know I haven't touched a cigarette since I have been over here until three nights ago, since when Mrs. Roosevelt and I have smoked every night in secrecy, even here tonight with the door locked and our heads up the chimney.

It is very late and I must go to bed but my heavy blessing on you and may I be with you your next birthday.

Always lovingly yours,
Edith

Evidently Marjory was writing to Edith with corresponding frequency, for on March 10 Edith writes from Aix to say that she received eleven letters that evening, "four from you." A "boy" who hadn't had a letter in three months "looked at me very enviously."

Today started off wonderfully with that batch of letters, but just after lunch Mrs. Roosevelt got a telegram that her brother-in-law, Captain [Archie] Roosevelt had been wounded—shrapnel in the leg and a broken arm – so she has gone up to Paris tonight and expects to be allowed to go to him at the base hospital. He is in her husband's battalion that has been in the trenches these last ten days so she will probably be able to see her husband. She is a corker and you are going to like her enormously. I have a feeling that this is the end of the pleasant part of Aix. For the present I shall be in charge of all the women here, and it's a heck of a job. We are expecting more men this week, which means more work, thank heaven. My principal difficulty is getting the milk transported here and doling out American flour to the French bakeries for our bread. I am anxious now to get my job here polished off—then go up to the Front. I am awfully sorry to be missing all the Paris air raids.

A busy day today. We took about eighty soldiers on a picnic to Hautecomme Abbey, an old Trappist monastery at the end of the Lac du Bourget. A marvelous spot and a beautiful day. The men were crazy about it and toasted hot dogs over the fire and forgot there was such a thing as war; awfully nice men, engineers and members of the Johns Hopkins Medical Unit.

. . .

Did I tell you that Captain Little had the band serenade us last night before Mrs. Roosevelt went up to Paris? It was quite all right until they played Auld Lang Syne, and then Eleanor and I both snuffled quite audibly, which pleased Captain Little enormously who was standing by me on the balcony.

In canteen this evening about 10:30 we got the word that…men were arriving in an hour's time and would we give them coffee and sandwiches, which we have just done. They had been on the train for forty hours, sitting up all last night, so bed is going to seem good to them.

I wish I could write more about the feelings and opinions but the principal emotion is one of absolute unreality on the one hand and absolute matter-of-factness on the other. Mrs. Deland is terribly blue about the war and its after-effects. I am sure she is right and yet it seems as if we must take things as they come, and if we go under perhaps that *may be the best thing. Better (?) peoples and civilizations than ours have gone in order to make room for us....*

This last remark offers a glimpse of the philosophical side of Edith's nature alluded to in the horoscope, but it also reveals the profound pessimism felt by the Allies not long before the war ended. Edith ends this part of the letter with a reference to the "powers at home," whose "present inefficiency…is appalling as seen from over here."

As the war on the French front intensified, Edith wrote to Marjory in an undated letter that she was

> *awfully keen to get up to Nancy or Toul but it may not be possible. I am scared to death of such little things as bombs and gas but I want to do it and then come home.*

As in the autobiography, Edith can be very hard on herself.

> *I haven't made good over here as I should and I'm afraid I never shall. I haven't the capacity for detail and monotonous work that Sylvia has.*

But the mood passes, and she returns to the describing the events going on around her, in all their variety.

> *I am enclosing three poems that won prizes in the Paris Herald competition for which Mrs. Deland was one of the judges. I think they are amazingly good, especially the second. You know life over here this summer is going to be hell. Things have happened already that aren't published, and the Germans are going to perpetrate one form of frightfulness after another.*
>
> *You should have seen me making chocolate frosting this afternoon for some dried up cakes we had—I made it up out of my head and it was darn good.... We are beginning to fill up again in earnest and life is getting more complicated. In the first place the war is terribly*

serious just now and it looks as if almost anything might happen. Paris is getting a frightful dose of air raids, and the French papers said this morning that the city has been bombarded by German guns that carry 100 miles. I think that is only a rumor but God only knows what is going to happen in the next month—the Front may be brought to us. We are going to have guards stationed around the Casino for fear of an attempt to blow it from the inside. That isn't likely, but it isn't impossible and it's well to be on the lookout. It's a last terrific drive on the part of the Germans, and they seem to be on the crest of the wave.

All her life, Edith was exceptionally skillful at devising "schemes" and getting others to go along with them. Here's one:

I doped out a wonderful scheme for a portable Ford canteen in which the exhaust would be used to heat a coil of piping to keep coffee hot, and which could be fitted up to carry fifty or sixty gallons of coffee and several hundred sandwiches. The Front is changing so from day to day that it is almost hopeless to station definite canteens in any place, and a portable one would help out amazingly. Some of the mechanics I have talked to say my scheme is practicable and I do want a chance to try it out. Mrs. Deland is a peach and she knows how restless I get. She speaks the hard truth to me but in love, and as Eleanor Roosevelt says, I "kiss the rod."

I had a wonderful trip to Lyon yesterday, about 125 miles. Came home by moonlight over Hannibal's Pass. The cherry and plum trees are in blossom now, and on the road going over we passed a beautiful big spreading bush all pink an white blossoms with an old gray stone cross rising up out of the center. It must have meant much to the pilgrims and travelers along the highroads in the old days.

. . .

I wouldn't have things different for the world and no matter what happens it's worth it. I am trying –for the most part unsuccessfully – to do what I ought to do rather than what I want, and it's good for me. There is a bully crowd of workers here now and we all mess together, which is fun. I bought two adorable salt shakers at Lyon yesterday for our table. My, it's a big time to be living in!

The last few letters Edith wrote to Marjory are from Paris, during the two weeks or so from mid-May to early June, shortly before her return to America.

Paris, May 18, 1918

Dearest Marj:

Always when I have other people to write to I leave them entirely in the lurch and begin with you.

I got back last night from a four days' trip with Mrs. Deland and Sylvia around some of the camps that I have previously visited. Every time you stir it means papers and then in these days it is often hard to find places in the [train] compartments and you have to fight for taxis. As I got out of one last night at 11 the alert sounded but nothing happened. They are laying for us this moon but so far unsuccessfully. I was dead to the world last night and dirty to a degree that might seem impossible. Anyhow I go up early this AM and had a bath in the bathing establishment near us on the Boulevard Montparnasse. I suspect it of being none too clean but what can you do.

I am coming home armed with all sorts of papers that will help to get me back next spring. It makes me feel terribly cheap when you talk about my having made good. Over here you realize constantly how inadequate and selfish you are and somehow or other I have managed to fall into more interesting jobs than have been good for me…. When I first come home spoil me a bit and then take a firm hand to me.

Going down on the train the other day the compartments were terribly crowded and a nice First Lieutenant gave me his place. He was one of about twenty…. Most of them hadn't talked with an American woman in months. One of them said they heard my voice in the corridor and began to make room for me and another one said, "you know I was afraid that you were going to read." Such attention you don't get at home I assure you. Anyway I asked them all to tea Sunday afternoon never thinking that any of them would show up. At four o'clock promptly twelve of them arrived and they stayed three solid hours…. They were very much pleased with themselves for having followed exactly my instructions as to how they should spend their time in Paris. They were wild to blow in a quarter's pay and I told them to go to the Tour d'Argent Saturday night for dinner—they could all spend enough there—and be sure to watch the crowds from a boulevard café Sunday morning and then to end up with the usual afternoon service at Notre Dame before they came to our house.

Afterwards Eleanor C. and I went on a real bat. We took a taxi to the foot of Montmartre. At this critical juncture the cab got a flat tire, so we consoled him with a few cigarettes which turned despair into joy and left him a radiant being. Then we climbed thousands of steps until the whole city lay before us in the late spring twilight. Beautiful beyond words with Sacre Coeur keeping guard over it all, queer and paradoxical in architecture but dominating everything. Supper out of doors at an out of the way place called the Cou-Cou. We were both in mufti – I in my purple dress which I have only worn twice, and we partook of a modest bottle of very good Italian wine and smoked innumerable cigarettes. The children played around and some chance musicians fiddled. The whole thing was as peaceful as if there were not war except when you looked at the listening ears on Sacre Coeur or saw the deserted studios and the Reformes. We walked down in the dark, very much disappointed not to have heard the alerts and had a chance to see an air raid from the front balcony.

Edith had her chance to see an air raid four days later, on May 22, at about 11:00 at night. After watching from a fifth floor room, she and Eleanor Cargin [the secretary to the chief of the YMCA] went down to the boulevard.

A watchman went hurriedly calling down to the streets "A bas les lumieres," and a French humorist leaning out of a window called back "A bas la lune," a quite obvious retort for it was a heavenly night and perfectly clear. We started up by the Boulevard Montparnasse to the

Observatoire, but the barrage was pretty hard and we heard bombs crashing, so we sat down on a bench under the trees and swapped remarks with an American officer and some carefree French citizens. They were all in the best of spirits, making fun of everything. An old man sitting with his wife said "Oh la la la, after forty years of married life, to have to put up with this?" The stars were shooting back and forth, and the barrage fire barked away in clean sharp shots… and then the heavy, louder more isolated crash of bombs.

This festive evening ended with a candlelight dinner of bread and jam and lemonade at a little restaurant in the quarter that "specializes in raids," and then home to bed. "Raids are all very well," Edith concludes airily, "but they leave you terribly sleepy in the morning."

Edith's letters suggest that beneath her breezy holiday façade there were troubling currents. Elsewhere in this long letter, after more descriptions of shops and scenes and walks around the city her tone suddenly shifts:

Marj my dear – I feel the need of a long jaw. You know over here it looks sometimes as if the end of the civilized world as we know it was close at hand with a complete overthrow of our present social and moral organization. I wish I could write you more fully. That is why it is so stupid writing home to people –from the objective point of view there is nothing to say. You feel so swamped by the inevitable big things.

. . .

There are little things that I'm always wanting to tell you or share with you. For instance, did I tell you about the very gaudy gilt diploma frames in one of the stores with a black band across instead of the diploma and the words "mort pour le France"?

The next letter, dated Paris, May 26th, describes a three day trip Edith took to the front, "all dressed up with two gas masks apiece and a tin helmet," past little villages in ruins where the soldiers are quartered in barns and cow stables.

At one of the places nearest the lines I met one of the lieutenants who had been there for tea last Sunday and it was so nice to see him. At another canteen I met D.F. [the husband or sweetheart of her friend Jane; she refers to him later as F.D.]. *and had such a nice time with him… when I see those camps at the Front and how much it means to the men to see any woman I feel guilty about coming home.*

She speaks of being kept up most of the night by the bombing and by the bedbugs in a peasant cottage where they were billeted, with the guns only five miles away. In a continuation of the letter the next morning she reports that

Bertha [the Allies' nickname for the German cannons] *began at 6:30 and barked every fifteen minutes for two hours. It was the worst yet and it is especially noisy over in our section. The French aren't afraid but it is a tremendous nervous strain to listen for that thing every fifteen minutes. The Germans have gotten to a pass where they don't care what they do….*

Edith began her last letter to Marjory the next day, after reading the letters Marjory had written on May 5th and 9th. The war news is so bad that the Paris papers aren't allowed to publish anything about the bombardment of the city, and Edith wonders "whether I'll ever get back to No. 4," their apartment in Boston. Marjory has sent her pictures, which she has been looking at "again and again." On May 30th she resumes writing:

South of Paris, May 30th
The whole world seems more upside down than ever. The war news doesn't get any better and even if the Allies hold where they are now, what is going to happen in the next offensive, which is as inevitable as tomorrow's sunrise? … Those brutes of Germans bombarded Paris on Corpus Christi Day when the English declared a truce in Cologne, but what can you expect?

. . .

> *I am a rank coward and every time Bertha goes off I feel as if she were walking up my back. I hate it all so. I wonder if I'll ever see you again but what difference do I or any other one individual make?*

Despite her fear of the bombing Edith can't stay away from Paris, even though she continues to wonder if she'll ever get home. Letters are censored, so she can't tell Marjory much about what is going on, and anyway, "you probably have more real news than we." "F.D.," [or D.F. – see above] has been killed,

> *probably by accident behind the lines. I can't tell you what a shock it gave me, and to think of my having had such a good time with him last week Friday. What a blow it's going to be to his family and how glad I am I had a chance to see him and slip him some cigarettes. The poor boy – but a brave and gay one. I shall try to find out something more about it for his family. I had promised him to take back some of his souvenirs with me. Rest In Peace.*

In this last letter Edith repeatedly expresses concern about Mrs. Deland ("Paris is no place for Mrs. Deland"). Writing from "all over France," she adds a final postscript about a week after beginning the letter, to say that she and Mrs. Deland and Sylvia have left Paris and are in a little town in Brittany.

To fill in more of the story, we must turn to Edith's autobiography, which describes the bombing of Paris at the end of May 1918. Here is her account of her last day at the YMCA's American leave facility in Aix, tending to a large crowd of exhausted engineers who arrived straight from the trenches and tumbled into bed.

> *Less than twenty-four hours later they were hastily recalled and had only fifteen minutes to make the train. We grabbed all the food in sight and rushed it to them. They scrambled in blowing kisses and singing "Where do we go from here, Boys?" As leaves were being cancelled I got permission to go back to Paris, thinking I might be of more use there—a*

rather dirty trick to play on Eleanor [Roosevelt] but she had her family to consider and I was unattached. I went up on the night train and stayed in my old quarters at the Rue de la Grande Chauiere where my special pals were living, Eleanor Cargin... [and others].

Edith tells the story of the first air raid and of being unable to find her clothes in the dark and then going down to the sidewalk to watch the show. The story of the old man and his wife is here, and the soldiers who were afraid she was going to read on the train.

Edith returned to America with Mrs. Deland and Sylvia at the end of June 1918, with the understanding that she would be discharged from the American Authors payroll, and hired directly by the YMCA, under whose auspices she would return to France. She tells an amusing tale of the journey on an empty transport ship, on which the only other passenger was Bishop McCormick, an army chaplain on leave.

In those days our soldiers wore yards of puttees around their legs and poor Bishop McCormick, who was dying to take a bath, was afraid to take his off. We told him to be a sport, that if he was going to be drowned it wouldn't make any difference to the Almighty, but I think he was more afraid of being captured by a U-boat and not looking like an officer. However he finally got up his courage, and of course at the critical moment came the call to Quarters. A more distressing object I have never seen than Bishop McCormick rushing towards his lifeboat, trailing yards of khaki webbing behind him, giving us a dirty look.

The Armistice was declared while Edith was on her way back to France, but she managed to get to Paris in time for the victory parade down the Champs Elysees with King George, the Prince of Wales, President Wilson, General Pershing, and "all the other Greats," as she put it.

The autobiography provides a somewhat different perspective on the time Edith spent in France than the letters to Marjory do, and the retrospective speaking voice reflects her many years of administrative and social service experience.

> *Mr. Carter, the YMCA Chief, turned over to me a traveling personnel job out of the Paris office. This meant visiting canteens all over France where there were women employed and listening to the gripes of the Staff, men and women. It also meant other things — usually sitting up all night several times a week on a train or sleeping in a bug-infested hotel bedroom or a cot in an Army hostel but there was little ground that I did not cover – the old battle fields of the Marne, Chalons, Mailly, Nevers, Toul, Chaumont which was General Pershing's Headquarters, and many others. Most of the huts were well run but in others there was friction, low morale and occasionally very sticky situations. The amazing thing is that there weren't more. The YMCA [staff] for the Army Overseas had to be chosen suddenly and in large numbers and the New York Office was no more infallible than any of the other organizers. The Directors of the camps were men – either over age for military duty – some of them were "do gooders" or pretty mediocre specimens – and the other group were the 4F's. Many of them felt terribly apologetic and were insecure or overly aggressive. As to the women, they were a mixed bag varying from the "lady bountiful"-type to the sweet young thing who "just loved our Boys" but didn't do a bit of work. The best of all, to my way of thinking were the middle-aged mums who had brought up their own children and were often widows. They sewed on buttons, worked long hours, and knew when a man needed a bit of mothering. On the whole, however, they were a grand bunch of people, hard working and anxious to give of their best. Oftentimes situations were easily straightened out by a shift to another canteen or, as in one case, finding another room for a woman whose neighbour snored. Sometimes the whole morale was so poor that the only thing to do was to suggest to Paris that the Director come up for an interview and there would be a general house-cleaning.*

Edith speaks of traveling alone with only a knapsack, of meeting soldiers of all ranks only to see their names posted later among the killed in action, and of "wrestling with recalcitrant canteen personnel who must have hated my guts."

> *It was a kind of vagrant life I have never known before or since*
> *– strange places, unknown people, delays of all kinds, red tape in*
> *unexpected places and having to improvise in any emergency. But one*
> *took it all as a matter of course. We were almost always tired and cold*
> *and hungry for sweets. But at the back of it all was the feeling that we*
> *wouldn't be anywhere else for all the world.*

It was now the winter of 1919, and she was sent to a small leave area in the Pyrenees, close to the Spanish border. The flu epidemic had begun, and she recalls that

> *One of the girls on the staff died of flu, and as our director was*
> *off with his petite amie, another YMCA member and I, according to*
> *French law, had to witness the sealing of the coffin, which took place*
> *at midnight, and accompany it the next day to Bordeaux to be shipped*
> *back to America.*
>
> . . .
>
> *Later on I had a slight case of flu myself and was sent to Hendaye for*
> *a week's convalescence. We were practically on the Spanish border and*
> *the temptation to go across the International Bridge was irresistible.*
> *Another girl and I persuaded two of the maids at the hotel to loan us*
> *some clothes, for being in uniform we risked being interned if caught.*
> *We stuffed our pockets with American cigarettes then hot-footed it to*
> *the Bridge. The cigarettes did the trick and the guard said if we could*
> *get into Irun and back, about six miles in all, before he went off duty it*
> *was all right with him. We made straight at full speed for the first sweet*
> *shop in sight, bought all the lovely chocolate squashy gateaux we could*
> *possibly carry and got back just in time.*
> *Anyway, I have been in Spain.*
> *In the spring of 1919, Leila Pugh and I were told that we were to*
> *be attached to the 29th division of the American Army of Occupation*

in Cochem, Germany, very close to our headquarters in Coblenz; the British were next door in Cologne. The transportation provided was an ancient Ford camion loaded with as much extra gas as we could carry and a lovely fruit cake, to say nothing of other supplies plus a small trailer. We thought we might as well do a bit of sightseeing on the way, but the roads of course were in shocking condition pitted with shell holes and bare of trees. At Chateau Thierry we had to ditch the trailer. It was just too much for the poor old Ford to take, so we repacked and followed the route of the great battles.

. . .

We were always breaking down, but usually someone would come along and patch us up temporarily. After we left Verdun the brakes failed us, so going downhill I had to drive in reverse and the only way we could get the wretched thing to start was for Leila to get out and push, and then make a lightening leap for the seat.

The thought of the fruit cake was so tempting that we finally cut a big hunk out of it and gobbled it greedily. As soon as it was down I began to feel queer so I said to Leila, "Didn't that cake taste a bit off?" At that moment we both began to be violently sick and discovered that one of the tins of gas had leaked and the cake was soaked with it. About ten miles out of Cochem everything gave out. The poor old camion had had it and we had to abandon it and get a lift into our station.

My recollections of our work there are a bit dim but it was a tough assignment. Our men were not allowed to fraternize with the Germans, and aside from drill there was not much for them to do except to get drunk. The result was that when I wasn't dancing with them at night I was overseeing them peeling potatoes under the direction of a bored noncom.

Edith ends this section of her autobiography with a brief account of her return to Paris en route home. Once again, she couldn't resist a bit of sightseeing:

Our travel orders were direct to Paris but we found that we could take in Brussels…. Unfortunately, when we arrived in Paris our times didn't quite agree with our passes but by a stroke of luck we got by the MP.

"Anyhow," she concludes with pardonable pride,

I ended up with three service stripes, the AEF Ribbon, and the Army of Occupation Flash. The uniform is now in the green room of the Loeb Theatre of Harvard, probably gathering moths.

Edith documented her war years in a large scrapbook with the title "War Clippings" printed on the front. It contains many postcards from the places she mentions in the letters and the autobiography, tiny blurred photographs one and a half by two inches, and some larger ones in various sizes. The war clippings are there too: one, from the Boston Sunday Herald, dated December 9, 1917, has the large print headline: "Mrs. Margaret Deland is 'Off for France'" and features photographs of the three women, all in rather imposing hats. Edith's hat is a tri-corner affair worn with a high collared shirt and string tie and overcoat, which makes her look rather like a soldier in the American Revolutionary War. The writer of the article, Ethel Armes, notes that the celebrated author is accompanied by Sylvia Annable and Edith Stedman,

…intelligent, capable and highly efficient women who have had several years of practical experience in their professions; one is a nurse, the other a business woman. They are not the sort of persons – of whom there are too many in France today – who go to fiddle while Rome is burning!

Some girls have gone to that torn and heroic land for sensations, or adventure, or to wear pretty uniforms – stage business, so to speak…. Miss Stedman, as vice-president of the Priscilla Sears Sweet Shop Company here in Boston, where she has fed as many as 1500 people a day, is particularly well qualified to look after the food end of the canteen work…. As for Mrs. Deland – "I can at least wash dishes!" she said.

Another clipping, from The New York Times Magazine January 12, 1919, highlights the "War Work of Roosevelt's Daughter-in-Law," Eleanor Roosevelt. Eleanor is quoted at length; she describes the creation of the leave areas at Aix and Chambery as a "gigantic experiment" which completely transformed the way American soldiers took their leaves.

> *"You see," she explained, "the men hated it, before they came. I suppose you know that they called Aix-les-Bains "Aches and Pains," and when they first gave it that name, before they got there, they meant it! In the first place every soldier wanted to go to Paris….. Then he didn't like the idea of being told to go to some definite place; he thought it was going to be a place with a lot of discipline and reveille and drill. And because they knew it was all in the hands of the Y.M.C.A. some of the soldiers were afraid that they would be expected to go to religious meetings all the time! … And as for us, having to invent it all, we were terribly afraid it was not going to succeed!*

The scrapbook also contains a large, detailed map of France, and Edith's very imposing passport, covered with seals and signatures. There are photos of the lavish interior of the Chambéry Club, of soldiers and YMCA staff, all in uniform, of spectators at a baseball game in Aix, and an especially good one that shows Edith in her uniform, accompanied by a soldier holding a cane and a young French boy who salutes the photographer in fine military fashion.

EIGHTEEN

The China Years
1920-1927

W HEN EDITH RETURNED to Boston from France she resumed her career in social work at the "Bureau of Illegitimacy," but soon became "restless and bored" and began casting about for something more exciting. One evening, she recalls in her autobiography,

> *I heard Elise Dexter, Director of the Nurses' Training School of the Church General Hospital in Wuchang, China, give an intensely interesting and vivid account of her experiences and their need of a medical social worker.*
>
> *It appealed to me strongly except for the missionary part – a career which had never had the slightest appeal for me.*
>
> · · ·
>
> *However, I was an Episcopalian by upbringing and a medical social worker by training; and Elise Dexter didn't fit any missionary prototype.... Her boundless sense of humor combined with her practical common sense and spirit were irresistible.... We began to see a good*

deal of each other, and after an interview in New York with Dr. Wood, Head of the Mission Board, and a physical exam, I found myself headed for Vancouver, where I was to meet Elise.

We sailed on the Empress of Russia on the 29th of July, 1920. I thoroughly enjoyed the trip except that, being a gregarious person, I was astounded to find that the business crowd would have nothing to do with the missionaries, and there was no use my looking longingly in at the bar. Our first stop was Yokohama, still showing the effects of the devastating earthquake, where I saw women loading the ships with coal in little baskets. As we neared Whangpoo, the blue of the Pacific began to show the brown silt of the Yangtzse River. My first view of the city was disappointing – almost like any other European city, with the Bund along the River lines with "go-downs" and office buildings and a park with the infamous sign, "No Chinese or dogs allowed." The only foreign sights were the rickshaws and the Sikhs, a tall, handsome, cruel-looking people, with their enormous turbans, who policed the British concession and scared the coolies stiff. We were put up for the night at St. Elizabeth's Hospital in the French concession and the next day were on our way up river.

Those river boats under the China Navigation Company were something to remember. Always with an English captain, a Scotch engineer, and Chinese stewards, they were extremely comfortable with all kinds of delicious curries, and the trip, which took four days to reach Hankow, was an ever-changing picture. In some places the river was a mile wide and in others so narrow that the little villages with their green rice paddies and water buffaloes with small boys on their backs were almost under one's nose. The prevailing colors were the green of the fields and the brown of the dusty foot paths connecting small white-washed houses tiled red or black with their lovely upturned corners. On the river there were innumerable boats, from little sampans to the full-sailed kwandos with eyes painted on their prows; some had their fishing nets out and others were loaded with blue-coated passengers and all kinds of livestock bound for various small villages along the river. Here and there on a hill would be a Pagoda, tiered in beautiful proportions, *and if the wind was right, the faint tinkle of its bells swaying in the breeze would come across the water.*

In 1920, Hankow was the largest of the three Han cities, Wuchang and Hanyang being the other two, and was a treaty port with foreign concessions. The population of all three was nearly 2,000,000. Commercially, industrially, and historically, it was a very important center and was labeled the Chicago of China. The three cities contained the mint, the big steel works, the largest branches of the Hong Kong, Shanghai, and other banks, offices of the British American Tobacco Co., many English and French shops, and cotton, silk, and oil mills. France, England, Japan, and Russia all had their own concessions in Hankow, won from the Chinese in the middle of the nineteenth century.

Although Edith had no way of knowing this at the time, the foreign concessions, those enclaves of residences, businesses, and missionary activities concentrated in an area smaller than a square mile along the Yangzee River, would be drawn into the political unrest that rocked China in the 1920s. By the time Edith arrived in Wuchang, the Chinese Communist Party was just beginning to emerge in the newly-formed Republic of China that had replaced the Qing Dynasty in 1911. Sun Yat-sen, the moderate leader of the government, had signed an agreement with the Russian Communists in 1923, but he was determined to remain on good terms with the foreign business interests. Unrest between the moderates and the leftists would increase through the 1920s, with students and labor unions opposing the concessions, particularly the British and Japanese ones (Russia had returned its concession to the Chinese government in 1920). The Han cities became a battleground between the northern Chinese warlords, who had ruled China for centuries and refused to relinquish their power, and the Communist-backed reformers.

Edith describes her entry through the Big East Gate into Wuchang (now part of the modern city of Wuhan), where she would be spending the next several years.

Wuchang was an ancient walled city, the capital of Hupeh province, with at least a quarter of a million inhabitants. It came as a bit of a shock when we finally drew up in front of the big red-brick hospital – the men's and women's sides quite separate except for the chapel – all walled around in two different compounds. The American and Chinese staff were all waiting for us with firecrackers wound around long bamboo poles, the length of which determined the degree of your welcome. When I considered how I had hoarded my 25 cents worth of firecrackers as a child on the 4th of July, I was aghast at such prodigality. We finally ended up in a small wooden house at the rear of the hospital, which Elise and I shared with Dr. Mary James and Anne Brown, the other foreign nurse.

. . .

Elise and I shared a big bedroom and bath, which, by the way, was extremely civilized. The john was a commode emptied twice a day by a special amah [personal servant] and the bath was a large zinc affair, made of Standard Oil tins in which were set at night and in the morning big watering pots of hot and cold water, the hot ones covered with outsized tea cozies to keep the heat in. I didn't see the like again until I happened to get a glimpse of a bedroom at Garlands Hotel in London in 1934 with a proper English hip bath. Anyway, the idea was the same and it worked beautifully. In addition, there was a dining room and living room with two small studies, all of which took three servants to maintain. The cook took his orders for the day and did the marketing with the implicit understanding that he was entitled to a 10% squeeze on the bills. The Number Two waited on the table, did the general cleaning and washing up, and the amah did the laundry.

For her first year Edith's job consisted of studying Chinese six hours a day with an elderly scholar, who arrived each morning at nine. The lesson began with a pot of tea, which he drank from the spout.

When he came into the room Mr. Yin took off his spectacles (a matter of politeness) and, with his hands in his sleeves, bowed to me. In return, I made a similar bow and said "Has the honourable teacher eaten his rice?" (more politeness). With that out of the way, we settled down to work at the dining room table. In addition to my Chinese grammar he had a stack of small 2 inch square cards on each of which in his beautiful writing was a Chinese character. As fast as I learned to repeat it successfully, I wrote the Romanization, the definition, and the tone on the back.

When he left at about 4:30 and after tea, I would go into the wards and practice my classical learning on some of the poor peasants who, when they finally caught hold of something familiar, would immediately turn it into the vernacular, which was alright with me.

Edith's lifelong ability to solve problems through small interventions and improvisations began to evidence itself almost immediately:

There was one old gnarled and cussed country woman whom no one could do anything with. She either clammed up or went into a temper tantrum. I got nowhere with her until in desperation I handed her a bunch of brightly colored glazed papers of every imaginable hue. The next time I saw her she was completely engrossed in turning out the most artistic and realistic repousse figures of peacocks, birds, and animals, all done with infinite skill and detail. The peacocks fairly shrieked, they were so lifelike, and old Huang Nai Nai had found release and an ability to communicate. We became tremendous friends and she would pull my head down to hers and ask why my amah didn't use proper oil to make it nice and shiny.

The hospital belonged to an enclave dominated by the American Episcopal Church, which had laid claim to Wuchow just as other church missions had done in other Chinese cities. There were about 150 Americans, mostly families or "spinsters," all required by the church hierarchy to pass examinations on the Prayer Book and phonetics instead, as Edith observed caustically, of being exposed to the history and art of the region. The Episcopal Church maintained separate schools for boys and girls and a university, along with a number of churches and the hospital. Of the faculty at the university, Edith remarks that too many were "second or third rate."

Hell could have been paved with their good intentions, but they were extraordinarily self-centered and lacking in curiosity, and many of the wives never bothered to learn Chinese, but conversed with their servants in Pidgin English.

By the end of her first year in Wuchow Edith had acquired a fair speaking knowledge of Chinese and, she adds, "an ability to understand Chinese sermons."

I taught English to a group of nurses by a method unknown to any pedagogical system and mostly by improvisation. Also, I could watch operations to my heart's content, and was even allowed to help Dr. James in a difficult obstetrical case by putting my arms around her waist while she pulled on the forceps. My own job seemed to clarify itself and the only question was how to get things started. There were at least a dozen "deadheads" occupying hospital beds that were sadly needed, but no one knew what to do with them, for they were more or less derelicts. Two of them, women in their forties, were blind and helpless and otherwise would have been turned out to beg. Two little slave girls about 11 or 12 years old had been abandoned at the Hospital Gate. Their feet had been bound in infancy and, because of cold or infection, gangrene had started and amputation of both legs was necessary. Obviously they were of no further use to their owners, but they were perfectly normal, healthy youngsters otherwise, and needed training for some kind of occupation. By some devious method, I wangled some artificial legs for them from the Peking Union Medical Hospital and got them on their feet. The owner of one of these children, when she heard about this, came to the Hospital demanding that Sz Ku be returned. Dr. James, with great presence of mind and courtesy said to the great lady, "But of course, we shall be delighted to return Sz Ku to you, but unfortunately she will have to leave her legs behind." The cook, meantime, had hidden them in the kitchen oven. So that was that, and Sz Ku and her legs were once more united.

There were other residents ranging from abandoned babies to old arthritics and arrested cases of tuberculosis. Occupational therapy seemed indicated, but as I knew nothing about it first hand, I had to rely on Providence and instinct. One day, when I was in a little village outside the City Gates, I saw an old woman making a narrow silk braid such as the Chinese used on their gowns for decoration or button loops. She was making it on a conical shaped bamboo contraption fitted up with spools of different colored silks, and by tossing them back and forth was turning out some fascinating patterns. With a bit of persuasion and a few coins, I induced her to let me bring her back to the hospital with her contraption and in nothing flat she was teaching the blind patients how to do a similar thing using just one color. It could be done very rapidly, but the question was how it could be used. One of the doctors said, "But that, sterilized, would make perfect umbilical tape." So we did it up in three-yard packages, and with a bit of advertising sold it up and down the Yangtze to the various hospitals. As the patients got more skilled, it was made in red and green to tie up Christmas packages. Ribbon lasted a very short time in the damp and mildew of that part of China, and the Christmas tape was wildly successful. Then someone produced a small cardboard loom that could be hitched at one end to the foot of the bed, and we turned out half inch tape as ties for the doctors' and nurses' gowns

What was obviously needed was a "Half Way House" where patients who didn't need hospital care could live and try to learn to make themselves self-supporting, plus a work room for the mothers of some of the children who were still in the hospital as free cases. Thanks to an anonymous gift of $500 and endless wranglings with the owner and the "go between" I managed to rent a house on the Tsang Kai which had several courtyards. We called it the House of the Merciful Savior, the name of the Hospital chapel, and after a terrific housecleaning and buying the minimum of furniture, benches, tables, bed frames made of rope, rice bowls, chopsticks, and kitchen utensils, we moved about eight of the "deadheads" from the hospital and had a feast to celebrate. The place soon turned into a three-ring circus, for, as the children needed a *teacher, we allowed some of the neighboring youngsters to join them, and before we knew it, we had a school on our hands. Then there was the workroom for the able-bodied, who turned out, among other things, the most beautiful Chinese embroidered tea cloths and napkins and bewitching children's shoes. The soles of these were made by sticking odd scraps of cloth together with a flour and water paste until they were thick enough to be cut and hand stitched into the right size. The tops were made of gay pieces of silk, and the toe in the form of a cat or a tiger's face with whiskers and bead eyes.*

In a report (possibly presented as a speech) Edith made three years after she arrived in China on "Hospital Social Service in China" she discusses the reasoning that led to the creation of the House of the Merciful Savior "in the hope that our experiments may be of some interest to others who are struggling with the same problems." Her report contains some examples of her successes:

For instance, of the original inhabitants I hope that the two blind cripples will be taken over by the Blind School in Wuchang as they have both learned a useful occupation i.e. making the umbilical tape and lingerie ribbon which your excellent magazine has been good enough to advertise for us. The footless youngster is now a big girl walking around perfectly fearlessly on two marvelous wooden legs…she has learned to do very nice embroidery and in a year or two ought to be able to take work as a sewing amah somewhere. The orphan is going to school and we hope in the future will be able to take nurses training in the hospital. This all may seem to have wandered far from the hospital but it is really very closely connected with it for it means that we, through the House of the Merciful Savior, have created a social agency to which we are able to turn to help for our patients. Let me give you another illustration. Some time ago a woman who was living in the Widows Home came to clinic bringing her little boy who had a bad spine caused by tuberculosis. For a long time she brought him for daily dressings and then, as that was too expensive, we urged her to let the child stay in the hospital. She said that she could not afford to—whereupon we sent her down to our general workroom at the House of the Merciful Savior to do embroidery. She has been working there now for nearly a year and earning enough to support herself and pay Lin T'ang's board in the hospital. In order to pay the board of the inmates at the house of the Merciful Savior we opened up a day work room where all kinds of embroidery, etc. is done by ex-patients or by members of the patients' families who in some way have a claim on us through the hospital.

Of course, with Edith, one thing always leads to another. The autobiography notes that:

The next thing I knew, we were running a clinic one day a week with the help of one of the Chinese doctors for the treatment of run-of-the-mill ailments—trachoma, scabies [an eye infection], *small pox, and leprosy.*

Edith preserved a folder of records from those early years of the House of the Merciful Savior. It includes a handwritten list headed Oct 8-Feb 1st:

Trachoma tests 1071
Dressings 391
Vaccinations 197
Teeth pulled 16
Old patients 114
New patients 98
Physical Exams 86

A list headed "School Children" categorizes according to "Tb glands," "tonsils," "Total gain in weight," "bad teeth," and so forth. Fifty-three percent of the children were underweight, and there were "only 7 out of 84 [who] have no defects." Another sheet of paper contains a pie chart showing the divisions among 65 births that took place in an unspecified period of time. Fifty-two percent were labeled "normal health," but a dispiriting

39% had died by the age of five and 9% were "living but sick." These are further subdivided as follows: "Hunch back 1, Blind 1, Leper 1, Weak 3." A similar list details the causes of death, which range from "Infected Hand" to cholera, small pox, convulsions, measles, and "cause unknown."

A report typed on the House of the Merciful Savior's printed stationery indicates an average monthly expense of $100 for salaries, food, clothing, etc. The school now has 33 pupils, and 33 women employed in the workroom. Here too, the children are categorized according to the "physical findings after medical examination": 33% are undernourished, 72% have tubercular glands, 18% have bound feet, 30% have temperatures above normal, and so forth. Edith concludes her otherwise impersonal and business-like report with the following observation:

> One of our fifteen year old pupils left school a week ago and came back yesterday married! Her lungs are affected, she has very bad trachoma. And her mentality is of the lowest. What can a poor child like this give or get in this world?

The folder also includes a draft of a document entitled "A possible General Outline for the future work of the House of the Merciful Savior and the Social and Religious Departments of the Women's Side of the Church General Hospital." It is clearly a public document, written with an eye to the Episcopal Church's sense of mission. The House of the Merciful Savior's primary school, she says, is intended "for the dissemination of Christianity and moral and social hygiene." The goal is for the inhabitants "To live a normal Christian, family life as far as possible in the midst of much ignorance and misery and to commend that life to our neighbors." The General Outline reports a budget for the year 1923, in which the $5,133.85 in expenditures is offset by sales of $6015.74. Edith was not only a social worker; she was a social worker who knew how to turn a profit!

With so much work to be done, the staff expanded to include two more American women. We get an oblique glimpse of the group dynamics among them from Edith's comments in her autobiography:

I think I was the most difficult and resistant member of the group, for I was impatient, critical in my judgments, and very headstrong. When an explosion seemed imminent, Elise would take me off for a long walk, and after I had blown my top I could generally see how badly I had behaved, and how ridiculous it all was, myself included.

Of course, we were a far too ingrown community, and hospital life is a small world, with its daily emergencies and self-centeredness – church services on Sunday were better for one's understanding of the language than for one's disposition. None of us had sense enough to realize the ferment that China was going through, and we were stupidly unaware of the volcano on which we were living. Wu Pei Fu and Chang Tso Lin were [viewed as] a pair of tiresome warlords in the north who seemed to be always swapping sides. When Feng Yu Hsiang, "The Christian General," appeared on the scene, he gave great comfort to the missions, but he soon got bogged down in the struggle for power. Strikes of all kinds were fairly common, and usually temporary. When anti-foreign feeling ran high, the house servants all walked out, but soon came back. Of course, there were intermittent boycotts on Japanese goods, and on one occasion, when things really looked bad, barbed wire was put around the Japanese concession in Hankow; and it was a familiar sight to see an English Tommy on guard on the porch of the Hong Kong Shanghai Bank, sitting in a wicker chair with a tea tray in his lap and a rifle and bayonet beside him.

Meanwhile, Edith continued to invent ways to make Chinese women self-supporting.

My work room was getting along very well, with a pretty steady demand for our embroidered products. I had hopes of extending the scope of workers, and was permitted to visit the women's prison, for, aside from the daily chores that had to be done, no effort was made to occupy the prisoners with any kind of industry or handiwork. I also tried my hand at the Widows' Home. To remain a widow was to gain great "face," and widows were respected and cared for by the

WHEN PEOPLE WROTE LETTERS

government. Each widow had her own small quarters built around a quadrangle with a tiny street through the center, a bit like an English medieval alms house. Each did her own cooking, and the only men allowed in were tradespeople, and they were carefully chaperoned. My efforts to get any kind of systematic work done there which might have added to their incomes were pretty ineffectual, but I think the widows thoroughly enjoyed themselves, quarreling with one another and basking in the sun of achieved merit.

I had a small office in the hospital compound, and every now and then would come back to find a live squawking hen tied to a chair as a gift from a grateful patient. We were often invited to birthday feasts and weddings. Presents in such cases were always in order, and they would be sent on an open tray carried by the hospital messenger, who was tipped according to the value of the present. It was a fair enough system, but, in order to give your boy "face," you often had to be unwillingly extravagant.

No letters home survive from Edith's years in China, but she did preserve a letter from Mrs. Deland, dated November 19, 1923.

Dear Edith:

Joffre has sent some candy off to China, in the hope that it will reach you by Christmas time. But the mails in our beloved land, (as well a several other things!) seem to be so uncertain that Heaven knows what will happen to the box from S. S. Pierce's!

Your package to me, which you say you have sent by parcel post, has not yet arrived, but it is delightful to look forward to it, and I am perfectly sure that the things that you have picked out will be just exactly what I want. The only thing that troubles me about them is that they may be so attractive that I shall not be able to give them away as Christmas presents – which would be most unfortunate, because I know that people would like them! I am, therefore, inclined to think that it will be the better part of prudence for me to send you some more money, and you can purchase things from your pupils as you think best.

That little table cover that you sent me sometime ago, with the little pagodas and rickshaws is in constant use, and has aroused the envy of many of my friends....

How far back those days in France seem to be, when you saw everything, and felt everything, and got so much out of living. I will never forget the significant thing you said about the soldiers coming out of church, and dipping their fingers in the holy water, and then exchanging lights from their cigarettes: "I thought of it as baptism—the water and the Spirit."

I hope you are keeping notes of things you see, and most of all of things you feel, because I am confident that the really important thing is not to make a record of events, but to make a record of the reaction of events upon the soul. To my way if thinking, it is the ability to do that which makes Literature. Certainly you have had lots of "events" popping about you, and I know how you have felt them – how you have felt the dew on the leaf in the early morning, or the smell in incense in a temple – or, for that matter, the smell of Chinese houses, which must be truly terrific! If you can tell how these objective things make you feel inside, we shall all owe you a debt.

After these eloquent words of advice from one writer to another, Mrs. Deland turns to other, more mundane domestic matters. The letter, which had been dictated to a typist, ends with a handwritten postscript announcing that the package from China had just arrived, but the duty was $7.00, far too much to allow for another shipment of gifts until the next year.

Edith took short holidays to Shanghai, generally with Elise Dexter, and in 1924 they were given a six-month furlough. They returned to Boston, where Edith found a small apartment at 96 Chestnut Street. Not surprisingly, she spent part of her furlough engaged in public speaking, recruiting new nurses, and energetically selling the embroidered products she had brought with her from China. She began her journey back to China in March, 1925, stopping along the way in Cisco, Texas to visit her brother Frank and his family, including ten-year old Betty. I am sure that Betty, with her vivid imagination and love of pirate lore, listened wide-eyed to Edith's tales of China. Back in Wuchang, Edith sent a large envelope to her namesake Edith, addressed to Miss Edith Stedman, Big Spring, Texas, USA. It contained three sets of delicate tissue paper cutouts of kitchen gods, "usually hung in the kitchen," according to a note on the back of the envelope.

Edith records in her autobiography that Elise had decided not to return to China. "I missed Elise terribly and, for reasons too complicated to go into, I was persona non grata at the hospital as far as Dr. James was concerned." Had Edith's famous temper gotten the best of her without Elise's moderating influence? To put some distance between her and the other Americans, Edith was given her own house to fix up and live in.

> The house wasn't in frightfully good repair, but it had a garden and great possibilities. I fitted it up as cheaply as possible with Chinese furniture, inexpensive curtains, and rugs of coarse matting, and the end result was charming. Two or three of the smallest children with an amah moved in with me, and I engaged a cook and houseboy. The first night I spent there I was scared silly. There were heavy clumps on the stairs, as if someone was going up and down…. In the morning, I discovered that the bindings of all my books had been nibbled off—the place was infested with rats the size of cats, and it was they who were galumphing up and down the stairs.

However protected and self contained the Episcopal Church compound may have seemed, the world outside started to make itself felt. By the spring of 1925, it had become impossible for Edith and her colleagues to ignore the conflicts brewing around them.

> I suppose I read a daily paper, but the pressure of work and lack of contact with the more politically informed Chinese blinded me to the clouds on the horizon, which were growing black. We, of course, knew a bit about the Kuo Min Tang, which was the People's Party founded by Sun Yat Sen, but our own immediate war lords and officials seemed more in evidence. On May 30, 1925, things began to happen fast. The

British-commanded police in the International Settlement in Shanghai fired into a crowd of students who were demonstrating in connection with a strike against some Japanese owned mills and extraterritoriality. Anti-foreign feeling spread like wildfire. On the 5th of June, two members of our mission were attacked, and the Bishop sent word that all foreigners were to stay off the streets. The next day, a representative from the Governor's office came early to my house to get any foreign names and arrange for police protection. Miss Tetley was with me at the time, and at 9:00 that night forty policemen arrived with rickshaws to take us to the Hospital. About half way there the crowds rushed us, the policemen and the rickshaw coolies fled, but somehow Miss Tetley and I managed to get there. At midnight, the Chief of Police notified the hospital that the students were planning to attack all foreign compounds at 4 a. m. However, it was only a scare, and the next day two or three of us went over to Hankow for a night to find out what was up. One of the Chinese nurses and I went back to Wuchang the next day with a guard fourteen strong.

The Bishop felt that this was only small stuff, but that a big push was under way, and we had better get things tidied up in case of a sudden emergency. A riot in Hankow followed with all foreign volunteers called out, and several Chinese were killed. There were sandbags everywhere, and American and British gunboats in the river. All the women in Wuchang were ordered to Hankow to the Foreign Concessions. Things were worsening rapidly, and it was a question of what to do or where to go until things quieted down.

Edith was prepared to leave China, if necessary, but eventually the crisis passed and she returned to her workrooms and classes. Life continued within the compound: the children sang Christmas carols under Edith's window early on Christmas morning, and a few days later set off firecrackers in honor of her thirty-seventh birthday, then bowed to her and wished her a long life in traditional Chinese fashion. Seven months later, however, when Edith and several friends were having a summer holiday in a rented house in the mountain-top resort village Kuling, the political situation worsening rapidly. The Nationalist Party had continued to grow in numbers and influence under its leader Chiang Kai Shek and the young revolutionary ideologue Mao Zedung.

It was obvious that Wuchang was one of Chiang Kai Shek's objectives in his all-out effort to conquer China. I decided that I had better get back to my job as soon as possible, in spite of the Bishop's advice that women and children should remain in Kuling.

I arrived in Wuchang August 30, 1926, and had difficulty getting through the City Gate. The Chinese were fleeing from what was ahead, and looked at me as if I were crazy. Actually, I was almost the last one in before the Gates were all barred. I found that my house had been broken into, and the head of a spy was hanging on a nearby telegraph pole. I took a canvas cot over to a basement room in St. Michael's Church, where I stayed for the next six weeks. Father Wood had taken in about three hundred refugees, mostly women and children, but I had next to me a very mixed group of companions. An old Chinese man who was sleeping in his coffin, among an assorted lot of elderly gentlemen including my teacher Mr. Yin, who had cannily picked out the safest spot in the building – a small hallway from which ascended a spiral iron staircase to Father Wood's quarters on the third floor. I suppose there were about a dozen of them, and the nightly ritual was fascinating. They would arrive in the early evening escorted by their wives or concubines, or both, the concubines carrying their tea pots, pipes, bedding, and a light snack. Then the old men would make themselves comfortable on the floor, each with his head under the staircase, so that the general effect was of an enormous cartwheel. After they had been settled, the women were dismissed to fend for themselves. The guns began to let loose, and we set up a clinic in St. Michael's to care for casualties or any obstetrical cases in that part of the city.

On September 6, Chiang's troops captured the arsenal at Hangong, and Hankow fell. For the first few days, there was complete confusion and a run on food supplies. For some strange reason, the telephone lines between us and Hankow were not cut, so we could ring up our friends and let them listen to the uproar. That didn't last long though, but by superhuman effort and bargaining with both sides, the Bishop and others managed to get about 1,500 Chinese women and children out of the city and across the river. The jails had no food, so they let the prisoners loose, and before long they were begging to be readmitted! I more or less settled into a routine – going back to my own house for a bath and change of clothes while both armies were having their breakfast, then back to St. Michael's and the clinic. Chiang Kai Shek was allied with the Russians at this time, and so Russian pilots bombed us during the day and we were under fire night and day from guns from the river and the south. Our artillery was fantastic – a lot of it consisting of old Krupp cannons from World War I, and the scene at night from the city walls was like a medieval painting. Chiang's Southern army used scaling ladders made of bamboo, and the defenders of the city dropped enormous blazing balls of cotton soaked in oil on them. Casualties, of course, were heavy, and we were kept on the jump in the clinic treating a lot of nasty shrapnel wounds. One afternoon, Father Wood and I went up to the hospital to try and scrounge some medical supplies, and on the way back we were caught in a heavy air raid. After we banged on the door of the nearest house, a frightened Chinese man let us in, and politely offered us a bench to sit on. The rest of the family were all huddled under a table. It was a tiny place, with nothing but a flimsy tile roof between us and the shelling. I was scared stiff, and for protection put an old Atlantic Monthly that I had borrowed on top of my head – a symbolic rather than a realistic gesture. Food for our refugees and ourselves soon became one of the greatest worries, and we spent a lot of time trying to get hold of any rice. Father Wood and I messed together two meals a day of a few beans boiled or stewed, washed down with a small amount of tinned milk flavored with celery powder. One night, two men came to him and offered two sacks of rice, which we bought at once. Alas, the next morning their heads were on poles outside the church – soldiers stealing from the commissary.

It was impossible to get much sleep, for the noise was deafening, so I used to go and sit with my cartwheel of old men and try to improve my

Chinese…. Of course, the racket kept the babies awake, and you could hear them yelling all over the place. This so alarmed the old gentlemen that they called out sternly, "Women, nurse your infants or the enemy will find us." How a baby could have been heard above that din was unimaginable, but the women meekly obeyed.

The time came when there wasn't a dog left in the city, and people were stripping bark and leaves off the trees. I helped the doctor deliver five babies in our small clinic using old copies of the London Times for mattresses. About 1,000 bodies were buried together with quick lime in one pit and another seven or eight hundred in another. Toilet facilities were very primitive – a row of buckets in a very inadequate make-shift lavatory – of course, cholera broke out. A bomb fell in the small pond behind my house, and there was a minor hit at St. Michael's. Negotiations were supposedly going on between the two armies. But the bombing continued, and we carried on as best we could. Early in October, they got a few of the foreign women and some Chinese out after a wild scene at the City Gate, where numbers of people were trampled to death. Sleep and food were pretty limited, and our clinic ran in high gear. We didn't have many rules for our refugees, but Father Wood smelled opium one night, and said he really felt he had to draw the line somewhere. On Sunday, the 10th of October, there was an unusually heavy bombardment and suddenly three of the City Gates were opened by the warlords' Northern Army, which had mutinied for lack of food and ammunition. Then all hell broke loose. The Southerners poured in on both sides and started looting….

After a tense few days the fighting seems to have subsided; Edith reports a "rather somber Christmas," with gifts for the children, although anti-foreign sentiment continued to run high, and on one occasion a rickshaw in which she was riding was surrounded by an angry mob yelling "Kill the foreign devil!" Rioting resumed early in 1927, however, and the British women and children were escorted to Hankow on gunboats under heavy escort from a Standard Oil launch. Edith left with them, and by the end of January she was on the "Empress of Canada" on her way to Vancouver. By

March, widespread looting of the foreign concessions had begun and the British agreed to surrender their Hankow concession to the Chinese over a two-year period. Wuchang continued to be a center of conflict among the factions, and the Episcopal mission was completely disbanded.

Much later, writing her autobiography from the notes she so carefully preserved, Edith reflected on those years in the twenties from the perspective of a very different era:

I hated leaving China, for I loved my job and working with the Chinese, but the door had closed, and that was that.

What did it all add up to, and where did we and foreigners of other nations go wrong? I can only speak for the hospital which I knew intimately. I am sure conditions were better in the concessions and the universities. It was a luxurious ghetto life in some respects – separate but equal. The Chinese Nurses' Home, from their point of view, was exactly what they wanted – their own rooms, servants, a dining room where they could spit the fish bones on the floor, and considerable freedom. We lived in a different and, from our point of view, more civilized, luxury—six or seven single females eating four meals together each day, with very little talk except hospital shop or gossip, and no rapport with the men's hospital on the other side of the wall. There was precious little mental stimulation and inevitably among the small group there was friction and irritation, with all of us in our different ways responsible.

Why didn't we have the sense to go to China as co-workers? The Chinese with their ancient culture had so much to teach us, but in our unconscious smugness we thought it was the other way around. There was much that we could have learned from each other – and the tragedy is that we learned all the wrong things and never thought of our debt to the Chinese, but only of what we were giving. Of course, we did some good, principally in the medical field, but there, again, it would have been better to train Chinese doctors in their own country, rather than spoiling them by western training and techniques which they felt they had to have when they came back disillusioned to their own country.

However, we foreigners of all nationalities were only a spot in the barrel of apples. After the Boxer Rebellion and the end of the old Imperial rule, China became chaotic, full of greed and corruption, split up by small war lords who disliked the merchants and businessmen and even the farmers until there was no security in times of danger except in the hated foreign concessions to which they would flee in haste. Famine and floods had always been with them, but with the westernization of so many of the young, one of the strongest pillars of China weakened – that of the family, and the military began to take the place of the scholars who had formerly had the highest rank. So the Chinese cynically turned around, learned what they could from the West in military matters, and then turned the tables. Once the handwriting was on the wall, one wonders if we shouldn't have gotten out with dignity and friendship rather than to have been kicked out.

Edith's bitterness is understandable, given the idealism with which she had worked to create a model society on a small scale. In a handwritten draft for an essay or speech entitled "Social Work as a Profession" included among her reports from the China years, Edith had written movingly about her profession. Social work, she said, "includes everything done by society for the benefit of those who are not in a position to compete on fair terms with their fellows: in other words, for those who can't quite make the grade for one reason or another, [like] the rickshaw coolie with a too heavy load on a slippery hill," his load the "load of ignorance, disease, heredity, illiteracy, etc." The report continues: "Now somehow in order to live in peace and security we must take care of the criminals, the insane, and the feebleminded in order to protect ourselves if for no other reason." The needs of others—the sick and the aged — are "an obvious appeal to the altruistic and benevolent instinct." Most people, however, are unlikely to look beyond their own families: "We may take care of our own sick and crazy aunt but we don't plan on taking in our neighbors' relatives as well." Later in the draft she observes that

The Social Worker is found wherever the lame dog is being helped over the stile; He may not know he is doing social work and he may be

doing it very badly. He has a place with the Educator, the Doctor, and the Priest (a rash statement to make here), and he not infrequently bridges the gap between them.

Edith illustrates her point with a lengthy example involving a sick school boy in a church day school who is sent to the hospital, discharged by the doctors, returned to the school, but once again falls ill. The social worker comes into the case, checks his hospital records and compares these with the school records, then makes a "friendly visit" to the home "to impress upon the family the need of building up the boy's health." Then, she notes,

> *...the real facts of the case come out—poverty, unsanitary living conditions, and unemployment or with equal truth it may be due to ignorance, indifference, and a variety of other causes. The fact remains that the connection between the home, the school, the hospital and the church is not in good working order, like our present telephone system, and it does the doctor no good to talk into the receiver if there is no one listening to him and transmitting his orders to the proper people.*

A few paragraphs later, she describes the social worker's job as "not only concerned with the relief of distress but with the investigation of its causes and the arousing of public interest to deal with it."

> *A kind heart and an open purse are not enough. We must be trained as the doctor is to look for causes and not be tempted to give sugar pills in the form of a few hundred cash. Social work is as old as civilization and has had many motives: Love of God, the desire to obtain merit for oneself, and the impulse for self expression, etc., but true social work it seems to me begins when the subjective impulse is sublimated and the complete welfare of the person at stake in his relation to society is considered. This isn't as easy as it sounds—but it certainly is an aim to be worked toward.*

And so Edith's China years ended on a somber note. With all the traveling she would do during the rest of her long life, she never returned to China. There is, however, a curious postscript to this part of the story. In September 1931 Mrs. Deland sent a letter of introduction to her publisher on Edith's behalf. Among the family papers in New Sharon, Maine, Edith had evidently come across a travel journal written nearly a century earlier by a neighbor and close friend of her great-grandparents, Stephen and Deborah (Mayhew) Howes. Edith seems to have thought the author of the journal, a Rev. Samuel Munson, was a relative of hers. This was an understandable mistake, since Stephen and Deborah had named their ninth and tenth children after Stephen Munson and his sister Eliza. Rev. Munson, a missionary, had gone on a journey to the Far East in 1833 that must have fascinated Edith, and she was hoping to publish parts of the journal because, in Mrs. Deland's words, "it reveals so strikingly the difference in the religious point of view of today and yesterday, so to speak." The journey's sad outcome is described in a letter from Samuel's colleague W. H Medhurst to Eliza Munson back in New Sharon:

Batavia, Sept 13th 1834

My dear Madam,

*   It is my painful duty to have to inform you, that your dear Brother, and my dear friend, the Rev. Samuel Munson, is no more. He left in the beginning of April for Padang, in company with the Rev. H. G. Lyman, on an exploring tour to the island of Nias, and the Battah country in the interior of Sumatra. At Padang they hired a Malay prow, and made the tour of the Batu and Nias islands, after concluding which they arrived at Tappanooly on the 17th of June, in good health and spirits. Having completed their preparations they set off for the interior on the 23rd of June, and in five short days they were met on the road by a band of 200 armed men, who fell on them and inhumanly murdered them. Their followers and one of their servants escaped to tell the tale; and to assure us of the melancholy catastrophe. The habitual preparation for eternity, and the unwonted love to the Saviour, & devotedness to his cause,*

which the brethren manifested, assure us that to them sudden death was
sudden glory....

Although the letter does not go further into the precise details of Samuel
Munson's death, family legend has it that, as Mrs. Deland's letter puts
it, "poor gentleman — he was attacked by cannibals and eaten up." The
journal (copies of which can be found in the Bowdoin College Library and
the Schlesinger Library) is addressed in epistolary fashion to Eliza and
begins on June 21, 1833, at which time Samuel and his young wife Abby
had been at sea for eleven days. Samuel is an eloquent and observant writer,
and his descriptions of life on shipboard and the many kinds of sea and
airborne creatures he observed are wonderfully detailed. Not unlike the
Episcopal clergy with whom Edith was associated in China, Rev. Munson
and his colleagues have set out for Java and Sumatra to bring about "the
salvation of those poor islanders." His journal entry for September 30th,
after one hundred days at sea, relates his first impressions of nineteenth-
century Sumatra:

> *Every thing is entirely new & strange. It is strange to see the half*
> *naked natives running thro' the streets. It is strange to see the Chinese*
> *shops filled with articles of merchandise, few of which I ever saw before,*
> *— & the doors covered with prayers & good wishes and charms written*
> *in Chinese. It is strange to hear such a babel of tongue,— such a jargon*
> *as few can understand. It is strange too to see the mosque & heathen*
> *temple, the followers of the false prophet, & the worshippers of "dumb*
> *idols." It is strange to hear the groans of the prisoner & the clanking of*
> *his chains — & the sighs of a people oppressed, despised and trampled*
> *under foot, destined to be Gibeonites, hewers of wood & drawers of*
> *water, till the gospel shall put an end to their captivity.*

On November 28, 1833, Samuel writes his last journal entry to Eliza,
for he intends to send it to her on the ship "Florence," which is sailing for
Boston the following week. He and Mr. Medhurst have set up a dispensary
in the town from which they distribute free medicines three days a week.

The men attend, at best they can, to "a most wretched set of mortals, some with ulcers, some with asthma, others with dropsy & Rheumatism, etc." Not being trained doctors, they "are almost constantly consulting medical books." While caring for their patients, they distribute religious tracts "which many of them receive with gratitude." Some of their tracts are evidently written in Chinese and Malay, and Samuel has begun to "chatter a little" in Chinese and hopes to learn more:

> *I find the only way to get the language is to go into the midst of them, & talk in the best manner possible. I get laughed at often; but I am daily getting new words & phrases. It is a most difficult language — it is in fact learning two languages instead of one.*
>
> *I am almost sorry that I promised to send you this Journal; if so it can be called. It is indeed a hasty thing — if it affords you any amusement then I shall feel quite rewarded for writing it. The posts of duty at which you & I are stationed place us far, far (!) asunder. We shall probably see each other no more during the voyage of life! But let us see to it, that we meet in the haven of everlasting rest!!*

No more is known of the remainder of Samuel Munson's stay in Malaysia. His wife Abby and their child Samuel, who was born in Java, evidently returned to Maine, and were living in Brunswick at the time of the 1850 US Census.

Unlike the unfortunate Rev. Samuel Munson, Edith left China unscathed and returned to New England to resume her career. In January 1927 she was thirty-eight years old and, after an absence of six and a half years, would be starting over again. From this point onward, there is less documentary evidence regarding her life — for when travelers stop traveling, the letters become less frequent. The story shifts, therefore, to another collection of letters, written by Edith's niece, my mother, Betty Stedman.

The Chores of the Modern Health Crusaders, New Sharon, Maine, c. 1920.

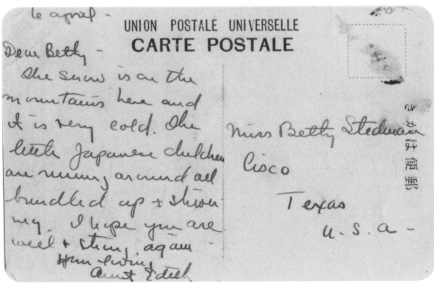

A postcard to Betty from her Aunt Edith, c. 1924

Frank, Frank Jr, Edith, and Betty Stedman and their Ford, Cisco, Texas, 1924

Betty and her sister Edith, 1930

Key West June 15th 1840

Respected Parents

It gives me much satisfaction to have the priviledge of answering another letter from you which I recd yesterday. It found me quite well as to health & tolerbly well contented. I should be well contented were it not for the musquetoes they are very troublesome. I have slept under a musquito bar this three months. Olive I was very sorry to hear that you was sick but I hope these few lines (which I am writing by lamp light) will find you & all the rest of the family enjoying good health & a decent flow of spirits. The mail is to leave Charleston the first of every month for this place & leave this place on the fifteenth of every month for charleston but the mail did not come last month so that your letter was a long time getting here. I have hardly yet made up my mind wether I shall stay here all summer or not I probably shall stay should I come north I shall start in about two weeks. The people here tell me that I have seen as hot weather as I shall see & as many varments I hope I have. I have been at work for about two months past on a fine house at $2.50 per day I have about two weeks longer to work there & then another job to build a piazza which will take three or four weeks more if I see fit I do in more here in a day than I used to there in a half day. I recollect you wished me to tell you of what order the church is in this place I spoke it in my last, it is the Episcopalian fashion that is preached here full of forms & ceremonies would keep one hopping up & down every minute. Through the winter season there was a Methodist Prayer meeting every sabbath eve in a gentlemans house after I found it out I used to attend quite often there was two or three that took an active part in the meeting there was one staunch old fellow like old

Vernal Stedman's letter to his parents, June 15th, 1840

Capt Butterfield he put it down by the word of mouth strong & heavy — helped them ~~bring~~ I do not remember telling any one that I had helped you except in conversation with Orren I wish he was here I should think if he cares any thing about me he would write me & let me know the state of his mind perhaps if he were in that place he never was in before & prison a stranger to him it might be pleasing to hear from old native home though we so lonely (the poet says) there is no place like home we had green corn from Havanna several weeks ago also new potatoes we have on this Key at this time ripe watermellons near two feet long till seldom that I have saved him some seeds — I believe I have told you before that this place is supported by the wrecking business mostly however the fishing is a help to the place here are almost all kinds of fish around this Key you can even from the wharfs catch almost any quantity of them that you wish to This place is called the Key of the gulf it has been settled about 15 years by the inhabitants which are now here but previous to this it was a complete rendesvous for pirates its location for that business must have been first rate for hardly a vesel can pass betwixt this & Havanna through into the great Bay of Mexico or betwixt this & florida within long seen There is about 10 wrecking sloops that belong to this port that constantly lay out ~~and~~ side up & down the reef watching for vesels that go ashore or strike the hidden rocks this reef extends from near two hundred miles the entrance of the gulf when a vessel gets on any where on the reef twill not be long before assistance will be offered if the capt excepts assistance the sloops go along side & take out enough cargo to lighten her & get her off in that way then if the vessel is not bildged they take vessel & cargo into this place put the cargo into ware houses built for the purpose throw out the vessel & examine her by a committee if she can be made sea worthy she is repaired if not they

Augustus Holt's Dairy Business, New Sharon Maine, c. 1850

Portrait of Gratia "Kitty" Holt by Edmund Messer

Edith as a child in Somerville, MA

Portrait of Edith with her parents, Kitty and George
Stedman, and her brothers Frank and Bert, c. 1898.

LEFT- Edith's Radcliffe College graduation picture, 1910

ABOVE- Edith in France with unidentified French soldier and boy, 1918

Edith in China, 1920s.

The House of the Merciful Saviour in the past year has undergone several changes although we are still affiliated with the Church General Hospital and our medical work is carried on with the co-operation and under the general direction of Dr. James. We are also still acting as a receiving station for disabled and homeless hospital patients but the scene of our activities has been transferred to the Ta Tsao Kai where the Bishop has kindly given us the use of an old mission house for our House of the Merciful Saviour family. Fr. Wood, whose near neighbour we are, offered us at the same time a large sunny room in S. Michaels Parish House as a work room for our poor women and a small gate house for a school and neighbourhood clinic. Our lease of the old property was up last year and a move had to be made. We tried desperately hard for over a year to buy a good-sized Chinese house where our work could be all under one roof and which we could feel was a permanent home. One must have lived in China to appreciate the difficulties attendant on buying property. A half dozen times we congratulated each other all around and said "well that is all settled". Each time the deal slipped through and we found ourselves fast approaching a state when we should be utterly homeless when the Bishop and Fr. Wood came to our rescue. When I was on furlough last winter, through the never-to-be-forgotten kindness and generosity of friends, we raised enough money to give us a substantial start on a building fund. In the interval while we are looking for permanent quarters this

A pamphlet by Edith about the House of the Merciful Savior, China 1920s

Edith wrote on the back of this photo:
"A forlorn little girl brought to us from
several hundreds of miles [away] in the
country. Her old 'pa' has come to take
her home. She was burned most fearfully
but now is quite well." China, 1920s.

Betty's passport photograph, 1933

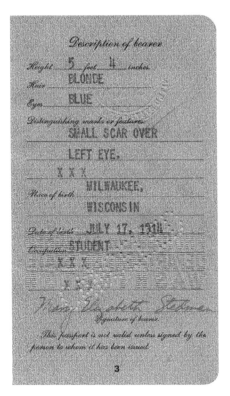

ACCION POPULAR

MUJER: ¡Vota la candidatura de derechas y contra el marxismo!

SI NO LO HACES

vendrá el COMUNISMO, que te arrancará los hijos de tus brazos;
la iglesia de tu pueblo, símbolo de NUESTRA SANTA RELIGION, será derruída y arrasada;
el esposo que amas HUIRA DE TU LADO, autorizado por LA LEY DEL DIVORCIO;
vendrá la ANARQUIA A LOS CAMPOS y a vuestro hogar el HAMBRE Y LA MISERIA.

MUJER: ¡Vota la candidatura de derechas y contra el marxismo!

SEÑORA: ¡Con tu voto ayuda a salvar a España!

NOTA.—Vota la candidatura COMPLETA. Si borras algún nombre das fuerza a los contrarios.
A las ocho de la mañana empieza la votación. Vete temprano a votar para que nadie pueda hacerlo por ti.

¡Votad a las derechas!
¡Votad contra el marxismo!

Imp. Palomeque. —N.° 23.

A political flyer Betty sent home from Spain, 1933-34. It urges women to vote for the right, against the Marxists.

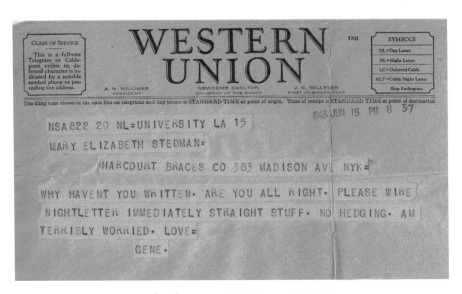

Gene's telegram to Betty, June 15, 1943.

LEFT- Gene Tuck at the U.S. Army Camp Upton, 1945

ROGHT- Betty and Gene's wedding portrait

PART THREE

Betty's Letters
From Spain

NINETEEN

Fall and Winter
1933

EXACTLY A CENTURY after Samuel Munson left Maine for the Far East, nineteen-year-old Betty embarked for Spain to spend her junior year in college studying in Madrid. Travel journals are rather like documentary films without the images, though if the descriptions are vivid enough, and the characters reappear with regularity, the "film" can begin to take shape in the reader's mind's eye. I feel that way about both Samuel Munson's account of the time he spent in Malaysia and Edith's adventures in wartime and post-war France. Betty was a different kind of traveler in 1933-34; her year in Spain was not nearly as exciting or dangerous as her aunt's, and much of what she recounts in her letters reads as a very personal coming of age story. The spirit of adventure links them, however, a spirit that seems to me to be part of their inheritance from the sturdy settlers of New England from the time of the Mayflower.

Betty's letters from Spain are extraordinarily detailed, particularly by twenty-first century standards, and the characters seem more lifelike as a result. They contain revealing character studies not only of the people she met in Madrid, but of her father, mother, and brother Frank back in Boston. Her family's letters to her (which we can only imagine, since they were not preserved) must have contributed to a lively, sometimes fraught conversation about the negotiations, misunderstandings, and accommodations that cross-cultural social interactions entail. Now, when so many college students study abroad with apparent ease, the frustrations Betty speaks of and the decisions she had to make speak to us across nearly eight decades about how different everyday life was in the 1930s.

Betty's year in Madrid was arranged by another remarkable woman who plays a small but important role in this story. Miss Alice Bushee, the head of Wellesley's Spanish department, took Betty aside at the end of her sophomore year and encouraged her to go abroad. When Betty explained her financial circumstances, Miss Bushee undertook the arrangements, as she explains in a letter to Betty's mother Marian. The letter gives a clear sense of the value of a dollar – or one hundred dollars – in the midst of the Depression.

> *My dear Mrs. Stedman:*
>
> *I want to write out a few things in black and white so that you will know absolutely about certain matters especially money. In the first place I was a little surprised to have to say the other day that Mr. Stedman did not want to give his consent at first and almost hoped she would not go now. Bettie was so enthusiastic about it all and came to see what could be done about scholarships that it set me to thinking out all kinds of ways and finally this little home suggested itself to me. I really should not have gone into it if she had not shown the interest. I will help her in every way possible but of course I cannot guarantee that nothing will happen. A steamer is safer than a train and a European train is safer than a Mass. Automobile! Doña Benigna has been connected with this mission school for over 50 years, first as pupil, then secretary and teacher and finally as director. She is a most unselfish, capable head and no one could be any safer with any director than with her.*

Now for accounts:

Tuition for 9 months is		*$450*
Of this you have paid	*$100*	
Her scholarship sent from Wellesley	*$250*	
The rest can be seen to later	*$100*	
Board		*$100*
A friend has already paid	*$50*	
I can get the rest	*$50*	
Allow for travel there and back		*$200*
I understand most of this she has earned or will earn this summer.		
Running expenses at the most (probably less)		*$100*
She thought an aunt might give her this		

According to the above there is really only about $100 to think about for the rest of the tuition sometime during the year. If she cannot borrow this easily without interest then please let me know and I can make arrangements to borrow in a way that will not be difficult to repay.

If I have made any mistake in my calculations please let me know in order that I may be set right also. I do not want her pleasure lessened by worrying about money nor do I want you to add financial worries to your missing her through the year.

If in any way I can help you or her please be free to let me know.

Very cordially yours,
Alice H. Bushee

History does not relate, as Betty used to say, whether her aunt Edith did in fact give her the $100 she needed for a year's "running expenses," or spending money. I hope Edith did contribute, for she may have realized that she had been a bit unyielding in the matter of the Radcliffe Scholarship Committee, even though everything had worked out for the best at Wellesley. The $100 for the balance of Betty's tuition may have come from her brother Frank's earnings at the Boston Public Library, for in one of her letters from Spain Betty admonishes her mother not to use a small inheritance to repay Frank the $100 she borrowed, since "that is to come out of my very own pocket just as soon as I can make it." It is touching to hear Betty telling her mother to "spend money on yourself for a change…blow it on something you want." Money was clearly in short supply and Frank was entering Harvard that September, though to economize he would live at home in Jamaica Plain for his first two years. It was understood that when Betty graduated, she would go to work and help pay his expenses, so that he could live at the college for his junior and senior years.

I wonder why my grandfather was so reluctant to let Betty go to Spain. I find it revealing that Miss Bushee's correspondence was addressed to Marian, not to both the Stedmans. It is unlikely that the Stedman family knew much about the political turmoil than was brewing in Spain, which would lead to one of the bloodiest civil wars of the century some two years later. Had they known, they almost certainly would have opposed the trip.

When Betty left for her junior year abroad she promised herself that she would write home weekly. Altogether, she produced roughly two hundred single spaced typed pages of correspondence during the 1933-34 school year, plus a few handwritten letters. The daily texture of her life emerges in extraordinary detail: Betty worries about money, describes her classes and classmates, her outings and flirtations; she darns her stockings, takes her shoes to be resoled, makes a few careful purchases, wonders about what is going on at home, and repeatedly expresses her love and gratitude toward her family. She is at once remarkably independent for a nineteen-year-old and still very connected to her immediate family, to whom she confides the most intimate details of her life.

Betty starts writing home two days after the S. S. Manhattan departs from New York Harbor, using the elegant blue stationery of the United States Lines. Travel abroad in 1933 was a momentous event; Betty dutifully reports that she received nineteen letters and cards and numerous gifts. After a tentative beginning ("I felt when I left you, Mummy, that a little of my confidence was slipping, but now I am all right") she begins to enjoy herself:

I, my dears, am one of the <u>two</u> girl students on board. There are some eighty odd men students so you can imagine we are pretty popular. Almost all are going to Vienna –medical students—and some are very nice, others not so nice. We two eat with four very nice ones (all Jews, I think!).... There are several others who hang around us – a funny little fellow named Sid Diamond who does a lot of things well, but, to offset that, sings (not badly) opera, camp songs, etc. in a dopey voice...There's a host of others—we have at least four clustered around our deck chairs (each) all the time! What a life!

Just as Samuel Munson had done in his travel journal, Betty mentions the sharks and porpoises and flying dolphins she sees and then writes "This last paragraph makes me think of our ancestor who wrote the diary a hundred years ago!" Evidently Samuel's journal was a well-known bit of family lore among the Stedmans. Interestingly, she is also "hearing plenty about the Nazis and Hitler and about the riots." She probably didn't realize that the Jewish students who were traveling to Vienna to attend medical school could not study medicine in the United States because of a widespread quota system in the universities; and the young men certainly didn't realize how dangerous a place Vienna would be within a year or two. Betty seems to have become quite friendly during the voyage with the waggish Sidney Diamond, for the bundle of letters contains one from him to her family:

My dear Mr. and Mrs. Stedman and Frank and Edith too,
   I am writing for Betty who is so tired of trying to write letters on the wobbly and rolling boat, that I have volunteered to write to you in your daughter's stead.
   There are some forty young men on board in 3rd class but one young lady other than Betty so you can easily see that Betty is enjoying this trip. Of course the accommodations in 3rd class are not very good, but Betty makes occasional trips up to Tourist and First along with 3 or 4 of us tagging along and succeeds in dazzling the passengers up there.

The letter continues in this vein for several more paragraphs. Apparently Sid and Betty keep in touch after the voyage but alas, none of his letters from Vienna were preserved.

Betty's next letter, dated September 21 from Paris, instructs the family to "look at a map of Paris when you read this." Betty reports that she has learned a lot about traveling from the medical students, and that "Sid took me around yesterday, two others (Hi and Nat) last night, and today yet three others, so…I haven't looked up those people Aunt Edith gave me letters to." Edith had referred her to a favorite hotel from her tour of duty with the YMCA fourteen years earlier. Betty takes leave of her escorts and travels by train to San Sebastian on the northern coast of Spain, where she writes her family another long letter on September 23rd. Everything is new to the traveler, and Betty is an observant one:

> *There are so many interesting things about Spain! This morning I walked out to the elevator and there on the steps was a girl scrubbing them with steel wool which she managed with her feet! Further down I observed the same thing. Everything is of wood, you know, and when it is scrubbed with the wool it simply gleams. The girls wear heavy shoes which look something like a wooden shoe but are more rounded and are of cloth. But I saw wooden shoes too—down at the fish market where the women carry baskets filled high on their heads.*

The family Betty will be living with is introduced in the letter of September 26th. Doña Benigna, on first acquaintance, is "a peach!" and Agapita, one of two Spanish girls who also board with Doña Benigna, would remain a good friend for many years to come. Betty's program in Spain has been organized by Smith College, which maintains a Residencia for its students, and some of the classes are located there, while the rest are at the University of Madrid. Betty reports that

> *We take painting with visits to the Prado, modern lit., Spanish civilization, Spanish language, phonetics, and a survey of Spanish lit. with supplementary classes at the Residencia and a host of famous*

professors. Truly we have rare privileges! The classes are from 5 to 8 in the evening! Those at the Residencia are in the morning, however.

Madrid continues to be vastly interesting, and I am realizing more and more how lucky I am to be living with Doña Benigna instead of in the Residencia. Every time I talk to Agapita or Doña B. there are little lessons in vocabulary and grammar. How agreeable to learn a language that way! And every time when we do something new there is a host of new words, all of which I can't hope to remember so I cling to two or three, and really, one gets along very fast that way.

Betty's devotion to her family comes through very clearly in a letter from October 11ᵗʰ, written just after the first long letter from home arrived.

My dearest ones,

At last a letter from you after waiting for more than a week after Mother's letter from New York came. The cartero or mailman comes every day while we are eating lunch. We can hear him coming up the stairs and stopping at each door, where he rings twice, and we wait, making conversation. Then two rings at our door and we become galvanized and gasp, "El cartero!" Or we hear his footsteps die away while we droop letter-less over our fruit.

All of that is by way of saying that I was terribly stirred by the letter, from Daddy's bit to Frank's…I signed for the letter, took it to my room, and read it while tears simply streamed down my cheeks. Don't be too alarmed, family dear. The other kids said they did too when they got their first letter or so.

Later in this letter Betty includes a few "Observations On Spain," starting with the curious observation that "there are many bow-legged people here." She is also struck by how small the Spanish women are; at 5 feet 4 inches, she feels tall. The women "really do wear mantillas…It's so convenient; you don't have to buy a hat, and they're always in good taste." She also devotes a long paragraph to the Smith students, who are "really nicer than I thought" at first. Each is described in the slang of the day: two are "pretty smoothy but nice eggs"; another is a "very swell kid"; two close friends are "the special society women; they've copped two good-looking Spaniards with money who take them everywhere and give them scrumpjous presents. But as Dot says, they have no principles at all about taking." Betty uses the word "mercenary" to describe the girls' attitude toward men and says that she too will "have to get me a caballero to walk home with me nights to save carfare. If that's not being mercenary, I don't know what is!" Although she isn't entirely comfortable with the arrangement, she realizes that she will have to be mercenary in order to experience what Spain had to offer. With very little money and an unfavorable exchange rate, she's "dying to see a bullfight" but won't allow herself to go until "somebody pops up and wants to take me." The Smith girls are similar to the wealthier girls at Wellesley, and Betty notes that "most all of them have seen a bullfight."

Betty continues to dwell on this theme in her letter of October 20th. One of the Smith girls, who is "rich as all get out" goes to "snozzy places to tea," and allegedly knows Ernest Hemingway, "who wrote the famous book on bull-fighting, *Death in the Afternoon*. He's in Madrid now; I'm going to see if I can't delicately wangle an introduction to him." Troubled about the morality of using people in this way, she asks her family to "tell me if you think I'm all wrong." Although there is no indication that she succeeded in wangling her invitation to meet Hemingway, Betty reports a week or so later that she is reading *Death in the Afternoon*, and finds the "very un-literary style" distracting at first.

Only one other girl in the Smith program is "po' like me," Betty notes off-handedly in one of her letters, and they will stay together in Madrid during the Christmas holidays "as it will probably be bad weather anyway, and, besides, money will be scarce. Then we will take a grand trip during spring holidays and see as much of Spain as we possibly can...." In a handwritten postscript at the end of her letter, she asks

Do you think it would be terrible, Daddy, if I didn't go to church every Sunday? Some of the other students make awfully interesting walking trips Sunday mornings some of which I'd like to join. You see, entries are free Sunday mornings to museums, etc. I'll tell you for your comfort that Doña B. reads the Bible to us every morning before breakfast.

There is no indication in subsequent letters that her father expressed an opinion on this subject. I'd like to think that that he did not object to her going to museums on Sundays from time to time.

Nine days later, on October 29th, Betty has been to tea "at the American Embassy, if you please!" a palatial mansion said to be the second-loveliest house in Madrid. Detailed descriptions follow, including an insightful description of "the ambassadoress herself" (presumably the wife of the ambassador):

> She was a surprise: a rather nice woman concealing more or less successfully the fact that she was terribly ill at ease, and that the house was as much a surprise to her as to us! But she saved herself from our utter pity by being very genuine (when she wasn't nervous). Poor thing! It's some trick, I imagine, to come into a huge palace like that where all the servants know more that you do about running it, and have to receive all sorts of people. I think the poor woman was absolutely petrified at the idea of having fifteen ultra-sophisticated college girls descend on her.... I wore my green wool dress and the little black velvet hat.

Although most of her letters are filled with details about classes, social events and day trips, financial matters, clothes, and food, Betty occasionally provides a glimpse of the political climate in Spain 1933-34, two years after the creation of a republican government and two and a half years before the outbreak of the Spanish Civil War. There have been student strikes at the university, and

> Every where you go you see posters or crudely painted signs calling the workers of Spain to action, to strikes, to meetings, to what-not. Socialists, Communists, Radicals, etc. Good old Spain! And the women take a huge interest in politics! Sometimes more than the men. It's amazing to see some perfectly domestic-looking creature get all hot and bothered over the coming elections (in November) while the men sit impassively by.

This last comment seems to make an implicit contrast to the women Betty knew in America, for whom politics may have seemed to be the province of men. A few weeks later Betty has more to say on this subject:

Poor Doña Benigna is very much worried about the state of her country. The elections which come off next Sunday are really going to mean great changes, history, in fact. You see, the women are voting for the first time. The ironic thing is this: they were given the vote by the Republic, but they are so under the thumb of the priests, that most of them will undoubtedly vote for the Monarchists! Besides, the Agrarios (the Monarchists) have more money than the Republicanos so they buy votes and do a tremendous amount of campaigning in the way of posters, hand bills, and radio. I'm enclosing one that was handed me on the busiest street in Madrid.... Doña Benigna has no hope for the salvation of the Republic. And with the Monarchy returns the persecution of the Protestants. You should hear D. B. on that subject: an ignorant woman was put in jail for three years for saying that Jesus had some brothers!

On November 15th, Betty sends her mother "a very special letter for you from your perplexed little da'ter." She has met a charming young Spaniard named Alfonso who invited her to cut her phonetics class and go to a movie along with another couple. When quizzed by Doña Benigna about why she was late getting home "in my excitement over the good time, I blurted out everything." Doña Benigna was quite indignant about the cut class, and then went on to tell her to be careful about going around with Spanish boys.

But, damn it all, what shall I do? The fellow wants to take me dancing sometime. Here I am at my first real fling into a good time stuck on the old narrow-mindedness of the Spaniards. How the Spanish gals ever get married is more than I can see! Though there are so many sweethearts promenading on the streets you have to walk around them.

What shall I do? Lie to her? For go out I'm determined to. Otherwise, I can't see Madrid, I can't go anyplace, etc. with no money. And these

> *people can show you a grand time. He makes plenty of money being*
> *a kidney specialist (surgeon) so I don't need to mind about being*
> *mercenary. And you can trust me, you know, as far as getting entangled*
> *is concerned. My only qualm is Miss Bushee, and I'm pretty sure D. B.*
> *tells her everything.*

This handwritten letter is utterly different in tone from the witty, detailed ones Betty has been sending to the family, filled with teasing for her brother Frank about his freshman year at Harvard, and affectionate asides to her beloved father. But her mother is her "pal when it comes to discussing things" like her current dilemma, and she asks "Gosh, Mummy, what would you do?" Betty is determined not to "sit at home and knit like the two Spanish boarders, Elvira and Agapita, during her Christmas vacation. She ends with "Answer by return mail, please!"

Betty writes her next letter four days later, on Sunday, November 19th. She has received a letter from Sid about "Germany's being under martial law," but passes over this to discuss other letters from family members and friends, and respond to her family's questions.

> *Yes, dears, there is a bathroom here and a very good one, all*
> *equipped with a little foot tub as well as a big bathtub. But we have hot*
> *water only twice a week, Mondays and Wednesdays, wash and iron*
> *days respectively. Usually I go up to the Res. (Residencia) once or twice*
> *at the end of the week and soak in luxury...*

She goes on to answer other questions, about her grades in her courses ("so-so") and a query to be passed along to Aunt Edith about the qualifications for the diplomatic service and the sample civil service exams ("All relative to vocation, of course. More of this later.")

On the fourth page of the letter she writes the words "Private from here" in parenthesis; presumably, Frank and Marian had been sharing parts of her letters with family and friends. The strain between Betty and Doña Benigna is becoming more intense: on Friday, she reports, Doña Benigna told her that

...I can not go out at night <u>at all</u> except once in a while with the group; that it was a very improper thing to do, and that Spanish girls do not do it; and that I can not make any dates without consulting her.... I took it in silence. Then she called me back to ask me what my mother said about my going out. I told her that you had confidence in my discretion! It didn't register.

The next day Betty talks to the Spanish girls about the situation, and gets "a storm of rebellion" in response. "They say it's not true. They go out at home." Doña Benigna has even been known to vet their letters, since all the mail passes through her hands. Evidently a girl was sent home the year before just for talking to some boys who lived upstairs, and "Agapita and Elvira were almost sent home for doing the same thing." Were it not significantly cheaper to board with her than to live in college housing, the girls would leave. "And the gals told me she snoops. They caught her red-handed once." Betty is mad, but she is wise enough to be diplomatic. She resolved to be on time for meals, "and do what is expected of me," without telling lies, but that "I'll be d——— if I'll consult her about everything I do in the daytime!"

I really do want to be docile, and not cause Doña Benigna any trouble, but I will <u>not</u> give up my liberty completely. Am I right, Mummy dearest? Don't tell me, please, that I have to be a prisoner like the Spanish girls, for that's what it amounts to. I'm willing to be adaptable, but not put in chains. For you see, that Doña Benigna simply lives in the social customs of her youth (She is now 73, the girls tell me). There is a Spanish book called, ironically, 'Doña Perfecta' about a religious fanatic who ruined her own daughter's life by busting up her marriage with a supposed atheist. Doña Benigna is a fanatic on men, and on people going out....

Poor Betty! She wants to live up to Miss Bushee's expectations, and she doesn't want to lie, but she also wants to see "a big part of Madrid that I couldn't possibly see alone or with girls alone."

Her first test comes the next day, on Sunday. The telephone rings, and it is one of her friends arranging an early afternoon outing with Alfonso and another young doctor. Betty tells a partial truth, that she is going to the Residencia, and they go out to a cafe for a drink. After Sunday dinner, she sits down to write her long letter, which ends by urging her family "not to get upset over this here letter of mine." A couple of weeks pass before she receives a letter from home, but when it arrives, it isn't the response she hoped for. In her December 10th letter she writes "You say that I must not do the slightest thing that Doña Benigna could disapprove of. That's impossible." Betty realizes that her family doesn't understand how different her situation is from what they are accustomed to, and that consulting Doña Benigna or bringing her men friends around to meet her would simply not work. "Please believe me when I say I can't possibly do that, but that I am trying not to do anything reprehensible, scandalous, or otherwise disgraceful."

Betty departs from her custom of writing on Sundays to send a special "EXTRA! Election News!" bulletin on Wednesday, November 22nd. The election results were inconclusive, since by Spanish law one party has to have a 40% majority. The Socialists and the Republicans had divided the anti-Monarchists vote, and so another election will take place in two weeks. She is spending a few of her precious cents on newspapers, "both Monarchist and Republican. Even then you don't get the truth; each one spends all his time talking about the other." There have been some disturbances in Madrid, but "No shooting yet!" The thirty deaths from election riots so far have been in the provinces (no doubt her family back in Boston was not happy to hear about riots and shooting). Betty displays a youthful fascination with the whole process, which she calls "wildly exciting":

> I have an imposing collection of handbills which I shall bring home and translate for your enjoyment. I should like to get hold of some of the harrowing posters they have: starving children are best for the Socialists; scrawny looking workmen for the Communists; deserted mothers with children for the Monarchists (who are for the repeal of the law of divorce). So it goes…. People don't quite know what will happen; nobody dares to prophesy. There is talk of a civil war, but our history

teacher says the Spanish are really too lazy at heart to get up and
have a complete turn-over, popular notions of Spanish hot-headedness
notwithstanding. Cheer up! We may be deported any old day! So don't
be surprised if I walk in on you for Christmas. No, but seriously, I don't
think anything violent will happen.

The second part of Betty's letter, ironically entitled "War News," deals with the ongoing strains surrounding the issue of her social life. Filled with military expressions ("I stuck to my guns," "I silenced my artillery," "I retreated gracefully having gained nothing but on the other hand having lost nothing," "My last gun fired…") Betty recounts her most recent discussions with Doña Benigna about male-female relationships and marriage customs in Spain. A subtle strategist, Betty realizes that "the way to handle her [is to] announce things to her weeks before and get her gradually [accustomed] to ideas." She has enlisted the help of Miss Sweeney, the faculty adviser at the Residencia, who has agreed to help in the "weaning" process. Betty becomes more than usually self-reflective in this letter. After reassuring her family that she's not changing, "becoming butterflyish" or boy-crazy, she observed that she is "getting normalized socially. No more rationalizing things out by blaming it on being a minister's kid, etc." As she continues to meet people, she is "beginning to find out that it isn't all my fault (as I often used to think) that I didn't go out, etc. Don't you see, dears, that it is imperative that I go out this year? ….It's so grand to find out that maybe I am rather attractive after all!" Being a blonde in a country of brunettes helps, of course. And so, despite the strains with Doña Benigna, she concludes, she is happy and "everything is hunky-dory."

Betty devotes about an hour and a half to each of her letters, she tells the family, using time that she could have spent reading for her exams,

…but this is such a satisfying thing to do. I can talk on at leisure, say
what I like sure of a reception which I can imagine will be good though
it might possibly not be, and not be interrupted by thumps on the head
from brothers who don't like the tenor of such paragraphs as the last!
Life is good, and peace is sweet.

There's a wonderful long letter about Thanksgiving Day, which the girls spent going to a German restaurant for a turkey dinner and then, after classes, rounding up some Spanish men and attending a dance where Betty, to her delight, waltzed and tangoed and looked very sophisticated "with my black velvet jacket on backwards," drinking ginger ale and cognac and singing "Daisy, Daisy, Give Me Your Answer True" and "Sidewalks of New York" as she and her companions walked home at 1:30 in the morning. There are more men in her life now, Fernando and Aurelio, who don't know about each other and see her home from her evening classes at the university on alternating days. Aurelio has a "novia," or fiancée, but that doesn't prevent him from occasionally taking Betty out on the town. In response to some anxious questions from home, Betty explains later (in her February 11th letter) that most Spaniards are "nominally engaged" at an early age by their families (Aurelio is only twenty years old) and that Spanish girls "are used to having their fiancés run around, it seems, just as Spanish wives [are]."

The first set of exams takes place in December, and Betty is concerned that her parents will be disappointed by her grades.

> They won't be at the bottom of the list, I hope, but I'm quite sure they won't be as good as my Wellesley ones. I hope that won't upset you too much. You know what that means, don't you? If, by any stretch of the imagination, I _might_ have had hopes of Phi Beta Kappa on the strength of last year's marks, this will KO said hopes. I wonder if you understand, though, that this year will mean more to me, I think, than a dozen Phi Beta Kappa keys....What I want most of all is to satisfy Miss Bushee that she hasn't made a bad investment in me. Don't you think there's something magnificent in the way she trusted me so much? And because of that I keep cheerful and try to keep from making trouble here in the household.

But try as she might, Betty continues to find it difficult to keep from making trouble, for her Stedman upbringing disposes her to be honest and forthright. In her December 17th letter the one-sided dialogue continues:

You say that you think me too honest to do anything under-handed. I feel some compunctions when you say that, <u>not</u> because I am doing anything that I ought not to be doing, but because even the most natural thing in the world seems wicked to Doña Benigna. Why, I come in from the Rezy [Residencia], after going there to study in the afternoon, with a guilty feeling just because I've been out of the house for several hours! Oh, please, <u>please</u> try to understand. I know it seems incredible to you; it would have to me too before I came over here and actually saw how things are. And it isn't that...I'm being 'treated just as if I were a Spanish girl', but rather as though I were a wicked little devil who had to be watched all the time. And, by golly, that burns me up. So I retaliate by simply omitting details which would incriminate me in my versions of entertainments to Doña Benigna. What else can I do? I have told her just one real lie, and that I had to 'cause she pushed me into a corner, metaphorically speaking.

The lie was a small sin by our standards; when pressed for details when she said that "we were going to the movies" Betty said that she was going with the girls when in fact she was going with Fernando. This part of the letter concludes by saying that "I really don't think any other Wellesley girls could stand it here though Doña Benigna has signified that she would like some next year. Don't say anything of this to Miss Bushee, tho...." In a postscript Betty adds "Doña Benigna says that Miss Bushee is the best person she ever knew! I'm inclined to think so too."

A week later, in her Christmas Day letter, Betty tries to convey to her family "what sort of person Doña Benigna is" in a spirit informed, perhaps, by Christmas charity:

[She] is a perfect lamb: she has a cute sense of humor, she takes wonderful care of us, she makes us eat so much we're losing all line (vertical, I mean) we ever had, she runs herself inside out doing things for you if you're sick. In short, she's a very motherly sort of person with a good strain of Protestant piety. So much for the person. But her ideas: Republican, good. Thinks saloons should be abolished, all right. Thinks Catholicism is pernicious, OK.

I paused briefly over the line about Catholics, and reminded myself that Betty had probably met very few in Texas. Surprisingly, there's no reference here to outmoded notions about how young ladies should behave. The next day, though, Betty continues her letter, and once again, we can see the strain imposed by the expectations her family is expressing in their letters. Despite everything she has told them, they continue to give her the impression that they think she is "just agitating for a cut-loose good time," and this hurts her deeply. She has become acutely aware of the distortions that are inevitable when people write letters, and articulates these with remarkable insight for a nineteen-year-old away from home for the first time:

> You say that I've been fairly decent all my life, and that I haven't shown any particular tendency to go hay-wire. Please try to comprehend that I still am. I have a very delicate and ticklish situation to contend with, and I have to do it all by myself. You people can't begin to understand how it is, because a lot of it is just plain subtle mental anguish and nothing else, things you can't put down on paper without magnifying them. I have purposely avoided doing that, so that you would not be able to say that I have exaggerated.... I have tried to be square about it. You say that I came to Spain to study. Of course I did. But I came to see Spain also, to learn new customs, to meet different sorts of people, to see a lot of new things. Miss Bushee would agree... in thinking that that is very important.

In her frustration, she succumbs to the exaggeration she has tried so hard to eschew and says "I might just as well become a novice at once and apply for admission to an order of nuns." What she finds most infuriating is that Doña Benigna seems to be holding her to the standards of her own youth, not the standards of present-day Spain: "And here I find myself in an atmosphere of frustration, of inhibition, which is not current in Spain any longer, which is on the verge of driving me crazy." She is hurt to the core that "my own father tell[s] me that I am the cause of mental havoc in my family because they no longer trust me or something." She begins to wonder whether she must "censor my own letters? Heaven forbid!" Her father's letter, she says, is "break[ing] my heart."

Her mother's letter, evidently, is somewhat more "reasonable," advising her to invite Doña Benigna to chaperone her to events. Betty summons a battery of reasons why this wouldn't work and then adds, in a handwritten postscript, "She wouldn't go anyway." Adept rhetorician that she is, Betty turns the tables on her mother:

> *Now Mummy, put yourself in my place. Here I am for the first time in my life being a little petted and adored by the other sex. Unlike you. Did your mother get upset when you were in love at sixteen with Archie Coynor, or at 19 with somebody else or at twenty with Will Sweet or at twenty-four with Daddy? (Correct ages, names and spelling. I can't remember too well all the details of your love affairs.) And that was when you were in love as well as the boys with you. And here I am not in love with anybody, but merely enjoying the feeling of being liked, and not doing anything to aggravate the situation, I assure you. Is that a crime? Or you, Daddy? Would you call it a crime? Or something of which you could not 'fully approve'? Don't go Doña Benignaish on me and say that all men are deceivers and are a bad lot and are to be avoided. You'll be taking a crack at your own kind! I have every intention of coming home 'heart whole and fancy free' to get a job of some swell sort and help Frank through college and show my family a little better time by help of the good salary which I shall be getting because I have been to Spain and can understand Spanish perfectly and speak it well and know the Spanish temperament from contact with lots of different kinds of people. There!*

This ten-page letter ("the longest letter I ever wrote") reminds me, in this age of cell phones, of how difficult it must have been to carry on these intense conversations with pauses of two weeks or more between responses. Would Betty have made her case so eloquently and in such detail if she had been able to pick up the phone or send an e-mail? Probably not.

The ten-page letter shifts gears after Betty's assertive "There!" for Betty wants to tell her family about Spanish Christmas Eve customs: the "fiesta de niños" at the Baptist Church where mothers threw little bags of candy onto the floor for their children, who had dutifully performed their "recitations"; the "real Spanish fiesta" at the home of Peggy's beau Alberto; the Nacimiento, or crèche, with its little figurines which the American students bought in the Plaza de Santa Cruz; the special afternoon feast of hot chocolate and lady fingers; the English carol service where the girls sang; and the late Christmas dinner at Fernando's with the traditional Nochebuena meal of white fish. Betty and her friend Peggy indulged in a fine English cigarette afterwards ("I didn't have the heart to refuse") and were each given a bottle of perfume by Alberto's family. And after all this, she finally went dancing, since she'd arranged beforehand to spend the night at the Residencia. Why, she asks wistfully, "doesn't Christmas Eve come more than once a year?" Christmas Day at Dona Benigna's was far more subdued, but there are more details about food and gifts, including a copy of *Pilgrim's Progress* from the Baptist minister, Mr. Rhodes, who asked Betty "How is your soul today?" and "hinted strongly that it was high time I got to thinking about asking God to save me." Betty slyly adds that "I had an irresistible impulse to ask them how they [Mr. and Mrs. Rhodes] could be so sure they were saved." This, her Episcopalian family would recognize, was a pointed critique of Baptist dogma. For us, reading this many years later, it is a reminder of the role religious affiliations played in Betty's judgments of people.

Betty's letters continue to reflect her complicated feelings about Doña Benigna. In her New Year's letter she is bitterly resentful about being forbidden to attend a Sunday football game with her admirer Fernando, and even more resentful because Doña Benigna suspects her of pretending to go to church only to sneak away. A week later, however, she is describing the Día de los Reyes festivities. In Spain, the day of the three kings, the twelfth day after Christmas, was when gift-giving took place.

> It is now after church and dinner, of course. The latter was very swell today: filets of beef, French fries, cauliflower dipped in flour and egg and fried in small pieces (a delicious dish), soup before all of course, and apple sauce and roscón to finish. Then we had mazapán and turrón [Spanish candies] for the last time. The roscón is a sort of coffee

cake with bits of fruit glace on top, and is a specialty of the Día de los Reyes. Furthermore, there is always a little surprise inside. We had one yesterday, but, alas, there was no surprise, and Doña Benigna was so mad that she bought another for today. She especially wanted one with a surprise for me. Wasn't that sweet of her? So we had it, and…I got the surprise which was a 'haba' or good luck bean. On the Día all the children put their shoes on the balcony, you know, to see what the kings will bring them. We, thinking we were pretty big children, didn't put our shoes out, but we found two little packages on the balcony nevertheless. Doña B., the cute lamb, had put some nuts and things in paper napkins and had written us little verses from the 'Reyes Magos'!…She is a dear about remembering things like that.

Evidently Betty's strategies for dealing with Doña Benigna's prohibitions are improving: when an elegant box of candy arrives from Aurelio, she reports that this time when interrogated "I came out on top for the first time, though in a perfectly nice way." First Betty diplomatically offered Doña Benigna some candy; then,

…I told her that I was not serious with either Fernando or Aurelio and that they both knew it (that being the thing that bothered her) and that they were very honorable, decent lads whom I like. That I do not go out at night so it is not dangerous. That I infinitely prefer that someone accompany me home to coming home alone at nine from classes. That all the boys we go out with have Miss Sweeney's and Miss Pierce's <u>full</u> approbation, etc. etc. Well, she had to admit that everything I said was right and that I was perfectly within my rights. So we parted amicably. OK? Hope so. Anyway, <u>don't worry about me</u>.

TWENTY

Spring and Summer
1934

H OW DIFFERENT MIGHT Betty's year in Spain have been, one wonders, if she had lived in the Residencia with the girls from Smith College instead of with Doña Benigna? In her letter of February 4th she responds to her family's suggestion that

> *Perhaps my blowing off steam to you helped me to adjust myself to Doña B. I don't know but that there's something in that. Though just when I think I've got things all figured out, my attitude adjusted to a nicety, and hopes of a full return to open conversations, etc., something happens to send it all haywire and I have to build it all up again, painstakingly, like the old Greek – was his name, oh, I don't remember, something with an x in it – who had to keep rolling the stone up the hill down in Hades only to have it tumble right down again. He had nothing on me…. But I am fairly adaptable, thank goodness, and after all I always keep in mind the fact that if it weren't for Miss Bushee I*

shouldn't be here. Though sometimes I simply writhe over the idea that she actually paid my board and room…. If there had been any way I could have earned it…. It isn't that my feeling of gratitude and affection for her would have been any less, but that my position here in Doña Benigna's house wouldn't seem so anomalous, so utterly dependent on the intangible thing called good will.

In Boston, as in Madrid, there are ongoing worries about money – this was the Depression, and the Stedmans were struggling. A letter from home has referred to "cuts and rearrangements," and Betty bravely tells her family that these "don't amount to a hill of beans to me. The prospect of having less money doesn't perturb me in the least. I only hope that Daddy will understand that we all feel that way about it, and will <u>stop worrying</u>." Elsewhere in the letter she says that the financial situation "doesn't scare me at all, but I do hate it for Mummy's and Daddy's sake." She is painfully aware of the sacrifices they made to send her to Spain, and jokes about a melodramatic old movie she saw in which the heroine grows her hair long and sells it to buy a crust to feed her starving family. In a subsequent letter Betty expresses her hopes that Wellesley will come through with a $400 scholarship for the following year so that she won't have to take Frank's money.

The Stedman family's extraordinary closeness is nowhere more evident than in the birthday letter Betty writes to her parents a couple of weeks before their February birthdays. There also a whiff—perhaps more than a whiff—of the kind of nineteenth-century rhetorical flourishes Betty has absorbed from her reading.

So, Mummy and Daddy, this letter is really yours. And it brings with it a heart full of love for you. Plus the assurance that on the 4ᵗʰ and 12ᵗʰ of next month I shall be thinking of you so much that you will surely sense it, even across a whole ocean of water which, usually insensible to people's feelings, will help waft my thought along to you. 'For there's one corner of a foreign field that is forever…' YOURS! And that corner is wherever I happen to be… Human love must be an awfully strong force; I always feel, when I sit down to write to you, as though you were right *here beside me, or I were there and that I could reach out and touch you or put my head on Mummy's shoulder or sit in Daddy's lap. As though time and space were nothing at all! Someone said something to me the other day about 'souls which, being together, are so far apart' and I can say just the opposite. I could talk to you now about other things – about how wonderful you've always been to us, how much gratitude we feel for your sacrifices, what luck we had in having you for father and mother. But those things are for other days. And besides, they strike me as pulling love down a little from its high, bright pedestal and basing it on material things. On birthdays you think of <u>people</u> and not what they've done for you. And you try to put into inadequate words some of the things you've thought all your life, but, coming of a race which conceals its feelings more or less, you rarely express.*

The paragraph goes on a bit longer, ending with "God bless you both, and keep you for us."

On some days, Betty receives half a dozen letters, and we get little glimpses of what they contain from her responses. Mummy's letter "made me feel all warm inside the first time I read it, and the sensation was so nice that I read it over again with the same result!" When no letters arrive, she feels "deserted." On February 18th she reports that her only mail was a Valentine's Day card from Sid. At other times, though, the volume of mail is oppressive. Betty frequently laments that "letters are piled up on my desk six inches deep" and urges the family to share her long letters with relatives who have written to her. On February 25th Betty thanks the family for their Valentines and tells her mother that "you seem to have an unerring instinct; you always divine when I'm a bit homesick, and send me some special bolstering bit of love." Evidently the family worries that she is not seeing enough "old-world treasures" and she writes to reassure them that she has been to the Prado but that the museums are often closed during her very few free hours each week. Daddy's letter "reminded me slightly of one Daddy has read to us that his father wrote to him—the style, etc." (How frustrating to read of a family letter that survived for a while, but has long since been discarded). In response to something her mother said, Betty remarks, "No, I don't think it's wrong to care so much for one's children," and adds, "have your deep sentiments, but never let them get completely beyond you," a cryptic reference to her growing realization, described later in the letter, that Spanish men are not to be taken seriously.

> *Spaniards talk a lot, threaten to shoot themselves with the slightest provocation (Aurelio and Ferdy have both at different times), make love better than most anybody in the world, I bet, but they aren't serious. In fact, I have just found out to my horror that Alberto is not serious with Peg. And I'm kind of upset about it because she is serious with him, and after all he's always talking about when he goes to America and when they'll be married, etc. I've wracked my brains thinking of some way to warn her, but it's too late. She wouldn't believe me, and besides would only get mad. She'll have to find it out herself in due time, if he isn't man enough to tell her. Aurelio says that what will probably happen is that she'll go home, they'll write a few letters and then Alberto will just sort of forget to write…. I should have known from the start, of course; Alberto's far too good-looking and spoiled not to be typically Spanish in regard to other things…." So you so see that if there were any danger of my getting serious with any of my pals, I have a living lesson always with me."*

Several weeks earlier, during the Christmas and Dia de los Reyes festivities, Betty had negotiated a delicate situation involving her beau Aurelio, who wrote her a letter in Spanish that translates, roughly, as follows:

> *My darling Betty:*
> *Since I can't speak seriously, at least when I write I am serious. That's why I prefer writing a few lines to you rather than speaking. If I were to tell you what I'm going to write you wouldn't pay any attention and perhaps reading this you'll begin to think that I am serious when I speak to you.*
> *It's possible that when you have finished reading this letter you will decide not to look at me again, but I don't believe it; it would be too*

much punishment for such a weak and human fault as falling in love. Is it my fault that I liked you from the first moment?

But let's get more concretely to the theme of the letter. First of all, I have to say, and you can believe it or not, but it is the truth, that I am sincere; I don't use double talk or false words. And for this very reason I assure you that whatever you decide you will always have a true friend in me, since I can't be anything else if you don't wish it.

After this rather elaborate beginning, Aurelio turns to the subject of his "novia," the young woman he has been betrothed to for some time. He says he will marry her because he has promised to do so, but adds that if Betty had been Spanish, or if she had planned to remain in Spain, he would have proposed to her. However, he continues,

None of these hypotheses holds – you are American, I am Spanish, and you will leave sooner or later…. Therefore I can't say to you I will marry you.

Aurelio goes on to say that

Today my strongest wish would be satisfied if during your stay in Spain you would love me just a little. You can imagine that if we could manage to forget during the time you are in Madrid that one day we will have to separate that we could only think about living for ourselves it would be the height of happiness. I know that is asking a lot, but when people love one another they try not to think about the obstacles.

There is quite a bit more in this vein, with more protestations about his seriousness and sincerity, and some rather flowery pronouncements about women's roles:

The woman is for man a sweetheart, a friend, a wife, but still something more –she is a bit of a mother with her friend, her sweetheart, or her husband, for there is nothing equal to a woman's

affection. I only ask you for affection – as a friend, a sweetheart, or what you wish, but affection. A woman's kiss gives one strength to undertake tasks one would otherwise pass up.

Aurelio closes with a request that she not share this letter with her friends and a repeated offer of true friendship if she cannot reciprocate his love. In a postscript, he reminds her to address her response to him using his entire name, since his father, also named Aurelio, might open the letter by mistake.

Betty clearly labored mightily over her response, as the extensively revised draft of her letter indicates (we can't know for certain that she sent the letter, however). She too approaches her subject in a roundabout way, with repeated apologies for her errors in Spanish and assurances that she will write with the same frankness and sincerity. She chooses to interpret his protestations of love as a "broma," or joke, in order to protect herself from becoming credulous or romantic, and tells him that she knows he has a "novia," and that she doesn't want to be responsible for ending his engagement. If he is sincere in saying that he doesn't love the young woman, then, Betty says, "I feel sorry for her, but this is not my problem." She informs him "frankly" that she is not in love with him and probably never will be, then ends her letter by accepting his offer of friendship, and expressing her hope that they will remain the best of friends. We don't hear much more about Aurelio in subsequent letters, so we can only speculate about how he received her gentle rejection.

Every once in a while Betty's letters home mention the political situation in Spain; there have been strikes, evidently, and in February she notes airily, that "We're threatened with a general revolution, but I refuse to get excited. We've had so many false alarms…" In a letter written on April 3rd she says

No need to worry about us when you read things in the paper. They always exaggerate things so and distort them so that you'd never recognize the same thing in two different accounts. As to the present government's being strong and holding the situation well in hand, I don't know. At any rate, the parties are so evenly balanced at this point that an upset is not expected.

A couple of weeks later she writes that

> *Sunday morning we woke up to a nice strike. More fun. It seems that 30,000 Fascists (extreme Rights) were having a convention in the Escorial, the huge monastery built by Charles V's son, Philip II, right outside Madrid. Well, the Socialists and the Communists didn't like the idea at all, so they retaliated with a bread strike. That sounds comparatively simple, until you think of a country like Spain whose main food is her 'pan y vino' and then you see the importance of such a measure. There were lines of people in the street all day trying to buy bread. You know, they can't buy enough stuff for more than one day. For perishable things they have no refrigerators; for imperishable things, no room. And so it goes.*

Betty adds a handwritten postscript: "Don't worry about me. These strikes are silly little affairs and don't amount to much."

The letters occasionally provide other glimpses of the Spain of 1933-34. On March 18th Betty writes

> *Typical March weather. The people in the markets gather around their braseros (little open fires in punctured tin containers), stamp their feet, rub their hands, and yell louder than ever to combat the cold…. Snow sits on top of the cabbages, and I feel sorry for the beggars that huddle, half-frozen, in doors. I do not see how some of them live.*

More characteristic of the letters is a passage like this one, which describes the festivities on St. Joseph's Day:

> *You know that here people celebrate their saints' days instead of their birthdays, and it is a custom to give elaborate pastries and things. So all the pastelerías were filled with the most fanciful cakes you can imagine made in forms of baskets and decorated with fruit, nuts, candies, flowers, ribbons, etc. And on top of each is a little figure of San José. Elvira says that they will be having great festivals in Valencia tomorrow,*

*called 'fallas.' They make huge effigies dressed in beautiful clothes and
representing historical or legendary figures and parade them through
the streets. Then they turn out all the lights in the town and every
one repairs to see the figures burned. And they burn them with their
lovely clothes and all. She says it's a beautiful sight from the harbor;
most people go out in boats to see it. Gee, I should like to see Valencia!
Alberto swears we will go there this spring, but I've gotten so that at
this point I expect nothing and am therefore proportionately joyful if it
really pans out. And I lose nothing in the way of disappointment. Good
philosophy – if one could only work it!*

Betty's long-anticipated trip to Andalusia with Peg and her beau Alberto
is described in great detail in the April 3rd letter. Peg and Betty embark for
Córdoba by overnight third-class rail coach, arriving at six in the morning.
They visit the famous Moorish mosque, tour the city in a horse-drawn
carriage, and then return to the train station to resume their journey, en
route to Seville. They find Alberto waiting for them in Seville, and they
"sally forth" to see the city and the famous Palm Sunday processions.

*This being Palm Sunday or el Domingo de Ramos they brought out
only four floats or rather 'pasos' as they call them. And I should not
call them floats for they are the favorite images in the churches which
are brought out only during Holy Week and are carried, dressed in
magnificent robes and with hundreds of candles burning before them,
through the streets followed by penitents. These penitents are organized
into what are called confradías, each one of which has the care of
one of the images and sees to it that it is in the procession. They are
something like our lodges but with a more exclusively religious motive.
The confradías are all dressed in a costume which looks like the Ku Klux
Klan, tall peaked cap, cord around the waist. Terribly picturesque, of
course. The pasos we saw were two Virgins, a Last Supper, and Christ
before Pilate. As they go through the street suddenly one hears from
the crowd an agonized wailing sort of song consisting mostly of 'Ay!'
which is called a 'saeta' and is strangely minor. Something like Gaelic
songs I imagine. Anyway, as soon as one of these begins—sung by*

some lone man—the paso is lowered to the ground and the people all listen attentively. When he finishes – and this is the oddest thing – all the people clap their hands, and the man swaggers a bit and looks pleased! And puts his cigarette back in his mouth. That's the part I can't understand about it; the whole thing is supposed to be the outburst of religious devotion yet they take it so matter of factly. I just can't understand it, that's all. And you should see the way they commercialize the occasion to sell everything under the sun from beer to peanuts – and even when the paso is passing!

The trip takes a dark turn late that night, when Betty awakes "feeling all stuffy" and opens the window.

The next thing I knew I was hearing a most ungodly yell from Peg and a lot of rumpus in the street. When I pulled myself awake Peg was still yelping and saying in a stifled voice, all at once, 'A man! In our room!' I, of course, was scared to death, but relieved that that was all; from her yell I had thought that at least she was being killed. Well, it worked out that the gent had climbed up the wall from the street and had gotten in the balcony, but just as he got there Peg woke up and yelled, also some gent from across the street. So the robber, startled, grabbed the first thing that came to hand and fled. The 'first thing' happened to be that blue and gray dress (remember the material Miss Carrie Hoke gave me?), my beloved red blouse, and that nice soft brown one. I hated to lose them, but I suppose we can be thankful he didn't get everything including the money. They tell gory tales of people being left without a stitch of clothes and without a cent. When we told the manager he was quite unconcerned and said, 'Oh, that's happened dozens of times; you shouldn't have opened your window.' So we got mad and said, 'Well, why in h—- don't you warn people about things like that?' but it did no good. We spent the whole of the next morning telling it to the judge, in the faint hope they'd get them back. You see, the police and the robbers are all tied up together in Sevilla; the police know everything that goes on.

Fortunately, the rest of the trip is just what Betty had hoped it would be, especially the long-anticipated visit to the Alhambra:

> For when I stepped inside the Hall of the Ambassadors, the first real thing we saw in the Alhambra, my heart just beat and beat and I couldn't say a word. And it was like that all the way through. Our guide would go on volubly explaining this and that, and I could only go wordlessly around drinking in enough beauty with my eyes to last me a good lifetime.

Betty has carefully numbered her letters, with the intent of "reading them again sometime and reminiscing." Her brother Frank has written to ask her to say more about "art, civilization, etc." and she responds to him saying that these are things she'll talk about when she returns, for she wants to "devote my letters to answering and asking questions and picturing my life here."

> Hence the here-and-there technique of my letters. I shall answer anything you want when I get home, that is, anything I'm able to answer. And darling, such 'elementary matters' as the Spanish sewage system and other items of that ilk which you are so fond of are not particularly interesting to the others. I shall be available to any and all and will talk for hours without the slightest encouragement when I get home. But don't start me in letters. I just do it for your sake, don't you see? I observe all I can, and I am even making a very creditable effort to understand something of Spanish politics just because I know I have to develop some artillery for your barrage of questions. And that you will admit shows that I am public-spirited, for Spanish politics are the most incomprehensible affair imaginable, take it from me…. I will answer your questions about Spanish temperament, whether they have rivalries in their schools, and the question of the social class when I get home.

For months, Betty's letters have been filled with details about the return trip; she plans and rearranges her itinerary, worries about how to pay for it, and tells her family how much she looks forward to being home with them. Then, on May 3rd, she writes to say that she has been offered a summer job in Spain:

> *Mrs. Moles, the mother of the girl who is in Wellesley this year in my place, runs a summer camp for little boys and girls…and her whole family goes up to help her…. This camp is up in Asturias on the coast at a place near Gijón, and is supposed to be a perfectly heavenly spot. Asturias is very mountainous, you know, and has the finest scenery in Spain. And they want me to go up with them to help with the camp.*

The "conditions," Betty explains, are that all her expenses, including travel to and from Madrid and laundry, would be taken care of, but there would be no salary. Betty provides a list of "Advantages" and "Disadvantages":

> *Advantages:*
> *1) The opportunity to speak absolutely nothing but Spanish for three months (counting June here).*
> *2) The opportunity to see a part of Spain I have not seen and would have no other chance to see, with no expense to me.*
> *3) A busy, healthful summer which would put me in the pink of trim for my senior year. (Not so racking as the last two summers, however).*
> *Disadvantages:*
> *1) No salary.*
> *2) Not coming home for three months more.*

> *Those things listed above are the advantages and disadvantages of the job, of course. These are the difficulties and how they can be balanced. Of course, if Daddy were* <u>absolutely sure</u> *of a pay job for me this summer, there would be no questions about my coming home. If, however, it were a case of deciding between this camp job and my last year's one, I should pick this one in spite of the $50. So much for that.*

Now as to what I would do in June, for you will be wondering about that. Miss Sweeney has got me a job to teach English to a little Spanish girl of good family [Lucila]. This is for this month (May) and will be a pay job. Next month, however, they would like to have me stay at their house (board and lodging) in exchange for lessons to the little girl and perhaps another member of the family. Also there may be the opportunity to give other lessons for pay, so that I would I have not only my room and board, but also pin money. Thus I would not be costing you anything during the month of June, and incidentally, very, very little in July and August. I know, lambies, that you would protest against that, but I am being very matter-of-fact and unsentimental and trying to figure everything squarely. And you have to count board and room as money, no? So in that case I would be earning a little, because I would be saving you some. See?

Betty begins and ends her letter by assuring her family that the decision is theirs, and that "I shall abide by your decision completely." She asks them to send her a cable saying "Yes" if she can stay and "No" if she's to come home, and reminds them that they will have to pay for each word, including the street name.

During the next couple of weeks Betty goes to classes (evidently, the teachers have added extra hours of classes at the end of the semester to make up for cancelled classes) and works furiously at a thesis she and her friend Peg are typing in multiple copies for a Vassar student to make some extra money, taking turns on Betty's typewriter, with the result that the ribbon is becoming so faint that the letters are hard to read. And, she breaks off her relationship with Fernando, despite the fact that this will mean that she'll never get to go to the bullfight he's been promising to take her to for months:

The other night when he brought me home from the Argentina and inquired as to whether I were in love with him or no, I said no in a surprised sort of way, and asked him if he didn't know it already. He did, there's no denying it. But he took that as a pretext to go and fix things up with his novia (the everpresent thing in Spain!) with whom he had broken up about a month before he met me. He told me that she, a poetess, was deeply in love with him, and had been sort of neurasthenic over their separation, a detail at which I could hardly repress a snicker. But I said, OK, swell, I think that's grand, etc. with that cheerful look that left him completely nonplussed. I have my suspicions, she said modestly, that he just did it to bring me around, but I fooled him. So he bid me goodbye in a tragic sort of way, retaining the privilege, however, of taking me to the bullfight…. I am not at all upset; I just think it was a darned funny time to do it—less than a month before I leave.

She ends her paragraph with "I didn't know he had that much backbone." The romance with Aurelio had ended a few weeks after the January exchange of letters, so Betty is now without romantic entanglements.

The cable finally arrives, and the answer is "Yes." In her letter of May 18th Betty says she had expected it to be "No" and feels a rush of mixed feelings, which she realizes she would have felt either way. She writes about how much she'll miss traveling with Peg and the others on the way home, and about important matters like sending her trunk to storage with her winter clothes and buying a white hat and a white summer jacket, since "you can't go around in Madrid without sleeves." On May 30th she writes her last letter from Doña Benigna's house on Alvarez de Castro, and reports on the last two exhausting weeks of classes, papers, exams, last-minute shopping, and farewells to her friends in the Smith program, who are leaving for home. Two gentlemen have signed up for English lessons with her in June, and she will be in charge of young Lucila for several hours in the afternoon and evening. "Life will be very sweet," she remarks, despite the fact that "Lucila is very lazy intellectually and not a little dumb in regard to her English." Ruefully, she says "I see clearly that I am no Rabelais or John Locke on this business of teaching." She has received some conciliatory letters from Fernando, but has not deigned to answer them: "Nuts to him. He can just go fry asparagus (freir espárragos) as the Spaniards say."

Betty doesn't describe her leave-taking from Doña Benigna and her household, except as follows:

I gave her the huge bunch of roses and orange blossoms and peonies Don Julio gave me and she seemed pleased. Marina (the maid) is crazy about coffee caramels so I bought her some of them and put a duro in the bottom of the bag. It wasn't much of a tip, but a little is better than nothing. She has been awfully good to me all year in more ways than one.

In a subsequent response to an inquiry from home she reports that

I parted as the best of friends with Doña B., and I go over there about every two or three days for a few minutes at least. I have had tea with her several times. I just drop in, she is alone and lonely, and we have tea. She's a darling as a friend. It's only difficult when one is living with her. As far as I can see, that is the trouble with most Spaniards.

Although she is not boastful, Betty is justifiably proud of her final term's grades. The university grades range from 80 in Lyric Poetry to 98 in Historians (she had taken a total of seven courses at the university), and she earned an A and A- in the two Residencia courses. She and Peg are "right together" for first place among all the students in the Smith program. Peg is on her way home, via Paris and London, and she writes to tell Betty of her adventures.

She has loaded me up with errands and things to give Alberto to take to her. The horrible part is that I'm as sure as death that Alberto is not going to America. In fact, I've been told that he's already going around with his old novia. I get all hot under the collar whenever I think of it. Peg's a fine person and he's very charming, but why in H—- did he have to talk about marriage when he knew it was practically impossible. He knows enough about Americans to know that everything goes for a joke until one begins to talk about weddings, and then things get a bit serious. But I really think, luckily, that Peg will pull out of it all right. Menos mal.

In the midst of the Depression, jobs are hard to come by, and neither Betty's brother nor sister has a summer job. Betty's mother is evidently making some clothes for Aunt Edith:

> *The dresses you are making for Aunt Edith will be nice because you are making them, lambie, and you sew beautifully. If you ask my candid opinion of the prints, I should say that they do not arouse any deep emotion in me. They are nothing new or original; the sort of things she has worn for years. You forgot to put in the voile sample. I hope the family is being adamant about making you keep the $25 for yourself, lady.*

Betty has begun her tutoring job, and the lessons with Lucila, or Luci, as Betty calls her, are frustrating.

> *I've never had such a desire to spank a child in my life! Apparently pleasant and nice, that kid conceals one swell character: sinfully lazy, disagreeable and commanding to the servants, determined to have her own way (and being an only child with indulgent parents, she gets it), and with a most useless habit of playing tricks which are not funny. It is like pulling teeth to get her to sit down and have an English lesson. If by superhuman effort I get her in a chair, the battle has only begun; she won't listen. She says she likes English, but she won't learn anything. So what can one do! I'm at my wits' end.*

Despite the recalcitrant Luci, Betty is in high spirits. In her June 25th letter she tells her family that

> *With a full moon like the one that's peeking in my window now, with a full, lush breeze in the trees, and with the comfortable feeling of having friends and a loving family, life is very sweet.*

Waxing philosophical, she observes that the Spaniards are especially noted for their tremendous pride.

> *Honor – pride, 'el honor, el orgullo' is the birthright of every*
> *Spaniard, be he gentil hombre (hidalgo) or peon, and he will sell it for*
> *no pot of lentils! As you can readily see, there's something magnificent*
> *about such an attitude, yet something fearfully decadent. In times of*
> *glory and the height of their power, the Spaniards were arrogant enough*
> *to take it as a matter of course; now they are indifferent in their fall.*
>
> *On the other hand, the dirty gypsy women with their dirtier babies*
> *(if possible) than ever, the sun in the middle of the day is baking hot*
> *(just like Texas!), and Lucila is very naughty. But you see how much*
> *importance I accord these things when I give them four lines as against*
> *the formidable paragraph above!*

Actually, Betty gives an even longer paragraph to the "more banal" matters of the white straw hat with a little black veil she has finally purchased after much deliberation and a Jantzen bathing suit she is contemplating purchasing—a bright blue low cut one, since "the Spanish scoff at mine for being so modest!"

During her last couple of days before leaving for Asturias Betty takes her leave of Madrid, a "huge place of adventure" where she has met many more people than she would have in "rock-tight Boston" with its "terrible system of cliques." She takes leave of Doña Benigna at a lavish lunch of her favorite foods, sends off her trunk, and packs her new bathing suit (red, not blue), is taken to tea at a restaurant by young Luci, who "paid everything, even the trams, and was very proud of the new red purse her daddy had brought her from Switzerland."

A few days later she is writing from Asturias, surrounded by twelve youngsters fascinated by her typewriter and making a horrible racket. She had traveled north in an autobus with other staff members and the camp children, through a landscape that reminded her of Texas—"vast plains broken by rugged bare mountains…tawny earth getting red as we went north," and then, after a stop in Burgos, along the Ebro river with "green hills on each side" up into the mountains and the cooler air, and finally to San Vincente de la Barquera,

...where we had our first sight of the sea. It is a most picturesque place, above all when you leave the town and ascend the mountain road and look back down at the village set down there with the sea in front, a river coming down just below us to meet the town which tries to connect its two parts but just can't quite make it, and the boats slip through into the river...Oh, it was something unforgettable!

We arrived at San Antolín at eight and just when we thought we had seen enough beauty for one day we had a whole new panorama: hidden in the mountains here we found a little white house with red tiles big enough, nevertheless, to hold all of us and more, and at its side a little 13th century, ivy-covered monastery quite as it was six hundred years ago....

Well, I heard all about the monastery and about Saint Antolín, who, it seems, was a French gentleman who was drawn and quartered by some unbelievers, and then, miraculously, the scattered parts of his body reunited. So they dedicated this little monastery to him. It was intended chiefly as a stopping place on the way to Santiago de Compostela, the grand pilgrimage in the 13th and 14th centuries.

The letter ends with a handwritten postscript: "Why doesn't Aunt Edith write to me? You will send me the money soon, won't you?" The money, presumably, is for her return trip, during which she is planning to meet Edith in Paris.

Betty writes four letters from the camp, describing the daily routine in great detail, the morning lessons and afternoon excursions, the other staff members, the food, and more details about the monastery, which, as it turns out, was already an accepted stopping place on the route to Santiago in the year 1000. She is clearly fascinated by the monastery's history:

Charles V, you know, came to Spain by sea to take possession of his kingdom. He was shipwrecked near here, and was brought in his hand chair to the monastery accompanied by his Flemish courtiers. The monks sheltered him, and then he set out on the long arduous journey to Madrid still in his hand chair, for the poor thing suffered terrible from gout. Some time later somebody put his coat of arms on the house

as a souvenir! And here they are to this day. All this was around 1520.
So the monastery has a continuous history, and we are just adding to it!

Here is an excerpt from the letter of July 22nd, written a few days after Betty's twentieth birthday, describing what she sees from her perch on a bench in the old church on a rainy day:

> *Now I see a little girl in a white skirt and red sweater, one of our*
> *'peques' or little ones. And there goes one of the servants shod in*
> *madreñes (the wooden shoes) and carrying a bucket of water on her*
> *head. She has the job of filling the barrels in our wash rooms. So you see*
> *that Goya's picture of the girl at the well is not just fiction.*

On her birthday Betty observes the Spanish custom of treating everyone else, "instead of the other way around as in America, so I ordered enough caramelos for the whole camp (only cost me 4 pesetas!) and put them by everybody's plate."

> *When I went in to supper they began to yell "Viva la señorita-miss!"*
> *(one of their names for me) which is answered by "Viva-a-a" by the*
> *whole camp. Then somebody started "hip! hip!" (pronounced 'eep' in*
> *Spanish, and struck me as uncontrollably funny, so I sat there and*
> *laughed and laughed) answered by "hurra" with the accent on the 'u'*
> *and a strong rolled 'r'. Mrs. Moles opined that it was "un gesto amable'*
> *(a kind or nice gesture), and Mr. Moles wished me five centuries of life. I*
> *demurred at that, but appreciated the thought.*

In her last letter from Spain, number 43, Betty is very excited about her plans to travel home via the Basque country, Paris, Brussels, and London. Her letter of August 7th is mailed from Brussels, and she begins by assuring her family that she is "perfectly safe" despite the news in the papers about strikes. She had arranged in advance to meet Edith in Paris, and reports that "Aunt Edith was telling me the other day that the thing she admired most was courage, possessed in large measure by her mother." Many of the letters deal with calculations about money, for Betty, much as she wanted to avoid it, has had to ask for money from home for her return trip. Fortunately, "Aunt Edith paid practically everything for me in Paris and says she is going to do the same in London, so I shall have plenty. She doesn't want me to get home without a red cent in my pockets." Betty promises her parents that she will make money as soon as she can and "sometime, Mummy darling, I shall carry you away on a vacation to the place you most want to go to, and we shall do the things you want to do. And then one for you, Daddy." When Betty arrived in Paris,

> Aunt Edith took me to Reid Hall, the American student house in the Montparnasse section where she used to live during the War, and installed me in a comfy little room....

Betty and Edith wander through Paris, visiting churches with war memorials and eating delicious "goozly (Edith's own word) tarts, and on to Malmaison, the chateau Napoleon gave Josephine as a wedding gift, and Versailles. "Aunt Edith and I agreed that there is something pathetic about seeing the clothes and trinkets of people long dead, much more so than their larger memorials like furniture." They visit other places Edith remembers from the war years—a "cute little place called Henriette's," for example. "Aunt Edith is a swell chaperone; she does not stay awake worrying about people. Parents please take notice!" The letter breaks off abruptly after an account of their visit to Notre Dame, with no space remaining to "start in on Brussels. Already written too much."

And so the Spain letters end. No other year in Betty's life will ever be described for posterity in such detail. She must have written to her parents from Chicago after she graduated from Wellesley in 1935, but the only letters to survive are three written five years later from Mexico City. She reports that she is studying Spanish shorthand from 12:00 to 1:00 each day and spending the rest of her time traveling around with three young men she met on the train, who serve as escorts, since "otherwise I could not go out after dark; at least, it is not wise to do so." She says a little about her travels, but these handwritten letters are much shorter than the typed Spain ones, and the "Betty" that speaks through them is clearly more independent from her family and no longer intent on leaving a detailed record of her travels. Years later she described the trip differently; she had gone to Mexico, she said, with some other people to make a movie about crafts and craftsmen. The movie never came to anything, but she had a grand time.

When people write letters, they never "write the whole story," as Betty put it in one of her letters from Spain. Perhaps because her family had expressed concern about the space given over to social events in the letters, Betty offers a little sermon on how she decided what to include. "I just sit down and write along… [and] it is a well-known psychological fact that one remembers one's pleasantest and most unusual experiences." She developed a strategy of waiting a week before writing about the "disagreeable ones… [and] chances are I will have forgotten most of them." What makes the Spain letters so full a chronicle of Betty's year abroad, though, is that she does include so many details, large and small. Perhaps she knew she was writing for posterity, and that the letters would be saved.

PART FOUR

"The Jewish Question"

TWENTY-ONE

Edith at the Radcliffe Appointments Bureau

I WISH I KNEW MORE about the Stedman family's feelings about Jews when Betty was writing her letters in 1933-1934. Nine or ten years later, after she had fallen in love with Gene Tuck she wrote to him that "the Jewish question," had been "settled" between them "long ago," although the fragmentary evidence their letters contain suggests that it remained not so much a "question," as a source of friction in the Stedman family. I wonder, too, what happened to Sid Diamond, the medical student with whom Betty kept up a correspondence during her year in Spain. Did he finish his studies and return safely to America before the war began? Did he and Betty continue their correspondence after she returned to Wellesley? There are hints in the letters from Spain that Betty's parents were alarmed by her references to him. A few weeks after receiving those first few letters in the fall of 1933 they must have written about their concerns, for Betty replies on October 20th that

> *I did __not__ get up a romance with a Jew on the boat! Although two or three made love to me* [readers, please note that Betty uses the

expression in its old sense of "court" or "flirt with"] *of various sorts, mostly fooling. I have heard from only one of them, Sid. His second letter came this morning—great excitement in Germany over withdrawing from the League* [of Nations]. *He (and I) wonder if we're going to have another war. Heaven forbid! Incidentally, Sid and I agreed that we could never fall in love with each other; the idea was too humorous. Seriously though, I'm very sane about romancing on boats…*

The family back in Boston continues to ask about Sid. Betty has sent home some photographs she took on the ship, and in the November 4th letter she says,

> *I'm surprised you think Sid so old! He's about 25, I think, and of course he does have an M. A., etc., but he looks a perfect babe…. Poor thing, he's no beauty, but he is funny. He is a Jew, as far as I know. I have no illusions about that. Don't worry, I'm not in love with him.*

It's hard to know what Betty means here, just as it's hard to know why her family continues to dwell on the subject. On another occasion Betty mentions a cousin who is interested in a Roman Catholic girl; she reports that "he has said that if he marries her in five or six years, he will probably turn R.C. too. I hope not." Mixed marriages evoke disapproval in the Stedman family, clearly. Betty is also not above resorting to ethnic stereotypes; in one of her letters she mentions in passing a new girl in the Residencia, "a German Jewess and a lot like Roz [a Boston acquaintance], but nicer because she's younger. But she's got all of Roz's propensities in embryo and some of them fully developed." The new girl is trying to make friends, employing what Betty refers to as "predictable tactics" which make Betty "laugh and laugh." It troubles me to think that Betty and her friends from Smith College were more open to the cultural differences between Spaniards and American than those between Christians and Jews.

During Betty's year in Spain, Edith Stedman had been back in Boston for several years. There is nothing in her letters home to indicate whether or not Frank and Marian Stedman shared the Spain letters with Edith, or whether Betty received any letters from her remarkable aunt. Her feelings of admiration, even awe, toward Edith are evident in one of the letters from the spring of 1934, before she received the offer to spend the summer in Asturias. Anticipating her return to Depression-era Boston for the summer before her senior year at Wellesley, Betty was hoping that Edith could find her a job, and the tone of her letter conveys a bit of uneasiness about asking for help:

> *Don't you think that with all the glamour of having been in Spain a year I should get at least a $200 job this summer? I do. Tell Aunt Edith, and when she says, 'Why, the conceited little wretch!' break it to her that I'm just fooling. By the way, tell her I think she's the nuts. What a brain! She just sits in her little office and the ideas come popping out, apparently. Wish I could be as successful at any one job as she has been at all of hers.*

The office Betty's letter refers to was Radcliffe's Appointment Bureau, where Edith is putting her entrepreneurial skills to work, skills that she had honed in the candy business and in China. Like all of her other jobs, this one came into her life fortuitously, when she was as a crossroads.

Shortly after she returned from China in 1927 at the age of thirty-nine Edith landed a job as the Executive Secretary of the Judge Baker Foundation. "It was one more job for which I had had no training or experience," she remarked in the autobiography. The foundation had been named for the first Juvenile Court Judge in Boston, and its purpose was

> *...to study boys and girls referred to them by the Juvenile Court before any disposition was made of their cases, but when I knew it several of the Childrens' Agencies were also asking for their services.... The Directors were Dr. William Healy and Dr. Augusta Bronner. The former had made a name for himself as a psychiatrist in the particularly nasty case of Loeb and Leopold in Chicago a few years previous.... There were [also] one or two full-time psychiatrists, two psychologists, several psychiatric social workers, various secretaries, and me. I had no more idea than a cat what an executive Secretary did, but I soon found out.*

One of Edith's responsibilities was to arrange three-hour conferences during which, she observed caustically, "the child himself never appeared but everyone concerned with him had to be present…." After a couple of weeks on the job, Edith was taken aside by Dr. Healy. She describes the incident in her autobiography:

> After a slightly embarrassed silence he said "I don't think you are very happy here, Miss Stedman, and something else might be better for you." When the idea sank in that he was really firing me, I, like a fool, burst into tears, which no man enjoys. Such a thing had never happened before. I needed the job and my pride was terribly hurt. After being mopped up, I discovered that I had been mistaken in my understanding of the word "Executive," and that no man wants an arranging woman around. In my zeal I had tackled his desk which seemed to be covered with the contents of a half dozen wastebaskets, and had tried to bring order out of chaos. He preferred his own kind of order, thank you very much, but if I was prepared to leave him alone to do his own managing, he would give me another chance. I thought very long and soberly that night and decided that I had got to change my ways if not my aims….

Edith resolved to leave Dr. Healey's desk alone, and stayed with the Foundation for three years, learning, as she recalls, "not only some of the jargon and the techniques of testing, but a good deal about human motivation and to recognize the significance of certain attitudes, my own included."

She and her friend from China, Elise Dexter, found a five-room apartment on Charles Street, which they shared for several years, eating their dinners down the street at "the New England Kitchen, that haven of pleasant memory for so many Boston spinsters." The spent summer holidays with Elise's parents in Ogunquit, Maine, until Edith located the perfect weekend cottage: a two-hundred year old blacksmith's shop which she bought for $125 and had moved to a piece of land with apple trees and stone walls which she "bullied some friends of mine into selling to me." Edith recalls the pleasure she took in restoring the cottage, and the weekends she spent there with guests from Boston for the next two decades.

In August, 1930, Edith received a letter from Miss Ada Comstock, the president of Radcliffe, inviting her to lunch. Although Edith had maintained only the most casual connection with her alma mater during the past twenty years, the community of professional women in the Boston area was a small world. She reports that

> It turned out a rather momentous and surprising meal, for during dessert she asked me if I would be interested in the job of Director of the Appointments Bureau at Radcliffe…. I came away with very mixed feelings; another situation for which I had no training! I didn't know what went on in the place or what my particular duties would be. I wondered if I hadn't been hedgehopping too long, and at the age of forty ought not to become a stable character, but when I thought of Miss Comstock all hesitations dropped away. The job, and she too, might give me bad moments, but I knew that I wanted to work under her more than anything and that I had come home to port.

Edith's job, it soon became clear, was to dispense advice and help students and alumnae find jobs. But, as Edith notes, the Depression meant that "it was a lean time for students and their families and obviously something had to be done, and done quickly." She began with the graduating seniors:

> Most of the Seniors came in eagerly to see me and I spent a good deal of time with each one. For some of them there was no financial problem but rather a question of what they wanted to do after graduation. Some were fairly clear in their minds…[but] the majority of them were a thoroughly worried and frightened lot. Family conditions were difficult, in many cases their fathers were out of work, there were brothers and sisters who also had to be educated and what chance did they have as an untrained B. A. against the experienced workers already job hunting.

Edith realized that a new approach was necessary, and so she asked Miss Comstock if she could create a summer secretarial course, to which the President responded: "You can do whatever you like, Edith, as long as you don't cost the college any money."

That was all I needed. I went to see Mrs. Katherine Gibbs, the founder of the best private secretarial school in Boston and quite an old lady at the time. Without preamble I said, "Mrs. Gibbs, I want to go into competition with you, and what is more, I want your co-operation." Her almost immediate response was "Of course I'll help you, go and tell Gordon (her son) that I said he was to do whatever you wanted." She was a great old lady and it ended with kind Gordon providing us with two of his best teachers and certain supplies for which we paid a minimum sum. We charged the students $25 for a six week, 9:00-3:00 concentrated shorthand and typing course, held five days a week in the basement of Longfellow Hall. It was open to all Radcliffe students and they came, cursed, and worked their heads off in the hot summer weather. With the result that several of the Seniors got jobs under the noses of other envious recent graduates.

That first summer was so successful that Edith was able to set aside money to begin another project. "It was individualist capitalism run rampant and it drove the business office nearly mad," she observed wryly.

Just as in China, one project led quickly to another and job creation and social work went hand in hand. Edith's Appointments Bureau began a summer day camp at the Dormitory Quadrangle, with experienced teachers supervising undergraduate student counselors and helping them develop an understanding of the children's problems. Edith recalls that "we did an enormous amount of scrounging" to equip the camp, and "it was wiser not to ask" where all the seesaws and wood blocks and orange crates came from. Then the Appointments Bureau, in tandem with a student, took over the college tennis courts and rented them out at fifty cents an hour. Another student was permitted to start her own soft drink concession at courtside. Still other students took a waitress course, with a staff member offering her home as a training site. After completing the three session course (cost: 25 cents per session) the waitresses were in great demand:

The Appointments Bureau bought uniforms and aprons wholesale and charged each student for the laundering, or, if she preferred, she could buy her own at cost. She was also expected to do the washing-up afterwards and I think got 50 cents an hour, and had to be escorted back to her dormitory after 10:00 PM. As many of the employers were Harvard Faculty wives, there were opportunities for 'faux pas.' In the midst of a juicy story the poor professor might get a vigorous kick on his shin from his wife which meant "Do for heaven's sake be careful – that girl is one of your students." It was equal fun for the students to see some of the Harvard Great in their own lairs and realize that they were vulnerable. Once the news of this service got around we were deluged with calls, and the course had to be repeated at intervals.

There were also baby-sitting and dog-walking services, and frank discussions about the students' and employers' obligations and rights. Edith was both arranging for the students to make some money during the Depression and preparing them for the world of work after graduation.

Meanwhile, Edith continued working with the seniors, preparing dossiers and soliciting letters of recommendation from the faculty members. Understandably, the students were bitterly resentful when she advised them to take shorthand and typing. Editth noted that some responded indignantly, saying "My father didn't send me to college to be a secretary." Edith secretly sympathized with these young women, who were "so young and full of unrealistic and glamorous thoughts of the future." She also worked with the graduate students, writing "endless letters" inquiring about teaching openings at a time when it was not unheard of for Harvard PhDs to be "working in gas stations at $15 a week."

Edith's most ambitious project was a one-year certificate program for women called the Personnel Training Course, begun in 1935. After much bullying on her part, three faculty members from the Harvard Business School (all male in those days, of course) were enlisted to lecture. For her first class, Edith carefully chose five applicants (from a field of seventy-six) who had some employment experience. Many years after Edith's retirement in 1954, her former colleagues and students contributed to a little booklet entitled "Twelve Years on a Shoestring," chronicling the Bureau's activities from 1930-1942 under Edith's leadership. Here is the authors' description of the first year of the Personnel Training Course (later called the Management Training Program, or MTP):

> It was a rollicking year of new and unexpected experiences, excitement, and discovery....One [woman] worked for a Cambridge laundry and had her problems making it to the plant along with the other 500 employees by 7:25 AM. Another learned what it feels like to be on your feet all day behind the counter in a hospital cafeteria. Another commuted to downtown Boston, where she interviewed candidates for unemployment relief and filled in endless forms. Still another started a college placement office, from scratch.... Near the end of the hectic first year, the five went off for a treat – a quick trip to Washington for cherry blossoms, dinner and conferences with executives from the U. S. Civil Service, the S. S. Employment Service, the Social Security Board, and the Census Bureau, and – incredible coup of the year – tea with Eleanor Roosevelt at the White House.

When "Twelve Years on a Shoestring" was being compiled, Ruth B. Drinker, one of the first students in the MTP, wrote a letter that gives us a good sense of the way Edith approached her job:

> I can't remember my first interview with Miss Stedman but I'm sure it was akin to so many that followed it. You never had to wait anxious days and hours for an appointment. Maybe she knew you were desperate to find ways to stay at Radcliffe during those grim Depression years. Or perhaps she was aware of how hard it had been to screw up your faith in your ability to get and hold a job before you even dared to apply for one....
>
> I remember her eyes. They were at once laughing at you, challenging you, and infinitely kind. Bombast, balm and boost. I never came away without a dose of each.... People didn't forget Edith Stedman.
>
> Far more than knowing the market, she knew her product. She knew us. She knew what we could do or saw to it that we were trained so that we could.... Her knowledge of us, her vision of what we _could_ do,

made her go so far as to change the very environment to which we were applying.... Who could conceive of a female personnel manager, market analyst, or company president? Edith Stedman did, and built the MTP to prove it could happen. She changed men's thinking.

Elsewhere in "Twelve Years on a Shoestring" Edith is described as

...impatient and possessed with a sense of urgency – everything she did was important to her – and soon became important to those around her. A good idea was to be put into practice – tomorrow if not immediately.... Persuasiveness came readily to her, and there were always willing volunteers – to hunt up jobs, to make ideas practical, to provide liaison, or organize, to teach, to lick envelopes.... Catherine Hiatt, who entered Radcliffe as a freshman during the fall of 1930 recalls her first impressions; [Edith Stedman was] "the epitome of the proper Bostonian....tall, tweedy, slightly brusque to cover great warmth, direct and energetic, and, of course, imaginative and determined that those who turned to her for help should find some practical next steps....

One of Edith's assistants during those early years recalled that

...Every day (we soon learned to be on time if not early) Edith would come in and as she hung up her coat and hat, she would say, 'Girls, last night I had an idea...." And we would hang onto something fairly solid and wait for the new idea to come.

One of these new ideas was an entirely new record-keeping system that recorded, on the infamous "blue sheets," every contact and interview with each student.

The "easy" girls and the monosyllabic ones had brief blue sheets which recorded simply jobs recommended, tried for, possibly refused; one blue sheet, one side. The others – worried or rebellious or "queer as Dick's hatband," as Edith Stedman would say – merited three or four

blue sheets, typed single spaced on both sides. Here there were recorded the adventures and misadventures of the girls and the salty comments of the director. These were the most intimate – and certainly the most amusing and vivid – stories of the girls that the college had. A quick glance at the blue sheet, and Edith Stedman would be able to go back five months or five years and recapture the tone and feeling of the last contact as she started an interview. No wonder her placements were successful!

The "pie plates," so named in whimsy or for a reason not recorded, were simply master files that showed the name of each job candidate in every field where Edith Stedman thought she might conceivably some day fit in…. One graduate has called Edith Stedman's set of interlocking files the forerunner of the computer – and indeed, they were. But they were more… the underpinnings and structure for an extremely human and perceptive placement service.

By 1935, the Depression was showing no sign of ending. Jobs were scarce, but the Appointments Bureau was doing remarkably well. Betty graduated from Wellesley that spring, and Edith called upon her old college classmate, Elizabeth Singleton, to secure Betty a teaching position. In the fall of 1935 Betty moved to Chicago to serve as a fifth grade teacher at the Girls Latin School, where Miss Singleton was the headmistress. After a year of teaching, she became the school librarian. In 1937, she must have written to her aunt about some difficulties she had encountered, judging from Edith's response:

February 2, 1937

Dearest Betty,

It is grand to hear from you at any time and of course it is the most subtle form of compliment to be chosen as the choice vessel for your woes. Human relationships are difficult. I quite agree with you and the worst of it is they always continue to be fairly complicated. I can only give you the advice which you have already given yourself—be as objective as you can and don't take yourself and the other feller too seriously. Most people don't really mean to be unkind or hateful but something goes wrong—the cream has soured or the boy friend hasn't written or money is tight—any one of a hundred tragic or comic reasons—and wrath gets poured out on the uncomprehending and innocent head of the nearest bystander. Heavens what a sentence! I have been nursing some horrid grudgeful feelings myself in the last few weeks toward a colleague and I have just about decided that I at least had better try to be decent—at least I can see the funny side of it all and he can't so to that extent I have the upper hand. It is amazing tho what a nasty batch of undesirable qualities can simmer in own's mind.

As for Barnard—I didn't mean to sound indifferent but I thought it was up to you to make your own choice without too much family advice. Selfishly it would be very pleasant to have you in N. Y. and in many ways I think it would be a good job for you and quite in line with future advancement. My only question is can it be arranged to be fair to Miss Singleton who has been such a brick. If it can and it is all right with her—more power to you. I expect tho that you will have to tell her pretty soon—won't you?

I have been laid low with the flu and have just gotten up after nearly a ten day siege in bed. As a result my legs feel uncomfortably wobbly and about four hours at the office leaves me limp as a rag.

You know I am terribly fond of you my dear and I have great respect for the honesty of your thinking and your spiritual integrity. Let me know what happens and I'll do any thing that I can be of any service— give my love to your chief....

> *Lots of love to you always,*
> *Edith*

I wish the letter had said more about what the job at Barnard consisted of, and why Betty decided to turn it down and remain at the Girls Latin School for another three years. Did Edith's letter exert a subtle pressure, with its references to her friendship with Elizabeth Singleton? Betty did eventually leave Chicago in the summer of 1940 to go to Mexico, not knowing what she would be doing upon her return. She recalls that at the end of the summer she went to Taylor, Texas, to stay with her good friend from high school, Clara. She traveled by train, for she had sold her little car, nicknamed "Little Henry" after Henry Ford, for $45 before going to Mexico. She remembers lying on a bed at Clara's house, fanning herself in the intense heat, when a call came from New York telling her that she'd been offered a job at the publishing house Harcourt Brace. "I never worried," she remarked years later, "even though it was the end of the Depression. I always knew I'd get a job."

Back in Cambridge, Edith was succeeding in getting women into "men-only" administrative jobs through her Personnel Training Course, and had created still another program, the Publishing Procedures Course, which continues to exist to this day, although it is now housed in New York at Columbia University. In "Twelve Years on a Shoestring," her former colleagues fondly recall that Edith was

> ...intensely practical. She could never abide waste – of space, opportunity, people, or money.
>
> A building vacant for the summer? Shocking waste! Let's use it.
>
> A need unmet? That's a new job market.
>
> A person underoccupied – worst crime of all! Get her busy; waiting is a waste of precious time!
>
> She was impudent, irreverent, imaginative, and brilliantly sensible. Ceremony, the academic robe, the Radcliffe image, and people in high places did not faze her in the least…. Who else would ring up the First Lady and suggest that she have a tea for five students in a still unknown personnel course.

Edith, in effect, also invented the idea of the unpaid internship. Unpaid training programs were "unheard-of concepts" in 1930, according to "Twelve Years on a Shoestring." But Edith reasoned that by offering to work without a salary a girl might get her foot in the door and at least get a reference. And so she set off on "a whirlwind sales trip in and around Boston in November, 1931." She located ninety organizations, hospitals, agencies like the Red Cross, museums, and social agencies willing to give the Radcliffe graduates a chance to work as "apprentices" in exchange for carfare. When asked by a newspaper reporter in 1932 whether "this might not be considered unfair competition in the form of dirt cheap labor" Edith had an answer. "Radcliffe girls do not compete. They take only jobs for which no salary is available…." Students worked two or three afternoons a week and shared their success stories, or worked full time after graduation. Eventually, the College gave Edith a budget line to appoint a staff member to handle the expanding program.

Student testimonials fill the pages of "Twelve Years on a Shoestring." One letter in the Schlesinger Library archives that isn't quoted, however, sheds light on "the Jewish Question" in all of its complexity. A grateful former student wrote this revealing note:

> What did Edith Stedman "do" for me? As with most [members of the Personnel Training Course], my first contact with Radcliffe was with her. After we discussed my career aims Miss Stedman, with no preamble said, "You are Jewish. I will not be able to find you a job—you'll have to find your own." Her bluntness helped me in every subsequent job interview.

The Jewish alumna's letter goes on to explain that later in her career Edith and the Appointments Bureau did, in fact, help her find jobs. But in the 1930s, the formidable woman who convinced men from Boston to Washington and beyond to accept the notion that women could do "men's work" firmly believed that, despite her wide circle of contacts, she would not be able to find a position for a Jewish woman. This incident, I think, can help us understand why Edith acted as she did, several years later, when Betty became romantically involved with my father, Gene Tuck.

TWENTY-TWO

Gene's Army Letters
1943

IN LATER LIFE, Gene always admitted that he had avoided military service as long as he could. He had been out of law school for ten years by 1942, and because of the Depression and the anti-Semitism widespread among the big New York law firms he had only just begun to establish himself in his profession. Toward the end of 1942, about a year after their courtship had begun in New York City, he writes to Betty that "I can't help feeling that my days as a lawyer are numbered…." His law partner has received his army commission and the firm may not survive his departure. In a letter sent a few days later Gene wishes he could place a phone call to her in Chicago, where her travels for Harcourt Brace had taken her, but in those days, people seldom made phone calls except in emergencies — they wrote letters instead.

The wartime scarcity of fuel put an end to Betty's travels, and so I assume that she and Gene had a few months together in late 1942 and early 1943. The letter writing resumes in March 1943, for the day Gene had been dreading finally arrives: he has been drafted into the U.S. Army. "This is by all odds the coldest goddamn place in the world," he writes in a hurried note on March 9th from Camp Upton on Long Island. "This is also the first free time I've had since arrival." Betty carefully notes the date on which she received the letter (3-10-43) and writes back immediately. Meanwhile Gene sends another, even shorter letter:

Dear Betty
    Shipping out of here today. Don't know where we're going. Will let you know.
    Working hard – sleeping little. Beefing plenty.
    Am waiting for train. Will write fully in day or two. Take care of yourself.

Love,
Eugene

Betty's letter, addressed to Gene at Camp Upton, has two postmarks, the first on March 10th, and the second on March 12th, and some pencil markings over the address. It was evidently forwarded to Gene, as his next letter indicates, and it is one of only three of her letters from this period that survived. The tone of the letter suggests that she is trying very hard to sound cheery.

Wednesday morning

Darling,
    Your letter came this morning and I'm calmly stealing office time –not to mention paper! – to write you so you'll have something before you're shipped out. Friday seems terribly soon. Have you any idea at all where it will be?
    I'm burning with curiosity, of course, to hear all the details – inoculations, tests, classification, etc. but I know you must be standing on your head most of the time still. Did you get the beautiful forest green fatigue uniform?! And how do you look and feel in a complete suit of your favorite color? I can hardly wait to pepper you with questions – and see you in your new regalia.

The letter continues in this chatty tone, with an account of a young man Betty had met in Mexico, who wants advice on how to become an editor and who takes her out for cocktails, Indian curry, and a movie. But she closes with details about the framed picture of herself she intends to send him (should the frame be brown or dark red, she asks), and assurances that she is thinking about him continually.

Gene writes his first real letter on the cross-country train to Arkansas, where he is being sent for eight weeks of basic training.

> Dearest—
>
> Now finally I can find time to write a real letter. It seems years ago that I left civilian life – literally years – and its only four days. I can readily see that in less than a month I will have forgotten civilian life entirely…
>
> If you can't read this, blame the Penn R. R. We are moving thru Indiana – traveling west – very far, I'm afraid – don't know where… I'll know when this is mailed for I'll mail it when I get there…
>
> Well, the first 2 days were a nightmare. It was bitter cold and we spent hours waiting on line for this and that. I have never been so cold.… What with the I.Q. tests and getting our clothes and getting inoculations ("the hook" – they call it at Upton) the first 2 days were hectic. I took the I.Q. test in a bitter cold room with my overcoat on – my hand shaking with cold. They shaved 15 minutes off the usual 50 minutes for the test and I, figuring on 50 minutes (they expressly refused to say how long they'd give) finished only 88 out of 150 questions. I was lucky to make 119 (110 needed for OCS) – must have gotten practically all my 88 correct. If I'd known I have raced through vocabulary and arithmetic which were really chickensoup and left the goddam cube-counting which really threw me. Oh yes they showed us a venereal disease picture which the boys call Mickey Mouse – very effectively done – rough too – some boys passed out at some of the scenes.

Gene ends with a postscript: "Just arrived here in Arkansas. Will be here for 8-10 weeks."

His first impressions of Camp Robinson in Arkansas arrive a few days later. Like many New Yorkers of his generation, he had never been farther away than New England and so Arkansas must have seemed like the end of the world.

Dear Betty,

Darling (I wish I had time to write you a decent letter. Unfortunately I haven't, and am afraid I won't for several weeks. They don't give us enough time to take care of our personal hygiene & at every odd moment we try to do something about that. There isn't much one can do.)

Briefly then, I am at a Branch International Replacement Training Center –a brand-new part of Camp Robinson from where I can be sent to any branch of service and will after 9 or 10 weeks. The place is a mud-hole –no sewage. – prefabricated barracks with no latrines. Arkansas weather is foul – putrid – rain –rain – rain –rain & the wind is really something.

Do you know – I am for the first time thankful that I was dragged up in NY gutters because nine-tenths of the kids here are dead end kids & I know how to get along well with them.

The Commanding Officer is an ex-football star & a great body-builder – or breaker — & I understand the 8 week process is hell on wheels….

Psychologically I adjusted magnificently – right proud of myself – all the dirt – inconvenience – hardship, rubbing shoulders and everything else with guttersnipes—sitting up in clothes for two days and two nights in a cattle car from N.Y. –no sleep for about a week. Things that bothered me most were a bad cold and the shoes –Oh God the shoes – they still hurt but not so much. Up to yesterday –every step was agony.

Darling when I read your letter and one from Mother today (forwarded from Upton) I came as close to crying as I have in 20 years. I've had to force myself to stop thinking of you and of what we've had this last year and a half because if I thought of that I don't know if I could have gone on. The horrible thing was comparing my old life with this one. I simply had to clear my mind of it all.

That old life, of concerts and parties and restaurants in New York City, his law practice, the synagogue youth group, the summer camps and hotels in the Poconos and Catskills, tennis in the summer and ice-skating in Central Park in the winter, must have seemed like a distant dream. Betty has annotated his letter in pencil, indicating which parts to omit when she reads it to someone else. This last emotional paragraph is marked "omit," as is the sentence about being "dragged up in NY gutters." Later in the letter he warns her not to tell his sister Jane "anything of what I've told you. She'll tell Mother and I've been writing Mother that I love the army –what the hell else can I do. She's so terribly worried about me." Except for his three years at Harvard Law School, Gene had lived with his mother until the day he entered the army. His letters to her must have required considerable creativity and suppression of the complaints with which he fills his letters to Betty.

When he has a chance to resume writing, Gene continues his account of the indignities inflicted upon him:

> I'm waiting now to have my hair cut –practically down to the bone – The C. O. insists that it be so short that he can't grab it. My moustache is gone already. I'm just a shadow of my former self – look about 10 years younger — & just as well for most of the lads are of the 19 year class and its hard enough to mingle with them on equal terms without looking old enough to be their father.
>
> Well baby it looks as if I'll not see you for 2 ½ months at least – after that God knows…
>
> I feel like a small boy – haven't felt this way in many years – always been so damned self reliant and sure of my ability to handle myself. Still can't get used to the idea of not making my own decisions.
>
> Well darling I won't write any more – I'm getting too damned emotional & it's just not good…I shouldn't write this way to you. I'm getting all right now—it's just this memory of those first few days of shock. I know you'll worry and there's really no need to. There are men here who can't adjust –I see them around. I can. But if I were 10 years younger and could keep up with these kids in all this mad rushing around, this would be an awful lot easier.

Write, dear, & by the time you get the answer to your next letter, I'll really be in good shape.

The letter is mailed on March 17th, and Betty's note indicates that she received it on the 19th and answered on the 21st.

Gene finds a moment to write again on March 19th, because

Its raining cats and dogs in Arkansas for a change – overshoes were issued but they didn't fit a few of us so we were denied the dubious pleasure of tramping with the others 6 miles in the rain down to the old post. So we are hiding in our barrack (hut, they call it here, but that word's so depressing)….

I don't know how much I have told you about this place…we are shipped out of here about June 1 for further training. Theoretically it's an 8 week cycle but actually you wait a couple of weeks more to be shipped out after your training is complete. I understand that the cycle is a nightmare – terrific physical training. They'll either kill me or make a man out of me.

Today I tramped several miles in the rain. Do you remember how I used to "rage at the elements" and how I wouldn't walk a block in the rain for fear of getting my feet wet? Well, I've really got my "comeuppance" now…

This morning they took all the high I.Q.s down for another classification test. This one was a peach – three hours worth. I could have knocked it for a loop right after college but my algebra and physics are 15 to 20 years old — Oh how rusty. So I don't suppose I did very well. I gather that they were looking for young geniuses to send them back to school for specialized training so I don't guess they'd be interested in an old codger like me. But it was fun anyway using my bean for a change.

After more descriptions of the bleak facilities at Camp Robinson, Gene closes by telling Betty to keep busy.

I honestly hope you will find yourself a couple of young men to flirt with so that you can keep your wits sharp. Do please dear. You know Papa won't mind.

Mama, you should see your hero now...can you imagine the old long-haired smooth New Yorker in a "crewcut"? What a come-down. Wall Street should see me now.

Betty answered this letter the day it arrived, March 22nd, according to her note on the envelope. Gene was writing nearly every day and Betty was keeping up with him, although evidently the mails were slow.

In his fifth letter (Betty numbers the envelopes in pencil, along with the date received and date answered) Gene reports that he has finally received two letters from her along with a good-luck rabbit's foot she sent ("Let's hope it performs traditional function," he says dryly). Now, nearly three weeks into his new life, he says

I have been much interested in watching my psychological reactions. During the first week or 10 days I couldn't watch myself objectively – Now I can. I'm beginning to feel things again and I hope I will be more coherent in my letters....

He is still unclear about what the Army plans to do with him:

Honey – a lot of my ideas about a place in the Army for my administrative ability have gone by the board. I'm just another guy in uniform – a pair of hands, a pair of feet, and a strong heart please God (if any).

Gene continues to write about every few days; there are 25 letters in all from March through the end of May. On Sunday, March 28th, he writes to answer some of her questions, with the answers neatly numbered 1 through 9. He also includes an account of the daily schedule at Camp Robinson:

Up at 5:45 out for Reveille

6:00 Breakfast

6:30-8:00 fix up barracks

8:00-9:00 calisthenics – with 10 lb. rifle – pretty tough

9-10 Either drill or some other work

10- 11 lecture, etc.

11-12 Bayonet practice – Disgusting and very wearing

All afternoon – Rifle work — My eye is good but I haven't yet been able to master that damned sling. You've got to tie yourself into knots and I'm still terribly stiff.

5:30 Retreat

5:45 Chow (terrible)

Evening usually devoted to cleaning rifle – which is a beautiful weapon – lots of fun to take apart and put together

Lights out at 9:45 — very tired.

TWENTY-THREE

What Did Edith Say?

O N A SATURDAY NIGHT in early April, "after cleaning my rifle, washing my socks, shaving and showering" Gene settles down to write a long letter to tell Betty how much he misses her, and how much it means to him that a self-confessed bad correspondent has written so many letters. There's a cryptic allusion to Aunt Edith in this one:

> *You may tell A. E. that – yea tho' I walk thru the valley of the shadow of Arkansas and tho she enlist the service of the whole goddam Army – that my head is bloody but unbowed and I will rise to haunt her.*

It would be just like Edith to "enlist the services of the Army" to get her way, but Gene doesn't provide any further details.

Later in his letter Gene apologizes for asking Betty to bake cookies, for he realizes that rations make it hard. But Betty had probably already sent them, for a week later Gene writes to say that the delicious cookies have arrived, and that he is "politely but firmly defending [them] from the frontal assaults of the dead-end kids in the barracks." Letters provide a moment for self-reflection, as Gene continues to examine his responses to this enormous change in his life:

> *Now more than a month since I left, darling. And just the last few days have I begun to be completely conscious. I was like a hurt dazed animal during the first weeks reacting to a whip and to cold and heat but with no real realization of where or what I was. I was still leading the kind of life I was used to and unwilling to accept this new life. Now the old life is becoming dim… and I am beginning to try to make the best of my new life realizing that it is to be fairly permanent – looking for ways to enjoy myself – becoming an ace goldbricker – thinking of my future in the Army in practical terms not in dreams. It's been a strange, strange experience and if I had had time to observe myself during this change it would have been something worth remembering…for it is like being reborn – suddenly.*

Gene, ever the strategist, has learned to "goldbrick," or appear to be working without exerting himself, reasonably well, but intends to develop more "chutzpah." He is really worried, though, about how to "keep my head above water." The infantry training is meant for younger men – jumping over 8 foot walls, for instance – and he says "We older men simply cannot do it." This may prevent him from becoming an infantry officer, he adds.

On April 11th Gene reports some "bright news"; only seventeen men in the whole company passed the I.Q. test and he was number 9. And so he will be interviewed for the Army Specialist Training Program (ASTP) and, if accepted, will "go back to College for six months." He continues to be pessimistic, though, for he has heard that the Army wants younger men for technical training courses. The letter ends with "FDR here on Sunday –twenty feet away from me. Will write you details in next letter." The next letter doesn't offer any details, however. There is another reference to Aunt Edith, though: "Tell her I'm still alive and kicking." And a week later he says in response to something Betty must have written about a conversation with her boss at Harcourt Brace:

Did you tell her the score re Aunt E. and Pvt. Tuck? When I have more time I will have to think up some ways of dealing with your incorrigible aunt. Maybe she's too formidable for me.

On April 26th Gene describes the ASTP interview.

Col. Milligan asked me about my practice, my associates, my political affiliations, my income, why I didn't go to Washington with the New Deal, etc. I'd had much more Physics and Math at school than most of the kids but they never even went into it on the theory I suppose that it was too long ago. Finally the Col. says that I'd make a good infantry officer. "Colonel," says I, "You're making a terrible mistake. I'd set a horrible example physically to the men." "Well," says he, "you'll make a good instructor." The trouble with that is that all the instructors here are also tactical officers. Well, I'll be damned if I'll be coerced into it. I don't want it and I wouldn't be any good at it.

What Gene really hopes for, as his letters repeat again and again, is a posting to the Judge Advocate General's Department (JAGD), a logical assignment for a Harvard-trained lawyer. His letters return again and again to his options, and to the Army's typically complicated and inscrutable procedures for application. There are interviews, and more interviews, and Gene is becoming increasing impatient.

Some men have already had a second interview and report that all men over 22 [years old] are being turned down. Looks like I'm an old man in the Army. Next interview I am not going to be respectful and demure and simply answer questions. I'm going in with fists flying and make the Colonels and Majors a little speech re Tuck vs. U.S. Army. I didn't do it last time because I thought they'd say "Smart N.Y. Lawyer – trying to sway us." But I figure now I've nothing to lose because the cards are stacked against me.

Just writing about this probably helped, for there is no indication in the letters that he actually did make that little speech. But in mid-May he is still using his letters as a way to review his options, wondering whether "I may outsmart myself" by turning down the Infantry OCS option.

Now that he can get an occasional weekend pass to go to Little Rock, where he has met some Jewish families who invite servicemen to dinner, Gene is determined to do something about his appearance.

> *The hair is all right now. I've worked out a deal. They examine carefully on inspections only the back and sideburns and I've a fellow here in the company who keeps them neatly trimmed for me and doesn't touch the top – so there.*

On May 17th Gene writes from the Hotel Frederica in Little Rock where he and some other men had a "wonderful drinking party." There's another letter a week later on Hotel Frederica stationery. He reports that 'We just live from weekend to weekend here."

> *Wasn't at all sure I could get away this weekend. I had the following hurdles to cross. 1) Had to get a weekend pass – had one last week and only half the men in the squad get them each weekend – got over that obstacle by financing the gambling activities of the squad leader. 2) Had to avoid KP on Sunday – just missed it and have it tomorrow. 3) Had to get by an inspection of all equipment – if pegged – no pass. Worked like a dog on my stuff – which took about two evenings – and got thru it. We never know until Saturday at about 6 p.m. whether we will get a pass. L. R. hotels are filled to capacity and reservations must be made days in advance. I shared a room here with a Lieutenant and a Staff Sgt. – just managed to talk the room clerk into putting a cot in and talked the Lieutenant into letting me have the cot while he slept with the Staff Sgt.*

Clearly Gene has learned how to work the system in more ways than one! His managerial and rhetorical skills are being sadly wasted on KP and rifle-cleaning.

Basic training finally ends and on May 30th Gene writes Betty to tell her that he is being transferred to Louisiana State University in Baton Rouge, the so called "star" center for A.S.T.P., where he will undergo further tests to determine which college he will attend for specialized training.

Since the beginning of May Betty has stopped marking Gene's letters with the date they arrived and the date she answered. Judging from his letters, hers have included news of mutual friends and accounts of some of her social activities. Gene begins writing on June 1st from Baton Rouge, and in each letter he describes the "good-for-nothing life here" where military activities consist of a few drills and some baseball and volleyball to keep in shape, followed by lots of "loafing" and waiting for something to happen.

> *The situation here is so laughable that the boys have made up a song to the tune of "Rambling Wreck from Georgia Tech" that goes something like this:*
>
> > *"Mother, take down your Service Flag*
> > *Your son's at L.S.U.*
> > *He isn't fighting battles*
> > *The way he ought to do.*
> > *Instead he's playing baseball.*
> > *And swimming in the pool.*
> > *Oh Mother, take down your Service Flag*
> > *Your boy's gone back to school."*
>
> *It's called the "Star Unit Song."*

On Saturday, June 6th Gene begins his letter rather petulantly with "I've been patiently waiting all this week to get a letter from you." We begin to get a hint that something is wrong in the next letter, though Gene doesn't. He is in a merry mood, and passes quickly over the signals he's getting from Betty.

> *My sweet little magnolia,*
> *Such a formal letter, little one. Not even a kiss or a dear or anything. Well now really. You haven't got me confused with one of your*

customers have you? A helluva thing.... Remember, I am a lonely male what needs affection.

Well, I went before the STAR Board today and they were immensely impressed with all my degrees.... Right off they asked me if I would like to study a foreign language and right off I tells them "Sure Mike." Then they tell me that I hit a high grade on the French exam and I tells them that this is a very surprising thing on account of I had French in high school 18 years ago. They pretends to be both surprised and pleased, and more pleased than surprised. Then they tells me that probably Spanish looks better on me than French on account of I had that more recently and I nods eagerly knowing full well that my Betsy would like very much I should learn Spanish without the pain of teaching it to me herself. Then my face falls as they say it will very likely be a new language. Howsomever I am pleased that it will not be engineering as I do not like to compete with a lot of science guys, me being a smooth talker and not much on figures (and talking of figures, the South really has something there. It takes practically all my restraint —-you know how active my hormones are). Then they tells me that lawyers are a drug on the market in the Army and I tells them they should tell me something new. Then I slips them the old harpoon. "Boys" I says, "how about this psychology deal? Look at all the psych I had at college – can't I sell that for something?" "Son," says the old guy, "we've been turning away guys with master's degrees in pysch." "Okay, okay," says I, "you don't have to hit me over the head with a hammer. I just thought there might be a chance for me to crash that racket."

You can see signs of Gene Tuck the amateur actor and comic playwright in this imagined dialogue. He ends with more pleas for letters – including letters written partly in Spanish, so he can brush up on his foreign language skills.

Three days later, on June 11th, Gene begins his letter with

I had hoped to get another letter from you today. Frankly I was disturbed by your last letter. It was so formal – so restrained – no chatty

little items about yourself – particularly since it was more than a week since the last letter. Is anything wrong?

After a couple of pages about how comfortable his life at L.S.U. is, he says he's lonely and bored, with a hint of nostalgia for Camp Robinson:

> *Crude and barbarous as Robinson was, hard and uncivilized, still there were men with a real cause – to build an army to win a war and no work, no exhaustion was enough to stop them. This place is a three-ring circus. You would never think a war was going on. It's hard to think of those lads across the water and us here wasting our time and our energy.*

This sounds a little odd from the self-proclaimed cynic who was so dismissive of the "dead-end kids" and the inept administration at Camp Robinson.

Finally, in response to an alarming telegram from Gene (see Illustrations) Betty writes a letter dated June 16th and postmarked the following day.

> *My dear love,*
>
> *Yes, something is wrong. It has been wrong for several months, but has only just come out into the open from its hiding place in the back of my mind. Unconscious suppression, I suppose, because I didn't want to face the implications.*
>
> *About three weeks ago it burst on me with all the force of an unleashed tornado, and I've been in agony ever since –wandering around like a sleep-walker, at times not eating, sleeping badly…. I've been trying to write it to you for days now – after that first period of hurt-animal blankness – and the letters I've written and torn up would fill a large paper basket. The ones not written would fill a still larger one. Your telegram this morning makes it imperative that I write now as best I can. My darling, I have to be honest with you – it's more than the best policy, it's a compulsion for me. And since I could not honestly*

write you as I had before, I could not write at all, except to answer your
requests for information, of course.

Probably I don't even have to tell you what this is all about; you have
surely guessed. You <u>know</u> it's not another man, and it isn't the Jewish
question which we settled long ago. Perhaps it's another casualty of war
for there's a curious parallel as you'll see. Anyway, I'll try to explain why
it happened so abruptly.

Your departure left me feeling taut and upset, of course, but
then I settled down to living your life vicariously along with my
own – following and <u>feeling</u> every difficulty, every new physical and
psychological adjustment you had to make, every strain and tension you
were undergoing. I knew you needed all the support I could give you,
and I wanted to give it to you so badly.

Then came the end of that period, your magnificent adjustment, and
your transfer to L.S.U. to begin a new, relatively easier phase of your
Army career – and with it an emotional let-down. For you too, I know;
I've seen it reflected in your letters....

Are you still wondering what this is all about? Very simply, then, it
began last November when you initiated a course of action – specifically,
meeting your mother, announcing our engagement, a ring, etc. –
and failed to follow through. That was a blow, but it was as nothing
compared to the second time it happened – just before you went away. I
wonder if you'll ever realize how that shook me....

Betty goes on to say that she feels as if Gene has let her down. I suspect, though, that while Betty thought that the Jewish question had been resolved, Rebecca Tuck may have felt otherwise. It is very likely that her resistance to her beloved only son's serious relationship with a non-Jewish woman was causing him to postpone announcing the engagement. Betty's allusion to "violent reactions" in this next paragraph suggests that she was aware that Rebecca Tuck had voiced her opposition. She speculates that either

1) you did not want me enough to be able to say to hell with anything
that stands in the way; 2) that you were so sure of me that you were

content to leave me in a suspended state indefinitely – neither maid, fiancée, nor wife – with the perfect assurance that I would be waiting with the same feelings I had for you when you went away; and 3) that you had, very humanly, chosen the path of least resistance. It was bound to rouse violent reactions otherwise, and you thought it best to leave it as perhaps an unpleasant piece of unfinished business to be coped with when there should arise the necessity for immediate action.

Betty, remember, is writing this letter a few weeks before her twenty-ninth birthday. She goes on to speak of how hard it has been to "withstand the constant, if gentle, pressure from my family, the unbelieving looks and queries of my friends…." All of them are expecting the engagement to be announced. She ends her letter, dramatically, with these words: "By all that you hold most dear, be <u>honest.</u> We are at a crossroad, and a perilous one. It is a question of you and me, and what's to become of us."

You can imagine how affected Gene must have been by this letter. He tries calling Betty immediately, finally gets through to her two days later, and then writes a long letter on Monday night, June 21st. For the first time since their correspondence began, he pays six cents to send his letter air mail (regular mail was free for the armed forces).

My darling,

That phone call fizzled out so. There were so many things I wanted to say that are so hard to say with an army milling around one's elbows. The only really important thing I wanted to tell you was that I love you so much I nearly went mad this last week at the thought of losing you.

I know that a great deal of what has occurred has been my fault but you know the other side of it. There's no use in repeating it and it isn't important. What is important is that nothing like this must ever happen again – ever. We must get married as soon as possible to make sure that it doesn't. I'll take care of handling my mother afterwards.

Gene realizes that "it must have been hell carrying this thing around with you" and asks Betty why she didn't say something earlier. He now realizes that those infrequent, business-like letters, with no salutation or signature, were sending a signal. But he can't resist the impulse to dramatize:

> *My imagination ran wild. I conjured up visions of a South American gaucho who had swept you off your feet, or your father exacting a promise from you never to see me again. I was really wild. After snapping off several dozen heads I was quietly pointed out to the new youngsters who arrived as an irascible old man who had best be avoided.... You really gave me a turn, young lady.*

The letter continues in a chatty vein, with an account of an evening spent in Baton Rouge with an acquaintance of Betty's and her roommate. Then there is more complaining – about the boredom, the calisthenics, and the young soldiers ("I am beginning to hate youth"). He ends with "Darling – write me very soon and tell me that the sun is shining once more on 47th St. I am worried about that strange voice I heard on the telephone a couple of hours ago."

Betty spends sixteen cents to send an air mail, special delivery letter two days later, on June 24th. She is all passion and reassurance, and eloquent on the subject of her emotional distress. There were four gauchos, not one ("And you will remember that your mother must have told you 'there's safety in numbers'") who have distracted her from herself but only confirmed "through the unconscious comparison with you – how unique you are for me."

> *I am pleased, in a way, to know that you are not omniscient – it makes you more human. But I really could not understand how you could <u>not</u> see this thing in me when you have seen and do see so many other things. And, of course, distance lends not enchantment, but exaggeration. The heart grows so fond that it bursts – and there are all the pieces to pick up again and pull together bit by bit.... When I have calmed down a little, I will write you again more moderately and more sensibly. Right now I am on fire, and I could go on like this for hours —-*
> *I love you so much that it is killing me —-*
>
> *Betty*

Gene's next letter, postmarked the following day, makes no reference to the emotional events of the past week. He has wangled a position for himself as company clerk, and now has the use of a typewriter. The Army continues sending conflicting signals: nearly everyone in the group who arrived with him from Camp Robinson has been transferred, and he fears that he won't be sent back to school after all. His name was posted for shipment, but "after a glorious 24 hours they cancelled the shipment."

Five days later, on June 26th, he writes to report on his weekend in New Orleans visiting Betty's friend Evelyn; they had dinner at two of New Orleans's most famous restaurants and he describes the food in detail. At the City Park Stadium he heard a thrilling performance of *Carmen*, but best of all was "being in a big city once more – seeing lights – ducking heavy traffic – milling with mobs … it felt almost as tho I had come home." Finally, after all the news, he refers to her letter:

> *Dearest, your note was so beautifully moving and so warm – I could almost feel you pressed to me.*
>
> *I shall always keep that letter by the way, and whenever you tell me you cannot write, I will show it to you. It was a throbbing piece of poetry…. I love you so my darling, it is hard to wait until I hold you again. But it will be all the sweeter for waiting.*

After a few more sentences in this vein, Gene permits himself a witty postscript, complete with a little funny face: "My best to the gauchos – all four of them."

There are more letters during the next few days including a very amusing description of Gene's role as company clerk ("I now have the entire company virtually eating out of my hand. It's really fun."). He has wangled a corner room with two windows for himself with only one roommate, although ordinarily the room is reserved for Master Sergeants and permanent personnel. When the Colonel heard about it "he looked mighty surprised. I don't suppose that during his 22 years in the Army any private has ever spoken to him that way."

Gene has organized a system whereby he is the first to hear the rumors, one of which is that men in his classification will be moved to the west coast. This, he worries, will interfere with their marriage plans. Betty has evidently written to him about the vexed issue of a religious ceremony, for he writes on July 8th that "you shall have whatever kind of ceremony you want… Of course I have no objection to an Episcopal ceremony and I know you will have none to a ceremony in some rabbi's study afterwards just so that no one can ever twit me about it." He still doesn't know where he will be sent, or when he will be able to expect a leave, "so if your father is to marry us we will have to wait…. I think you should tell your parents that we planned to get married next month but that we are delaying it for that reason." At the end of the letter there's a reference to Aunt Edith:

> So your Aunt Edith is at it again. Very well, she is simply piling up inexorable vengeance for herself by heaping new coals of fire on my head before I have a chance to even the old score. But even it will be – I promise you – and all in the smoothest and most unobjectionable manner. I shall never forget that scene in her office when she asked <u>me</u> how I would like the idea of your joining the Waves. Of all the effrontery. That was a year ago – still comparatively early – when I wasn't too sure how you felt about me and tho the restraint nearly killed me, restrain myself I did.

I have often thought about Edith and her motives, and wished that I knew how she would have explained what Gene regarded as her repeated attempts to disrupt the romance. Relations between aunt and niece had been a little strained ever since Edith, in her position of influence at Radcliffe, refused to help Betty win a scholarship when it seemed that she could not afford to remain at Wellesley. True, Edith and Betty had a delightful time traveling together at the end of Betty's year in Spain, and Edith had helped Betty get her position at the Chicago Girls' Latin School. Perhaps Betty embraced this offer enthusiastically, though she may have been hoping for a career with opportunities to use her fluency in Spanish. Certainly, she could not afford to turn down a position during the Depression.

The laudatory accounts of Edith's role at the Appointments Bureau, as well as her own words, indicate that she could be forceful, stubborn, and calculating when she set out to accomplish something. And it is clear, too, that in the Protestant New England culture in which Edith and Betty were raised, Jews – and Catholics, for that matter – were regarded as quite distinct tribes, interesting, perhaps, but not "our kind." The war was bringing people of different classes, regional origins, and religions together in an unprecedented way at places like Camp Robinson, and Betty, in her travels for Harcourt Brace, was undoubtedly meeting a wide variety of people as well. But Edith, despite the fact that she had been to China and back, remained, in 1943, a self-confessed New England spinster of strong opinions and a firm allegiance to the Episcopal Church. I would hazard a guess that she wanted Betty to follow in her footsteps, perhaps without admitting this to herself. Little Edith was married by now and a mother, as was Edith's other niece, Bert's daughter Gratia. Neither could have joined the Waves and gone off on an adventure analogous to Edith's in France during World War I.

Betty was not in the least tempted by the Waves, however, and in July 1943 she was still working in Harcourt Brace's New York office. On July 9th Gene sent her a telegram with news that he was on his way to Stanford University: "ON MY WAY TO STANFORD TOUGH BREAK BUT WE'LL WORK IT OUT WILL WRITE FROM THERE LOVE GENE." The rumors about the west coast had been true, and Gene has begun a five day journey by train that will take him through Big Spring, Texas, where Betty had lived as a child, to El Paso and Los Angeles and finally to Palo Alto. On the back of the Western Union envelope Betty wrote in pencil: "RT – San Francisco – United Airlines $329.90 – 18 hours." So although Gene's letters continue to counsel waiting, Betty was evidently ready to take her long-awaited summer vacation and fly to California, although it would have cost her an enormous sum of money.

Gene writes a couple of long letters between rounds of bridge and poker on the train:

I glance out of the window every now and then. It is hard to believe that I am really in Texas. For so many years my life followed its smooth routine – doing the same things day after day. Then you came and my life changed. Then the war – then the Army – so many new experiences – so many new places – so different a life. It's a strange, strange sensation – indescribable – all with the flavor of combat constantly near. In Shreveport today we passed a unit just come from maneuvers – steel helmets, packs, leggings, dark, sunburnt, dirty faces.… I realized quickly how soft I have grown, how easily I had slipped back into the current of my old life, — and how dangerous that was.… I shall try to harden up again at Stanford. When I left Robinson, I felt as tho I had been reborn – there was an exhilarating feeling of physical strength, of limitless endurance, of confidence in my ability to do things.…

Sometimes I think that this War with all its tearing of men and women from their close ones – with what it has done to you and me and to my career – has its compensations. At least one does not grow old with the desolate feeling that he has seen nothing, ventured nothing, had none of the romance and excitement of adventure. Maybe it's childish – but I feel it.

This last paragraph sounds remarkably similar to the way Edith felt during her time in France during World War I. Gene ends his letter by asking Betty to be patient and wait until he knows more about his assignment.

As soon as he arrives at Stanford Gene writes again, and, as in the past, his letters serve as a way for him to think through his options. There is no program in Spanish or French, so he will have to either study Italian or German, where he'd be competing with native speakers, or opt for Chinese or Japanese. He will be tested in geography, and he is busy studying an atlas. Students who don't do well are sent back to the rifles and packs, so there is terrific pressure to succeed. As of July 14th he hasn't heard from Betty and worries about "the ominous silence." But her letter must be on its way, because on the 17th he writes immediately "so as not to keep you too long in a state of suspense." He will be at Stanford for a three-month course, with no furloughs longer than a weekend. And so, he says, the wedding will have to wait.

Sweetheart, please try not to go to pieces over this. We've had a tough time. – but no tougher than many others…. I've gotten a break which if it follows thru as indicated will keep me out of combat and in one piece – will present lively and interesting work and may solve in part the problem of economic adjustment that I would have had otherwise to make after the war and which might embitter our first years together with economic hardship. Most of the able-bodied men have been separated from their women and they manage to adjust….

Darling, we are neither of us youngsters and the war almost caught up with us before we found each other. There is that, too, to be thankful for. All these obstacles will make it so much sweeter afterwards…. Please, sweet, have faith in us…

On July 21st Gene announces that "the die is cast." Although he had made up his mind to try for the Chinese language program, he has been assigned to the Italian one instead. He will be studying the Italian language and contemporary history in an intensive course of study until early October, when he will get a week off. Had he been classified as "fluent," he'd be on his way overseas by now; this program, instead, is designed to prepare him as an administrator in Allied-occupied Sicily. For the first time, he says, "I can breathe easy…after more tests, interviews, and red tape than I ever conceived possible." The airmail letters are flying back and forth between New York and California nearly every day. Gene tells Betty that the wives of some of the other soldiers have joined them in California and though he is jealous, he warns Betty that if she comes west for her vacation, which she apparently has said she'll do, he won't have much time to spend with her because classes and drills fill up every day except Sunday. It would make more sense, he says in his next letter, for her to delay her vacation until the week of October 3-10, when he'll have his furlough. The Italian course is very tough, particularly since Gene and the men who arrived at Stanford with him were added to a class that had already been in progress for a couple of weeks. He is working incredibly hard to catch up, and reports on August 2nd that "I can now read anything that is not too difficult and understand a lot of speech – even fairly rapid" – amazing, when you consider that he has "been at it only a week." He ends his letter, "con molto amore, mia amabile ragazza."

Gene preserved Betty's letter of July 20^{th,} which was probably among a batch forwarded from L.S.U. to California. Aunt Edith, evidently, had come up with another scheme, and Betty writes:

> *My Darling,*
>
> *Things are happening, and I want to know <u>exactly</u> how you feel about this problem. So send me an airmail letter right away...for I think you most certainly have a right to express yourself as strongly as you feel about this.*
>
> *I am referring, of course, to the Embassy job in London. Aunt E. is really putting the screws on me now – on the basis of patriotic duty, etc., and not just personal wishes. She just called me up long distance from Cambridge for a half-hour's intense supplication that I consider it very <u>seriously.</u>*

Edith claims that the State Department is desperate for people who know languages, including Spanish, and that Betty must decide right away.

> *Here are the considerations: I see no possible way for us to live together whether we do or do not get married now or soon, for at least the next 6 months (on the basis of what you've been able to find out) and most probably not afterwards either. Isn't it likely that you will be sent overseas...?*

Betty weighs her options carefully; on the one hand, she likes her work at Harcourt Brace. She's intrigued by the Embassy job, though, "if only to do something new," but would like to do it as a temporary form of war service, with the assurance that she could return to Harcourt Brace after the war, to give Gene time to "get straightened out economically" before they start having those children he's been fantasizing about.

> *What I'm saying is that this is a hell of a decision to have to make, and I am thrashing around like an eel trying to evade it, rationalize it, etc, because I have a feeling it's more than just changing jobs, that it's a*

very important thing. It might affect you and me much more than one can see on the surface, and I react violently from anything that might jeopardize our future. Yet I can do nothing for the duration of the war to have it as we both want it. In other words, I really want to be told what to do (if only women were drafted like men…) by someone who can see it more clearly than I can at this point. This is pure weakness, I know, but you'd better know about it.

. . .

Sweetheart, I hope you are not going to feel that my even considering this proposition means that I don't love you enough to stay here and wait, hard as it is. You do understand, don't you? So don't be hurt by it whatever you do.

Betty ends by asking "Does it make any real difference whether I'm here or in Europe for that period of time? If you think it does, tell me." Betty has also written to her boss asking for advice, and she encloses a copy of that letter.

Gene responds to the Embassy proposition in his letter of July 27th:

I think it very doubtful that Spanish is in very great need in London…. You know that I view anything that emanates from your Aunt Edith with suspicion. I'm sorry darling, but there it is.

He goes on to speak about how little time off he has, and how much he needs to study to keep up, but then adds: "one never knows about this goddam army. Anything can happen and usually does." He might be in the program for three months rather than nine; he might even be transferred to a post within week-end distance of New York. And so,

The upshot of all of what I have said is this: I am selfish about it and on the chance that we might get a break during the next six months I don't want you to take the job. But I realize 1) how slim the chance is and 2) how tough it is for you to stay in N.Y. – So if you want to do it very badly do it –provided you can kick it over. But if you don't want it _badly_ don't take it because I live in hope that somehow I'll get some assignment that will enable us to live together.

. . .

Darling – We seem so far away from each other. When I think that I'm reading what you thought 5 days ago – it seems terribly far... In the few hours I take off I just wander around aimlessly. I'm glad I've lots of work to do.

TWENTY-FOUR

At Last – A Happy Ending

WHEN I THINK about the decision my mother had to make when presented with the tempting prospect Edith had arranged for her I wonder what I would have done. It would have been exciting, certainly, to spend the war years in an overseas Embassy position rather than waiting on the sidelines, particularly with all of the uncertainty about Gene's next assignment. But Betty seems to have made her decision quickly, for in his August 6th letter Gene writes, "I'm glad, dear, that you've decided to chuck the Embassy job." Three days later he adds "don't under any circumstances commit yourself to staying with Harcourt Brace for the duration if such a commitment will keep us apart at any future time. I find it increasingly hard to get along without you and just as soon as I get somewhere where my evenings are free, you have simply got to come for good." On August 11 he addresses his letter to New Sharon, where Betty is evidently spending her summer vacation with her parents.

Betty has written from New Sharon, and Gene writes back to say that

Your description of Cape Cod Hill makes me really want to see it. And the good people there sound fascinating – a small world in itself.

So you went the last round with Aunt Edith – good for you. Only you shouldn't have mowed her lawn. Very decent of her to concede that everyone should do as she thinks best. The stubborn egotism of parents and those who fancy themselves in loco parentis who are determined to relive their lives vicariously in the next generation is one of the saddest of human instincts. Not that I am convinced that her motives are even as high-minded as that, mind you. Or am I being too unforgiving? I know that you are fond of her and perhaps I ought to shut my face.

If this were a novel, the confrontation between Betty and Edith would have been the climactic scene, and oh, how I wish I could write that scene! But since I've chosen to record only what I found in the letters, I will have to imagine what Betty said, and what Edith said, and the roles played by Frank and Marian Stedman, whether present or not at this meeting (presumably at Edith's summer cottage in Ogunquit, Maine). Betty, as Gene realizes, is indeed fond of Edith; it is her nature to be affectionate and loyal to family, and she has in some ways viewed Edith as a role model and inspiration. But I doubt that their relationship ever entirely recovered from Edith's interference at this critical moment in Betty's life.

As far as Gene is concerned, the decision to marry as soon as possible has finally been made, and his letter goes on to refer to their plans for the October furlough:

So your mother is afraid that we will get married in S. F. Good for her – she's right on the beam. And I was rather surprised by two things [you said]: one, that it would give her a stroke – I thought by now that your mother, at least, was resigned to me as a son-in-law; and two, that you are "doubtful that we will be able to resist it." I didn't think there would be any resisting. On the contrary – I have assumed for some time now that that will be the first order of business on our agenda – or am I wrong? As a matter of fact I have gone so far as to announce it to this segment of the Army.

This passing reference to Frank and Marian's feelings hints at the unpleasantness Betty must have endured during her vacation on Cape Cod Hill. The "Jewish question" may well have been a subject of repeated and contentious discussion. When I think of how much Betty sought out her parents' advice and expressed her devotion to them in the Spain letters, I can begin to imagine how painful this must have been.

Gene's letter dated August 28th makes another reference to Aunt Edith, whose "dirty tricks" he deeply resents:

> Little one, you are being very sweet about my pot-shotting at Aunt E. I have always momentarily expected that you would one day say – "Now look here –dammit – I can criticize my family but you can't. I'm fond of the old grizzly bear, and you lay off." But your restraint has been magnificent and I will accordingly keep my face shut on said topic until she plays the next dirty trick on me.

With only a month to plan for the October furlough, Betty has been working on Harcourt Brace to send her to San Francisco on a business trip. Gene's letter of August 30th indicates that her efforts have been successful: "I think it's really terrific that H B & Co is doing this for you. Almost makes me change my mind about employers generally." The letter continues:

> About the wedding – you have got to remember that your folks will be in Florida most of the year and that we can scarcely depend upon the Army giving me leave just at the time they pass through New York – it seems a little impractical to count on anything like that while I'm in the Army. But I don't want you to have any regrets about anything – so let it ride until you get here and we can talk it over at length. You did rather put a fright into me in your last letter although I noted that you worded same with scrupulous care. I rather got the impression that you weren't quite sure you wanted to marry the Tuck of August 1943 vintage at all until you examined the merchandise carefully and made sure that there had been no deterioration. I gather from Thursday's letter that the issue is _only_ whether to postpone same until your Daddy can perform

the ceremony…you are quite right about my erring in assuming that we would go ahead without consideration of that factor. What I am trying to say is that for a horrible moment I thought that your doubts went deeper…. Glad to have the record clear again.

The letter ends on a somber note. After a Saturday evening drinking with the boys, Gene worries about the state of wartime morality, and "the retrogression to the primitive." How, he wonders, "will the adolescents of 1943 ever grow up to be decent men and women after opening their eyes in such a world?"

Gene writes on September 4th in response to a highly emotional letter from Betty:

My little Poochie,

I object violently to your characterizing yourself as wayward, emotionally immature, unstable, etc. You are none of those things and I'll not have you say you are. It's entirely natural and understandable that you should feel the way you do with so many miles between us.

Sometimes I think of those early days when you were getting it on all sides from your father and Aunt E. and you never showed it. I remember one letter you got…. Nothing in your conduct indicated what I later found out – that the letter was from your father imploring you to give me up. I think that emotionally you're tremendously stable so we'll have no more of that.

Did Betty save that letter from her father, or was it too painful? I looked for it in the shoebox, but couldn't find it. There are a few more letters from Gene to Betty with accounts of weekend leaves in San Francisco and long hours studying for exams. Something conclusive must have happened during the next few days, for Gene sends a telegram to her on September 15th that says:

LETTER RECEIVED MONDAY AND ANSWERED IMMEDIATELY. BURSTING TO SAY I DO. MUCH LOVE= GENE.

On September 17, Gene's letter says "I went to town yesterday and canvassed the red tape situation and I think that we can unravel it over the weekend and be married on Monday." There are lots of complicated details regarding blood tests, which have to be done in California, not New York, and very little time to line up a minister or get a ring. Gene adds that "You're right, it's not possible to get a phone line thru to N. Y. from here," so from this point on, they communicate by telegrams. There are three of these:

> HAVE TO BE TUESDAY IF MARRIED HERE BECAUSE BLOOD TEST. MAYBE MONDAY IF IN FRISCO WILL FIND OUT THIS MONDAY AND WIRE YOU. YOU GET RING PREFER TO SEND ANNOUNCEMENTS LATER LOVE=GENE.

The next telegram, dated September 20th, says

> SET FOR MONDAY SEND RAILWAY LINE AND ITINERARY… FURLOUGH STARTS NOON LOVE = GENE.

On the back of the telegram, Betty has drafted the wedding announcement, hesitating a bit over the wording and settling on a simple "Announce" rather than "Have the honor of announcing":

> *The Reverend and Mrs. Frank Holt Stedman*
> *Announce the marriage of their daughter*
> *Mary Elizabeth*
> *To*
> *Eugene Tuck*
> *Private First Class, Army of the United States*
> *On Monday, the fourth of October*
> *Nineteen hundred and forty-three*
> *Palo Alto, California*

One final telegram, sent September 23rd, completes this batch of letters. It is an important one, for it serves as a reminder that "the Jewish Question" wasn't simply a one-sided affair. There was also the matter of Gene's mother, who may not have been privy to the discussions of the past three months. The telegram suggests that Gene was struggling with the letter he was going to have to write:

> SIMPLY WANT TIME TO WRITE MOTHER CAREFULLY AND WILL NEXT TUESDAY WHEN EXAMS OVER WANT HER TO HEAR IT FROM ME FIRST....HAVE ANNOUNCEMENTS MADE. MAIL FROM HERE. HAVE ARRANGED TESTS. WEDDING MONDAY AT 4 PALO ALTO LOVE =GENE.

The wedding did indeed take place on October 4th, and Betty and Gene had a brief honeymoon in Carmel, on the California coast. Betty did not return to New York; instead, she arranged for a position teaching Spanish to undergraduates at Stanford for the remainder of the academic year. In her characteristically scrupulous fashion, she reimbursed Harcourt Brace for her train fare to California. By April 1944, according to a letter forwarded from Stanford, she was back in her apartment at 333 East 47th St. in New York and working at Harcourt Brace in the children's books department. Gene was in Fort Warren in Cheyenne, Wyoming, where the unpredictable whims of the Army had sent him, rather than to Italy, as he had been led to expect. There are many more letters – twenty-five in June 1944 alone – but our story ends here, as stories used to do, with a wedding and the familiar words "they lived happily ever after." Which words, for the most part, are true – Betty and Gene had a long and happy marriage, and once the war ended, were never apart for more than a couple of weeks for the next forty-seven years.

Afterword

THERE IS A TRADITION among nineteenth-century fiction writers – and some twentieth-century ones as well – of telling the reader what happened to the characters in the years following the events of the story. I've always enjoyed those postscripts or afterwords, and so here is mine.

An Anglophile to her very core, Edith began spending summer holidays in England in 1949. The summer of 1950, she recalls, was "a particularly grim time. Elise Dexter, the person whom I cared for most in the world, died in March and I felt as though the bottom had dropped out of everything." Fortunately, a new project came along which would occupy her for the rest of her life. Some English women friends had purchased the Manor House at Dorchester-on-Thames, with eight acres of land adjoining a twelfth-century Norman abbey. Edith, with her experience in rehabilitating old buildings, pitched in and helped them. After her retirement from Radcliffe in 1954, she spent eighteen months in England, and then, for the next dozen years or so, she divided her time between Dorchester and the little house on Farwell Place, which Radcliffe allowed her to remain in after her retirement. The abbey, a magnificent structure, had fallen into disrepair, and so Edith adopted it. She formed a British-American committee and set about raising money for ongoing restoration of the buildings and grounds, starting with the great stained glass rose window above the altar. The monastery guest house became a gift shop, where Edith sold sweet biscuits and other items designed to appeal to tourists, including copies of the booklets she wrote for the purpose containing recipes, rather sentimental stories and poems, inspirational essays and prayers, and so forth. After two decades of energetic fundraising, the Friends of Dorchester Abbey surprised her with a sculpted stone corbel, which adorns the abbey to this day. And thus it was that Edith Stedman joined the ranks of angels and saints who customarily adorn medieval religious buildings. Without a doubt her proudest moment came in 1977, a year before her death, when the Order of the British Empire, one of Great Britain's most prestigious honors, was conferred upon her in an elegant ceremony at the home of the British consul General in Boston. From that point on, Edith was entitled to sign her name "Edith G. Stedman, O.B.E."

Betty and Gene visited Dorchester Abbey in the 1950s and 1960s while Edith was in residence there and undoubtedly made a financial contribution to the restoration efforts. Gene kept his distance, however, and I am quite certain that he continued to feel ambivalent about her. He assumed that she had decided to approve of him because he was now a successful lawyer, although in all fairness I believe that she became more open-minded as the world changed around her.

My visits to Aunt Edith in my college years always seemed like a way into the New England past, and I have often wished that I'd written down some of her *bon mots* and pronouncements on the world at large. I had never met anyone quite like her before, though in the years since then I've read about women of her generation who in their own way paved the way for the women's liberation movement of the 1970s that became very much a part of my world when I was in graduate school. In comparison to her younger self, Edith was on her best behavior when I visited her;

I think she was determined not to make the mistakes with me that she had made with my mother. The only time she attempted to "manage" my life occurred in the spring of my junior year, when, in her peremptory manner, she told me to go the Appointments Bureau, where a summer job on Wall Street had been set aside for me. I accepted it without a murmur.

I saw much less of Edith after I graduated and left Cambridge. As her old friends died and her health declined, her life became more circumscribed, although she remained adept at getting people to help with her projects to the end. She spent her final years in a nursing home in Boston; by then she was almost completely deaf and blind, but true to form, she prevailed upon the staff to let her use a supply closet as a makeshift office where she could listen to books-on-tape and record letters to friends and relations on cassettes.

Betty and Gene had almost, but not quite, acquired the large family of two girls and two boys whom Gene had invented in his letters. I was conceived at the Retreat on Cape Cod Hill, just after Gene was discharged from the Army, and was born a few months after the death of my grandfather Frank Stedman. My brothers, Jonathan and Daniel, joined me in 1947 and 1949 as part of the first wave of the post-war "baby boom." By then, my grandmother Rebecca Tuck was thoroughly reconciled to my parents' marriage, and she was a frequent presence in our home until her death in 1956, mending our clothes and looking after us when our parents traveled. Like so many families of that time, Betty and Gene moved to the suburbs when I was four years old so that their children could attend Long Island's public schools. Commuting to his law office in the Chrysler Building each day on the Long Island Railroad, Gene read the New York Times and wrote comic light verse and the Tuck family "Annual Reports" which a large circle of friends looked forward to at Christmastime every year. Each Valentine's Day, he would present Betty with a poem, a tradition that began in 1945 with the witty acrostic poem on the next page:

M ilady, there is comfort in the ever-present thought
    That among the other miracles that wedded life has wrought
    There's no need for the query "Will you be my Valentine?"
    Nor the vernal admonition "Come and seek and ye shall find."

Y ep, no long need I purchase scores of garish cardboard hearts
    No longer need I pierce them with those phallic Cupid's darts
    For my auricle and ventricle have found a place to beat
    And are palpitating gleefully on Forty-seventh Street.

W hen hostilities are ended and the chicken's laid to rest
    When I drag this beaten carcass home to our domestic nest
    When I've finished playing soldier, I romantically believe
    That you'll let me wear it for you on my custom-tailored sleeve.

I must confess it's always been a mystery to me
    Why Valentines are shrouded in such anonymity
    For if you garner more than one, my love, you soon will see
    That I'll have no one tamper with my sex monopoly.

F or others far less fortunate today's the day to write
    Corny second-handed sentiments, "hormonious" and trite,
    But for me the hunt is over and the quarry is at bay
    And February fourteenth's just another working day.

E ver since embracing marriage, I know that you have tried
    To eschew the "Texas Beauty" and become "The Battered Bride"
    But you're still the choicest morsel, and it's still the "bottom line"
    That I'd like to sink my teeth in my curvaceous Valentine.

Here is another, a birthday poem from 1957:

Iambic Pushover

Some gals want jewels and furs and dough
Some love to crow, "I told you so"
Some live for style; some store up bile
Some yearn to run the whole damn show

Some buck for dear old hearth and home
Some like to flirt; some like to roam
I've got a new variety
My gal's a sucker for a "pome"

Tho' there are "pomes" of various kinds
The kind that suits my bride
Is the kind that scans and the kind that rhymes
And's a bit on the sexy side

Now, I can't turn a pithy phrase
Or write immortal lines
But I do know prose from poetry
And poetry's gotta rhyme

You don't need furs or jewels or gold
To keep your sweetie merry
All it takes is a stomach strong
And a rhyming dictionary.

Betty settled into a routine of child-rearing, gardening, shopping for second-hand furniture, going to P.T.A. and Wellesley Club meetings, serving as a Cub Scout Den Mother, and speaking Spanish whenever she could. She maintained a correspondence with Agapita, her housemate at Doña Benigna's, and fostered a lifelong love of the Spanish language and culture in two of her three children. She and Gene traveled frequently as soon as they could afford to, and sent home picture postcards by the dozens to their children and friends. We children were expected to write letters as well, and during the summers, we would go off to camp with several thin fold-up airmail letters addressed to hotels in Europe. Betty had carefully written the dates on which they should be mailed in pencil on the back of each one. I remember those airmail letters so clearly, their onion-skin papery feel, the way you folded the sides in and then the bottom and sealed the top flap after writing on every available surface. Thinking about them now, I realize that they were just like Vernal's folded letters.

If my mother kept any of those airmail letters from her children in the 1950s and 60s, they were thrown out long ago. No small wooden box could have held all the pieces of paper that accumulated in our household, and thus, ironically, it was the very abundance of letters and cards and clippings and school art projects and essays that doomed them to oblivion. Living as I do, now, in the age of abundant and ephemeral cell-phone photographs and e-mail messages, I sometimes wonder what will survive for the next generation and the ones after that. Will anyone miss those verbal traces of the everyday past that were occasionally preserved back when people wrote letters?